Best-Kept Computer SECRETS

How to Do Everything on Your Computer the Fast, Easy, and Low-Cost Way

Publisher's Note

The editors of FC&A have taken careful measures to ensure the accuracy and usefulness of the information in this book. While every attempt was made to assure accuracy, some Web sites, addresses, and telephone numbers may have changed since printing. This book is intended for general information only. It does not constitute medical, legal, or financial advice or practice. We cannot guarantee the safety or effectiveness of any advice or treatment mentioned. Readers are urged to consult with their personal financial advisors, lawyers, technical and health care professionals. The publisher and editors disclaim all liability (including any injuries, damages, or losses) resulting from the use of the information in this book.

"For I know the plans I have for you," declares the Lord, "plans to prosper you and not to harm you, plans to give you hope and a future."

— Jeremiah 29:11, *New International Version*

FC&A Publishing®
103 Clover Green
Peachtree City, GA 30269

Produced by the staff of FC&A

ISBN 978-1-932470-89-5

Table of contents

i

How to use this book

For best results, read this book in order, as each section builds on the previous one. Unless otherwise noted, all information relates to:

✦ Windows XP operating system with Service Pack 3

✦ Microsoft Office 2007

You will frequently be given keyboard shortcuts — also known as hot keys — as quick ways to perform tasks and navigate around on your PC. You will see the name of the keys, all in capital letters, separated by plus signs (+). This means you press all the keys indicated together. You don't actually press the plus sign. For example, CTRL + C means you press the Control key and the "C" key together. CTRL + ALT + DEL means you press all three of these keys at once.

chapter 1

Hardware nuts & bolts

❝Improvements to computer processors seem to come at breakneck speed. Hold on to your mouse, because they're about to come even faster. ❞

University of North Texas Computer Science Department
1998 press release

Do you really need a new computer?

Most home computers last about two to five years. If your system is nearing an important birthday and you're considering buying a faster, sleeker model, decide if you can save a few bucks by extending the life of your old machine.

One great feature of many personal computers (PCs) is how easy they are to upgrade. There's a lot you can change out, depending on how you use your computer.

◆ Need more memory to store digital photos or music files? Solve that problem by buying an external hard drive.

◆ Want a larger monitor so you can really appreciate your movies, photos, or game graphics? You can buy a new flat-panel monitor for less than $150.

◆ Like your neighbor's fancy peripherals, like a CD burner or ergonomic keyboard? Those are easy enough to add at little cost.

◆ Tired of watching your computer slowly grind through operations? Try the simple tune-up tricks throughout this book that will help you get the most speed from your old system.

But don't try to make a silk purse from a sow's ear. Some experts say if the cost of upgraded parts is more than half the cost of a new system, you shouldn't bother upgrading — replacing your old system is smarter. And if you want to join the ranks of those running a new operating system, your best choice may be to buy a new computer. Windows Vista, in particular, may have trouble running on an old machine.

For information on what your computer needs to run Windows Vista, see page 141 in the *Operating system upgrades* chapter.

6 ways to shop like a pro

So, you're ready to buy a new computer. You want the most up-to-date technology, but you also want good value. It's got to be fast and powerful, yet easy to operate. It should last at least five years, and that means you'll need good technical support. You want only the features you want, without paying for add-ons you don't need. Doesn't sound like too much to ask.

Paint the big picture first. There's no point in going shopping until you've given this purchase at least a little thought. Without a game plan, you're likely to either get frustrated by all the choices out there and leave the store empty-handed, or — even worse — buy whatever the salesperson decides is the flavor of the month.

A mainstream desktop computer will suit you just fine if all you want to do are some basic things like:

◆ surf the Internet

◆ send and receive e-mail

◆ instant message

◆ do some basic word processing

◆ listen to CDs

◆ store personal photos

◆ watch an occasional DVD

◆ play a few games

Jot down any additional tasks or interests that might require a little more PC power. For instance, if you are really into editing DVDs, you will want to upgrade certain areas.

Find your computer a home. A dedicated home office space probably means you've got room for a nice-sized monitor and a conventional tower housing your processor and all the inner hardware for your computer. This option gives you the widest range of prices to choose from. If you're short on space, however, or just want to cut down on clutter and wires, then consider an all-in-one unit — the processor, memory, sound card, etc. are all stored inside a slightly thicker monitor. These are generally more expensive and can be harder to upgrade.

Special needs, like a PC for your kitchen, can require special technology — a water-resistant monitor and keyboard, wireless options, and others. These are fun and convenient, but can be pricey.

Don't waste money on an extended warranty for your computer. Most cover problems only during the first one to three years — when it's least likely to have trouble anyway. Save those bucks for repairs later, since the cost usually balances out. A better bet is to buy your computer using a credit card that automatically extends your warranty for free.

Technology at any price? Experts say two things:

◆ Spend money where you'll get the most bang for your buck.

◆ Buy as much PC as you can afford.

This means you should put your purchasing power into the main system — the processor, memory, disk space, and perhaps the monitor. You can always upgrade the peripherals and add on software later. Just be realistic. Do your homework before you go shopping so you'll have a good idea just what PCs are selling for.

> A home computer can add a bundle to your electricity bill — as much as an extra $50 a month if you leave it running constantly. Keep that cost down and help the environment without sacrificing performance by buying green. Choose a computer that has been certified as "80 Plus." This means the power supply is at least 80 percent energy efficient — 60 to 70 percent efficiency was the standard in old models.

See how the brands stack up. If this is your first computer, stick with known brands — Compaq, Dell, Lenovo, Sony, HP, eMachines, or Gateway. You're going to want reliability and good tech support. But before you spend one cent on a computer, check these three places:

Consumer Reports	*www.consumerreports.org*
PC World	*www.pcworld.com*
PC Magazine	*www.pcmag.com*

These organizations publish computer reviews and buying guides supported by field testing. Go to the library to peruse back issues or visit them online.

Hit the road. You've got several options when it comes to where you want to shop. Knowledgeable sales personnel can be a factor, but if you've done your homework, you shouldn't have to rely on outside help. Otherwise take into account price, return policy, shipping charges, selection, product availability, hands-on testing, how long the company has been in business, access to a service department, and whether or not you can customize your own system.

Types of vendors	Examples
Online retailers	www.Amazon.com www.Overstock.com www.Newegg.com www.TigerDirect.com
Online auctions	www.eBay.com; www.uBid.com
Electronics stores	Best Buy; Circuit City
Big box retailers & price clubs	Costco; Wal-Mart; Sam's Club
Manufacturer direct order	Dell; Gateway; HP
Mom & Pop retailers	(check your local Yellow Pages)

Know when to go. You can save money just by timing your computer purchase with care. According to *PC World* magazine, check out prices during these times:

✦ around the holidays

✦ during back-to-school sales

✦ throughout January or February inventory clearances

✦ when new products are launched

For information on buying refurbished computers, see page 245 in the *Internet deals & steals* chapter.

When a Mac makes sense

Microsoft Windows is not the only flavor of operating system, although it's what runs most PCs. You could choose an Apple computer, which uses a Macintosh operating system. Consider these issues before you buy.

	PC	Mac
Who tends to use it	typical office workers, serious computer gamers	artists, musicians, videographers
Great features	lots of add-on software available	not typically targeted by viruses, lots of helpful software is included, easy to learn and use
Problem areas	usual target for viruses and malware	some add-on software is not available
Price	lots of variation due to competition, but some fully loaded models are less than $600	initial cost tends to be higher, but better repair history according to *Consumer Reports*
Customer support	varies greatly depending on where you purchase and type of warranty	Apple Stores are known for great customer service

Don't overspend on CPU speed

Computer central processing units (CPUs) are getting faster and faster, meaning the brains of your machine can do complex calculations quickly — and can multitask, to boot. But just as you don't need a Ferrari to run errands around town, you may not need all that CPU speed.

To help your computer run faster without creating extra heat or using too much power, developers put two processors on a single chip and called it the dual-core processor. Then came the quad-core processor with — you guessed it — four processors on one chip.

These configurations allow your computer to multitask, or run functions in the background while you work with a program in the foreground. That's great if you work your computer hard — perhaps watching streaming video while you listen to MP3 music with other programs open. Some applications, like fancy, high-end games, may need to utilize more than one processor at once for best performance.

Most new PCs today come with dual-core processors. *PC World* magazine suggests quad-core processors are great for serious game players, but are not necessary for typical Internet, e-mail, and word processing users. Save some cash and buy a nice dual-core processor for about $100 to $400.

Shift into high gear with a memory upgrade

Even if you bought the fastest model in the store, over time your computer may slow down as you add more programs and files. But you can make your computer work like the latest model — without buying a new one. The secret is in the upgrade.

Don't blame the CPU. You might think upgrading your central processing unit (CPU) would make your computer run faster, but it's usually not worth the trouble or expense. That's because a computer is only as fast as its slowest part, and adding a slightly faster CPU won't make much difference. Instead, pick the cheaper solution and upgrade your system's RAM.

Remember your memory. You may be the top bridge player in your weekly group, yet you have trouble remembering your son's cell phone number. Same thing goes for your computer. The reason is, there's a difference between memory on the computer's hard drive and random access memory (RAM).

◆ Hard drive space is memory used for the physical storage of your data on the C: drive inside your computer's tower.

◆ RAM is the working memory that helps your computer process information faster.

Adding RAM is a pretty cheap upgrade for your computer, and it can make a big difference in how your machine works. A computer running Windows XP works best with at least 1 gigabyte (GB) of RAM. Some experts suggest you don't buy a new computer with less than 2 GB of RAM.

Try a DIY upgrade. First, decide what kind of RAM you need. RAM is sold in "sticks" of various types — SDRAM, RDRAM, and so on — but not all will fit your computer. Contact your computer's manufacturer to see what will work with your machine and whether you need to add memory sticks in matched pairs. You can also get help using tools at the Web sites of one of these memory vendors.

Crucial	www.crucial.org
Kingston	www.kingston.com
SimpleTech	www.simpletech.com

Once you have your new RAM stick, follow the installation procedure carefully so you don't foul up the inner workings of your computer or damage your stick. You'll need to open up the computer tower, so be ready before you start.

◆ Check the computer's manual for full instructions. If it's not complete, go to the manufacturer's Web site to download and print instructions.

◆ Turn off power to the computer. Better yet, unplug your machine.

◆ Wear latex gloves when you handle the memory stick to avoid damaging it with static.

If you must completely replace your memory stick, ask the vendor about getting credit for your old one.

◆ Be careful to properly orient the memory stick in the correct slot on the motherboard.

Adding memory is one of the simplest upgrades you can do. But if it sounds like more than you want to tackle, contact your local computer repair shop for help. You can also pay the repair department in an electronics store to install.

Most people are perfectly happy with the standard graphics card, or video card, that came in their computer. New systems typically have graphics cards that are integrated, or share memory with the rest of the machine. Sharing is fine — unless you want to play graphics-intensive video games or do lots of video editing on your computer. Then you may prefer a discrete video card which has its own pool of memory. No sharing is required, so your graphics-intensive programs should run faster.

Save money with the right CD

Your CD drive is a wonderful thing. Pop a shiny silver disc in and your computer "reads" the information off of it so you can install software, listen to music, or view photos from your kids. But there are different kinds of CD drives. A CD-ROM drive is common in older computers. ROM stands for Read-Only Memory — which means it can only read the information off discs, not transfer information to new ones. But if you have a CD-RW drive, you can also put information onto a CD — a process called burning. Once you know what your computer is capable of doing, it's time to run out and buy some blank CDs.

CD-R discs are recordable — once. They are best for permanent storage. At less than 25 cents each, they are pretty cheap. Use them for making backup copies of files for safekeeping or holding a stash of your favorite tunes. Most commercial music CD players can play CD-R discs.

CD-RW discs are rewritable or Read/Write. You can copy information to the disc, erase it, then copy to it again. That's why they are best for temporary storage, for instance if you need to make a daily backup copy of a document you're working on. But most CD players, like the stereo in your car, can't read CD-RW discs, so don't use them for music. CD-RW discs are more expensive than CD-Rs, but you don't need as many since they are reusable.

DVD burner = smart investment

A DVD burner can replace a CD-ROM or CD-RW drive because, in short, it can do everything a CD burner can do, plus more. You can use it to:

- ✦ burn CDs.
- ✦ install software from a CD or a DVD.
- ✦ store files to use as a backup or for sharing on other computers.
- ✦ play music CDs as well as DVD movies.
- ✦ copy CDs and DVDs.
- ✦ record home movies.

But if you plan on taking advantage of some of these wonderful features, make sure all your multimedia will be compatible before you buy. The type of disc you burn movies to must match the type of disc your DVD player can read. Check the manual.

Fix a scratched CD

Don't waste money on an expensive repair kit. You can probably fix your damaged CD with items you have around the house.

If a CD or DVD refuses to play, it may have fingerprints, dirt, or scratches on the shiny side — the side the laser reads. First, try cleaning it to see if that solves the problem.

◆ Use a lint-free cloth and a mild solution of soap and water.

◆ Wipe gently in a straight line from the CD's center toward the outside edge — not around in a circle — to avoid damaging the data.

◆ Let the CD air-dry, then try playing it.

If it still doesn't play, try polishing out the scratches.

◆ Use either toothpaste — paste, not gel — or Brasso and a soft, lint-free cloth to polish any scratches you can see on the disc's shiny side.

◆ Again, always move from the center of the CD toward the outer edge in a straight line. You're actually polishing down the plastic coating in an attempt to make the scratches more shallow.

◆ Rinse off the toothpaste or thoroughly wipe off the Brasso, let the CD dry, and try playing it.

The future of computing is at your fingertips — literally. Someday soon, you'll be able to accomplish all your computing tasks by touching the screen and manipulating windows with your fingers. Manufacturers are still refining the technology, but there are groundbreaking units available. The HP TouchSmart computer has a touch-controlled user interface that lets you check messages and calendar items by pressing the screen rather than using a keyboard. Other manufacturers are following, with Microsoft unveiling its own interactive surface and building software code for multi touch into its operating systems.

If all else fails and you really need that data, take your CD to the professionals for repair. A store that sells used CDs probably has good equipment and can do the job for less than $5. After you get the CD playing again, make a backup copy of the disc in case the problem is not permanently fixed.

Monitors: bigger not always better

You could spend thousands on a fancy monitor that's as wide as a small refrigerator, but experts say, don't.

No matter how big a monitor you buy, nothing on it will look good unless it's compatible with your computer's graphics card. This very important component lives inside the computer tower and basically translates data into images made up of tiny dots called pixels. The graphics card sends this image information to the monitor through a cable. Every monitor has a "best" screen resolution that signifies the number of pixels on the entire screen.

For example, an average resolution for a basic monitor could be 1024 pixels by 768 pixels. The higher the resolution, the better the picture. So unless you also invest in a high-end graphics card that matches your monster 30-inch monitor's resolution, the picture won't look good anyway.

But that doesn't mean you have to settle for small potatoes. Instead, look for the largest monitor you can afford that still gives a sharp picture. You'll almost certainly buy a flat-screen liquid crystal display (LCD) monitor, since those bulky old CRT types are nearly extinct nowadays. According to the experts at *PC World*, your best bet is a 22-inch wide-screen monitor. Prices are coming down fast, and you can find one with DVI (Digital Visual Interface), a feature that means you'll get the sharpest picture possible.

When is a PC a TV?

For about $100, you can watch your favorite TV shows on that beautiful new flat-screen PC monitor. The simplest, cheapest way, is to first buy a TV tuner card. This small component simply plugs into your computer's USB or FireWire port. A slightly more complicated option that some say will give you access to more bandwidth and provide a more stable connection,

Be sure the tuner card is compatible with new ATSC format TV signals.

is an add-on TV tuner card that uses an empty expansion slot. In either case, you'll then need to install the tuner's software.

Next, get your TV signal into the computer. Disconnect the cable that goes into the back of your TV, then connect it to a cable splitter — a little metal box that allows the signal to go in two directions. Then connect cables from the splitter to both your TV and the back of your PC.

For information on other ways to watch television on your computer, see page 271 in the *Use the Internet for fun & learning* chapter.

User-friendly accessories keep you feeling good

Don't settle for a plain, flat keyboard and a mouse that slides around like a bar of soap — especially if you suffer from muscle aches, joint problems, or even some kind of disability. Specialized keyboards and mice can make you more comfortable while you compute.

Cut the cords to move freely. Wireless keyboards and mice are wonderful inventions. Instead of sending signals through wires, these gadgets send them through the air to a receiver plugged into your computer. You've probably seen this technology at work — people talking on a cell phone with just a little bug in their ear. This is one popular type of wireless connection called Bluetooth. That earpiece talks to the cell phone using the same radio waves that carry information between a wireless mouse or keyboard and your computer. You can think of this type of wireless as a little personal area network (PAN), sending and receiving signals up to about 30 feet.

Wireless accessories mean fewer cords to tangle, plus you have the freedom to move your keyboard

Don't confuse a PAN with Wi-Fi, the higher-speed wireless connection that lets your computer connect to the Internet.

off the desk and hold it in your lap. Now you can surf the Internet from the comfort of your easy chair. The drawback of going wireless is, of course, how quickly you can drain batteries. Remember to power these gadgets off when they are not in use, and if they stop working, plug in a charger or install fresh batteries.

Type and click with ease. Whether you want your keyboard curved, split, or tilted, there's one out there to fit your hands comfortably. Some even have a padded shelf to rest your wrists on. Ergonomic keyboards like these are built to let you type for longer periods without stressing your hands and arms.

Example of a split keyboard

For information about using an on-screen keyboard, see page 95 in the *Accessibility options work for you* chapter.

Mice also come in varieties to better fit your hands.

Example of a trackball

◆ A trackball looks like a golf ball sitting in a holder. It gives you finer control and lets your hand rest on a surface rather than hovering.

◆ A touch pad also lets you make finer movements. You simply slide your finger across a flat plastic rectangle to move the pointer on your screen.

◆ Go totally hands-free with a foot-operated mouse, and never lift your fingers from the keyboard.

For information on making your mouse work more efficiently, see page 72 in the *Control panel: customize your PC* chapter.

Special keys make great shortcuts

You paid for all the keys on your keyboard — may as well use them. Save time and hassle with these shortcut keys.

✦ PRINT SCREEN. Capture an image of your screen at any given moment — sometimes called a screen shot. Then you can paste this image into a program like Microsoft Word or Paint, or Adobe Photoshop. Very useful when you need to communicate with technical support. ALT plus PRINT SCREEN captures only the active window.

✦ SCROLL LOCK. Press this key and your arrow keys now allow you to scroll quickly up and down in an Excel spreadsheet. Press again and this feature is turned off.

✦ PAUSE/BREAK. Press while holding down the Windows logo key. It opens the SYSTEM PROPERTIES dialog box in Windows.

For more information on pasting a screen shot into Paint, see page 175 in the *Top tips for popular programs* chapter.

Big sound comes with small price tag

Using old stereo speakers with your PC may seem like a frugal way to get sound from your computer, but experts say it's not such a good idea. First, stereo speakers are not made to work with computers, so they're not magnetically shielded. This means they may cause interference with your computer monitor or other peripherals. Second, the sound card in your computer generates a weaker sound than a stereo, so you probably won't get strong, rich tones from the speakers. If listening to music on your PC is important to you, consider buying specialty computer speakers — you can probably find some for as low as $30.

chapter 2

Everything laptop

" 1981: Adam Osborne completed the first portable computer, the Osborne I, which weighed 24 pounds and cost $1,795. The price made the machine especially attractive, as it included software worth about $1,500. The machine featured a 5-inch display, 64 kilobytes of memory, a modem, and two 5 1/4-inch floppy disk drives. **"**

Computer History Museum

Mythbuster: 5 reasons to love a laptop

Laptop computers aren't just for the work-obsessed road warrior anymore. These handy all-in-one machines, also called notebook computers, offer benefits anyone will love.

Using a laptop means you can easily move your computer to any room in the house — even out to your deck or front porch. Most come with wireless Internet connections, Wi-Fi, so you can check your e-mail or look at online photos of the grandchildren without plugging in cords. When you travel, take along a laptop to find local restaurants or check your airline flights without having to rely on your hotel's computer. And some airlines are now offering in-flight Wi-Fi hookup, so you can surf the Web from the friendly skies.

In the past, certain issues may have kept you from considering a laptop purchase. But just see what's happening in today's industry that may change your mind.

Price. Laptops used to be more expensive than desktop systems. But prices are falling. You can find some simple, sleek models for less than $500. Meanwhile, desktop prices have stayed about the same.

Battery life. You are limited by the life of your rechargeable battery if your laptop is not plugged into wall electricity. However, that's less of a problem now that some batteries can keep you running four hours or more.

Upgrades. Greater demand has brought more laptop options, so you may find it easier to buy exactly the machine you want.

Ease of use. Smaller keyboards, dimmer screens, tricky mice — all are part of the territory with a machine that's been shrunk. You can solve some of these problems by adding your favorite mouse, connecting a larger monitor, or plugging in to a docking station when you're at a desk.

Size. A 16-pound computer may not seem portable to you, but you can also find models as light as 2 pounds.

Laptop options: when to save and when to spend

Experts say you should buy your laptop just the way you want it — don't plan to upgrade it later, since this can be difficult and expensive. So consider these choices as you design a machine that will be your perfect electronic companion.

◆ If this will be your only computer, ignore the tiny new models. Some have screens less than 10 inches in diameter and cramped keyboards. And don't run to the other end of the spectrum. Jumbo laptops with screens larger than 17 inches are mainly for serious computer game-players. Midsize is just right.

◆ Test drive the keyboard and mouse. Some new models are easier to use, with tilted keyboards and keys that don't feel mushy. Also be sure a touchpad mouse has comfortable buttons and is large enough to use easily without having to lift your fingers repeatedly.

◆ Don't pay extra for upgraded processor speed. Standard options are fine for most users.

◆ Most laptops have a battery that will run the machine for two to five hours before it needs to be recharged. That's important, since you'll be disappointed if you can't watch an entire movie on DVD without running out of juice.

◆ Consider the new draft-N version of Wi-Fi, which brings in your data lightning fast — in one-third to one-fifth the time of standard Wi-Fi connections. Even if you plan to use your machine at home and plug in using a cable, why limit yourself? A laptop with wireless Internet access is the best way to take advantage of high-speed connections at airports, libraries, coffee shops, and hotels.

Put your battery on an anti-aging plan

Your laptop has a rechargeable battery. Don't waste it. Help it keep its power longer with a little TLC.

Discharge monthly. Whether your laptop has a nickel cadmium battery or the new lithium ion variety, you need to drain the power completely about once a month, then recharge it fully. This process extends the life of nickel cadmium batteries and recalibrates the fuel gauge on laptops running on lithium ion batteries. Same process, different purpose.

Turn it off. If you're not using your laptop, turn it off. You can also use the sleep, standby, or hibernate mode whenever possible to conserve battery life.

Turn it down. Dial down the screen's brightness to as low as possible while still allowing you to function. You could save up to 30 minutes a charge.

Limit the drain. Downloading large items while on battery power uses it up fast. Wait to start operating system or program updates until you're plugged into electricity. And watch those behind-the-scenes goodies. Streaming radio or playing CDs while you work can really consume the juice.

Keep it cool. Don't leave your laptop in a hot car. Lithium ion batteries like to be kept between 68 and 77 degrees Fahrenheit.

Unplug the extras. When you're not using your USB-attached items — like that external disk drive or extra mouse — disconnect them. They cause a battery drain whenever they are plugged in.

Cyber-surf safely — even in public

Your laptop probably connects to the Internet using a wireless network, or Wi-Fi. That's convenient in hotels, airports, or coffee shops — but there are risks. Public Wi-Fi networks are shared, so other people are also connecting. While you're at a public hotspot sending e-mail messages and shopping online, mean-spirited computer hackers may be stealing personal information. You should assume there may be a hacker listening in to your every move.

Some hackers set up an evil-twin network, posing as a legitimate connection. You think you're using the hotel's connection, but you're actually talking directly to a stranger. A similar trick is the man-in-the-middle network, in which a hacker captures your information, then routes you on to the legitimate network. Either way, your passwords, credit card numbers, or other sensitive information are up for grabs. Here's what you can do to stay safe in public.

◆ Some Internet providers, including T-Mobile and AT&T, offer free software that verifies you're using the genuine company network.

◆ Be sure your operating system, firewall, and anti-virus and anti-spyware programs are up-to-date.

◆ Save your banking, stock trading, and sharing of sensitive company information for when you're at home, on a network you control.

◆ If you must shop online, use a credit card that you keep just for that purpose. And check your balance online often. Don't wait until the end of the month.

◆ Plug into a high-speed connection — using a cable — rather than the public Wi-Fi. Your laptop is happy using either method.

For more information on wireless network security, see page 49 in the *Home network options* chapter.

Thief-proof your laptop

You're out more than just the price of your portable computer if your laptop is stolen. Your personal information is also gone with the wind. Safeguard both with these common-sense steps.

Lock down your equipment. Treat your laptop like the expensive item it is and it won't walk away.

◆ Use a cable to connect it to a table or chair leg in a waiting room, bathroom stall, or restaurant. Some cables emit a piercing siren if they're cut.

◆ Don't leave your laptop in a hotel room. Put it in the safe instead. And never leave it in the car, locked or not.

◆ Buy a motion-sensing alarm that attaches to your laptop. If someone tries to move it, you'll be the first to know.

Science fiction is turning into fact. Some computers come equipped with biometric devices — gadgets that read your body to be sure you are who you claim to be. Fingerprint readers require a valid fingerprint swipe in order to log in. And facial recognition software will do the same based on a scan of your face. Now, that's a clever password.

◆ Use a laptop case that doesn't advertise what's inside. You can find backpacks that don't look like they hold a computer, yet they have a protective compartment for your machine.

◆ At airport security, wait as long as possible before you place your laptop on the conveyor belt. Even if you're delayed going through, your laptop has less time to wait unattended.

◆ Sign up for a service that can trace your laptop if it's stolen. Some have software that sends a message to the security company when the computer goes online — a virtual call for help.

LoJack for Laptops	www.lojackforlaptops.org
Phoenix FailSafe	www.phoenix.com
zTrace Gold	www.ztrace.com

◆ Make labels with your name, phone number, and e-mail address and attach them to every piece of your equipment — laptop, power adapter, and so on. If you leave your stuff behind, a good Samaritan has a chance of getting it back to you.

Secure the contents. Let's say the worst has happened, and your laptop goes bye-bye. Be sure the thief won't have access to your personal information and documents.

◆ Set up passwords for all accounts — including Guest. Be sure to keep this and all your passwords stored separately from the laptop.

◆ Check out encryption software to scramble data on your hard drive. It may be worth the $30 to $100 price tag.

If all else fails, the tracking services listed previously may also be able to erase certain files or your entire hard drive remotely. How high-tech is that?

For information on how to set up account passwords, see page 77 in the *Control panel: customize your PC* chapter.

Help your machine keep its cool

Warning: laptop may burst into flames. You've seen the pictures and you've heard about the recalls. But, admittedly, the risk of actual fire from defective laptop batteries is very, very low. Lithium ion batteries produce electricity through chemical reactions, and in order to produce enough to run power-hungry devices like your laptop, they have to pack a lot of energy into a small space. Even a small defect can allow the heat to get out of control.

Water and computer circuits don't mix. And water, in the form of condensation, can form inside any electrical device when it's taken from a cold environment to a hot one — or vice versa. If your laptop gets too cold, let it warm up to room temperature and dry out before you turn it on.

So when is there reason to worry? Your laptop normally produces heat even if you don't have a defective battery. But it shouldn't feel uncomfortably warm, and its plastic case shouldn't melt or become discolored. If it does, turn it off and contact the manufacturer.

To help it stay cool, avoid overworking your laptop and if you must use it for a long time, place it on a flat surface. Don't put it on anything soft, like a bed, blanket, or even — yes, that's right — your lap. And don't block the laptop's vents. You can buy a special cooling stand to raise your laptop for good ventilation, but a free solution — if you like to use it in the case — is to place a couple of pencils under the back of the laptop to raise it just a bit and let air flow freely.

Prop up your laptop to keep it cool

Add-ons take the worry out of laptop life

Slosh coffee on your desktop computer's keyboard, and you only have to replace the keyboard. A wet spill on your laptop is a much bigger deal. Liquid that drips through your laptop keyboard may reach the machine's sensitive components. Prevent the problem with a flexible keyboard cover for less than $20.

Consider these other handy laptop accessories.

◆ A privacy filter for your screen makes it harder for strangers to read over your shoulder.

◆ A "real" mouse is easier for some to use than the touchpad or eraserhead pointers that come on laptops. Plug in your favorite mouse and your laptop will recognize it right away.

◆ Turn one USB port into four with a USB port hub. This lets you plug in your camera, extra mouse, optional keyboard, and memory drive — all at the same time.

For information on how to clean your keyboard, see page 27 in the *Hardware hazards* chapter.

chapter 3

Hardware hazards

❝RAM disk is not an installation procedure. ❞

Author unknown

Compute in comfort

Using your computer should be fun — not painful. Learn smart work practices so you can enjoy your time on the machine without having to pay for it later.

Protect your peepers. Blurry sight, dry eyes, headaches — they're all part of something called computer vision syndrome. It's difficult to focus on images on a computer screen, and your eyes end up paying the price. Tricks to stave off this problem have to do with avoiding eye overwork. Remember to blink often, so your eyes don't get dry, and look away from your computer every 20 minutes or so. Finally, adjust the room's lighting so you're not battling glare on the screen.

Practice good posture

Save your joints. Repeated motions and too much stress on your hands can lead to problems with the nerves in your wrists — carpal tunnel syndrome. In addition, people who wear bifocals often tilt their heads back to see the screen better, causing neck and shoulder pain. Set up your work area for the greatest comfort.

◆ Place your screen about arm's length away with the top of the screen slightly below eye level.

◆ Support your arms with some kind of cushion.

◆ Adjust your chair so your thighs are parallel to the floor and your knees, hips, and elbows are at right angles or slightly greater.

◆ Use a footrest or keep your feet flat on the floor.

Take care of your ticker. No matter how comfortable you feel at your computer, too much sitting is too much. Research has found that office workers who stay at their desks for hours at a time have a greater risk of developing blood clots. Stand up and walk around every so often to keep your blood flowing.

For information on ergonomic keyboards and mice, see page 13 in the *Hardware nuts & bolts* chapter.

Bust the dust: save money with a clean PC

Dust — tiny particles so small, you can hardly see them. But they're enough to take down your computer by causing a head crash. Sound painful? It will be when you pay to have your hard drive replaced.

Inside your computer, a read/write head hovers over — but does not touch — a rapidly spinning disc called a platter. All your data is stored on its surface. If even the smallest bit of dust gets onto the platter, the head crashes into it, scratching the platter and causing even more dust and debris. That can mean damage to your system, lost files — you may even need to replace the drive.

But dust and dirt can harm your computer in other ways. Too much dust acts like an insulating blanket that can clog your vents and make your computer heat up. It can also create drag on moving parts, causing your computer to run slower and use more energy.

Come clean. Inspect your computer tower for dust bunnies every three months, and clean it carefully. Pay special attention to areas around the vents and other openings. If it's so dirty you need to open it up to clean inside, be sure to unplug the power cord first. Just be aware that opening the case may void your computer's warranty. Read your documentation to find out.

◆ Don't use a dust rag or vacuum cleaner inside the machine — you can damage the delicate parts. Instead, use a can of compressed air to blow the dust out.

◆ You may need to clean the foam or metal mesh filters that keep dust from clogging the fan. You can wash the filters unless they're made of paper, but dry them completely before you put them back.

◆ Never spray water directly on your computer. This can short out the electrical components. If you need to scrub gunk off the outside of the case, use a bit of water or rubbing alcohol on a cloth.

Go for good ventilation. Try these TLC tricks to keep dust at bay and your computer dirt-free longer.

◆ Keep the tower off the carpet, so less dust, pet hair, and fibers get sucked inside.

◆ Don't block the air vents. Even storing the tower in a closed cabinet may prevent it from getting the air it needs.

◆ If you do ever open the case, don't leave it open. The cover keeps air circulating over the hottest internal parts.

Quick tricks for a clean keyboard

You get your morning coffee and shuffle over to the computer to check e-mail. Then — oops. Coffee's too hot, and you spill it right on your keyboard. Even though it could happen to anyone, a spill is bad news, especially if it's something more than just water. First thing to do is unplug the keyboard and use your mouse to shut down the computer. Then you can worry about damage control. Dry off what you can, and use a damp lint-free cloth to lightly wipe down the keys. Let everything dry completely before plugging it back in.

But even if you never spill, keyboards pick up dirt, oils, and germs from your fingers. Give yours a good solid cleaning by turning it upside down and gently shaking out any crumbs. Then use compressed air in a can to blow dust from between the keys. Finally, if there's serious gunk underneath the keys, take a picture of your keyboard so you'll remember where everything goes. Then you can gently pry off the keycaps — but never the spacebar — with a small screwdriver. Clean, dry, and push the keycaps back onto their pegs.

A keyboard cover will protect from the next spill. Better yet? Don't eat or drink near your computer.

More tidy up tips for your peripherals

Don't forget about cleaning all those things you plug into your computer — monitor, mouse, printers, and all the other gadgets. Just bypass the usual household cleaners, since some can harm the finish on components. Stick with water or rubbing alcohol. Unplug the device and check for advice in your owners' manual before you begin.

Mouse. An older mouse may have a ball on the underside allowing it to roll about on your mousepad. You'll want to remove the ball so you can clean off accumulated lint and dirt. Once clean, things will move more smoothly. Newer optical mice don't need to be opened up, but you can wipe off the bottom with a cotton swab.

Monitor. If your screen looks dusty, polish it carefully with a dry, lint-free cloth. More serious messes call for a water-dampened cloth, but don't press too hard. And dry off any moisture rather than letting it air-dry. Treat your monitor as carefully as you do your eyeglasses.

Printer. Get out that can of compressed air to remove dust from inside your printer, then wipe off the paper tray and outside of the machine with a damp cloth.

For information on running a Windows utility that can clean your printer for you, see page 126 in the *Fast fixes you can do yourself* chapter.

High priority: dodge electrical dangers

A surge protector can't take on lightning, but it can protect your computer from more common — but just as troublesome — electrical spikes.

Lightning is so powerful it will override almost any surge protector, so the best way to protect your computer during a thunderstorm is by simply unplugging it. Don't forget to also unplug the cable or phone line from the wall, since those can transmit a lightning strike as well.

But you do still want to use a surge protector, because sensitive electronic circuitry that's connected to other equipment is prone to damage from sudden changes in power levels. Simple spikes from home appliances cycling off and on can cause more havoc than lightning. Just remember, certain features are worth the price.

◆ Pick a surge protector that's certified to UL 1449 standards.

◆ Check the ratings on it to be sure it can handle your equipment. And don't overload it.

◆ Look for one with an indicator light so you can tell it's working. Surge protectors sacrifice themselves in a large rush of current, and you're not protected afterwards.

◆ Get one that includes a phone line or cable connection to protect all your wires.

That tiny red switch near the power cord on the back of your computer can keep you out of serious international trouble. It allows you to select a voltage to match the country you are in — 110/115 volts in North America and 220/230 volts in most of Europe. Set the switch incorrectly, and you'll permanently harm your computer. If you're not sure what the voltage is from your electrical outlets, call your local electric company or check travelers' information. If your computer doesn't have a switch, then it works only at the voltage in the country where you bought it.

Plug and play safely

A tangle of unruly cords. A grab bag of power bricks, plug packs, and AC adapters. An avalanche of prongs, and plugs, and outlets. It's enough to make anyone flee in frustration. But unsnarling this puzzle means a safer work environment for you and less damage to your equipment.

◆ Use only the power cord and adapter approved by the manufacturer to work with each item.

◆ Don't wrap a power cord tightly or treat it in other ways that may make it fray, crack, or crimp. If it looks damaged, don't use it.

◆ During use, unwrap any hook-and-loop fastener designed for storing or traveling with cords and adapters.

◆ Arrange your power cords so they're not in areas of traffic, and don't let furniture press on them.

◆ Don't modify or bend the computer cord's plug to make it fit a socket. For example, a three-pronged plug needs to have a grounded electrical outlet. Don't alter it to fit a two-hole outlet. Instead, call an electrician to get an approved outlet adapter.

◆ Never overload an electrical outlet.

Tame that mess of jumbled cords behind your computer. Use an old curly phone cord to wrap the bundle and keep them organized. They'll also be less likely to pull out of the machine.

Simple fix solves puzzling problem

You sit down at the computer and start typing, but nothing happens. Don't call tech support before you do one simple check — make sure everything is plugged in properly.

1. Turn off the power.

2. Unplug and replug in all the cords — keyboard, mouse, monitor, printer, and power adapter. Are they in the correct locations?

3. Turn on the power and see what happens.

4. Still out of order? Try borrowing a different keyboard.

If all this fails to fix your problem, you may have to replace your motherboard.

Perk up your picture in 3 simple steps

Use the buttons at the bottom of your monitor to adjust various aspects of your display — color, brightness, contrast, and window shape, among others. Your buttons may be labeled with a number 1, a down arrow, an up arrow, and the number 2. Some monitors have MENU/SELECT and AUTO/EXIT rather than the numbers. Yours may have even different labels, but chances are they perform the same

Example of standard monitor buttons

functions. Here's how to use the buttons to improve your picture.

1. First press 1 to enter the menu, then use the up and down arrows to find the function you want.

2. Press 2 to select that option. Use the arrows to make changes.

3. When you're through making changes, press 1 to exit. Your new settings are saved.

If you decide later the screen looks worse than when you began, go back into the menu and select an option that allows an auto adjustment or says it will reset to factory specifications.

For information on improving your monitor's color using the Control Panel settings, see page 68 in the *Control panel: customize your PC* chapter.

Heed warning signs to avert disaster

When your car makes a strange sound or doesn't seem to be running properly, you take it to the shop. You know better than to keep driving until it quits and leaves you stranded. Same goes for your computer. Don't wait until it breaks down to react to a problem that's been brewing. That will cost more in the long run.

Funny sounds are no joke. No computer is perfectly silent, but new or odd sounds may mean hardware trouble. A whirring or rattling could be a sign there's trouble with the fan, which keeps your computer cool. If you sit back and wait, the sound may eventually go away. Don't assume that means your problem has gone away — your fan may have simply stopped working and now your computer is overheating. A high-pitched whirring could mean your fan is rotating too fast because another internal component — perhaps the CPU or motherboard — is

31

about to go bad. And a clanking, grinding, or ticking sound from the hard drive may mean it's on its last legs. Get it checked straightaway.

Don't get hot under the tower. If your computer feels uncomfortably warm to the touch, or if the plastic case becomes deformed or discolored by too much heat, there's a problem. Along with that, a strong odor, smoke, or a hissing or popping sound may mean an internal component has failed. It could be a safety problem, so shut down and call in the experts.

Free 911 for your computer

You're not alone when your computer goes kaplooey. There's plenty of help out there that won't cost you a thing.

First, check your computer's warranty and support plan. You should have free technical support by telephone for a certain length of time — often one year. If your machine is still covered, call the toll-free number. Your warranty may also include free in-home service. And some cover the expense of sending the machine back to the company for repairs.

If you're not in a big hurry, you may be able to get good advice from online help desks or user forums. Of course, this option will only work if you can access the Internet. First try the manufacturer's Web site, then check for help at these sites.

Microsoft Help and Support	*www.support.microsoft.org*
Windows Users Group Network	*www.wugnet.com*
Google Users Group	*www.groups.google.com*

Finally, some computer stores have help desks that will give you advice about your computer problem for free — as long as you don't leave the machine to be repaired. Start with the Geek Squad inside Best Buy stores or FireDog in Circuit City stores.

Let your old PC rest in peace — safely

Did you know you can get lead and mercury poisoning — from your computer? It's true, but only if you toss it in the trash improperly. Lucky for you, there are safe alternatives.

Sending your old PC to a landfill means poisonous materials end up leaching into the ground and water table. In fact, some trash services won't even pick up computer equipment from the curb. But you can find it a new home.

Put it up for adoption. Your local senior center or public school may be able to use your old computer. Give them a call first to be sure they need what you have to offer. If your machine is too old or doesn't work, it may be more of a burden than a help. The best donations are computers younger than five years old with operating system software and peripherals, like a mouse and keyboard, included. Send along your user manual if possible.

A professional refurbisher acts as a sort of middleman — making sure your equipment gets to schools and charities in good working order. They can install legal software, wipe hard drives, and dispose of expensive e-waste. Locate a refurbisher near you by going to **www.techsoup.org** and clicking on FIND SERVICES.

Another easy method is to donate through the National Cristina Foundation. This nonprofit group provides technology and training to children and adults in need. Your gift is tax deductible. Contact the foundation at **www.cristina.org.**

Find yourself a rebate. Even if your computer is no longer useful to you, it may have some cash value. Some computer manufacturers will take away your old computer for free or even give you credit toward your next purchase. Others offer no incentives and charge a fee for pickup. So get all the details before you decide. Check out recycling services like Gazelle at **www.gazelle.com**. You can find out if your old machine is worth something — or if you'll just get free help disposing of it responsibly.

Scrub your hard drive for security

Whether you sell, refurbish, donate, or recycle your old PC, you'll need to strip important data from your hard drive first. Delete doesn't always do it. Here's how to wipe private information off your computer for good.

Placing items in the RECYCLE BIN on your computer — then emptying it — doesn't truly get rid of them. It simply deletes a reference to the files. Someone who knows how can still see what was there, whether it's your Social Security number, bank information, or passwords. Experts found it frighteningly easy to retrieve deleted information using common recovery software. Take the right precautions to truly clean off your computer.

Light wipe. If you're giving your computer to someone you trust, simply reinstall your operating system using the original CD. This makes files harder to find, but it doesn't remove all information.

Extreme erase. Go this route if you're giving or selling the computer to strangers. The idea is to totally wipe out all information on your hard drive. You can use free or for-fee disk-erasing software to do this. The best products work by writing over each piece of data with random numbers or letters. That's like erasing words on paper, then writing over them repeatedly so they can't be read. Check out these tools.

Eraser	*www.heidi.ie/eraser*
Darik's Boot and Nuke	*www.dban.org*
Active@KillDisk	*www.killdisk.com*
Blancco PC Edition	*www.blancco.com*
WipeDrive	*www.whitecanyon.com*

Heavy hitter. If your machine is so out of date it's not useful to anyone, physically destroy the hard drive. Get out your hammer, power drill — whatever it takes.

chapter 4

Accessorize your computer

“A printer consists of three main parts: the case, the jammed paper tray, and the blinking red light.”

Author unknown

Cheap printer not always a bargain

That rock-bottom printer isn't such a deal anymore when you see the price of a replacement ink cartridge. Surprisingly, if you pay a bit more for a printer, you may find the cartridges are more

reasonable. Always check out the specific replacement cartridges you'll have to use for each printer before you buy.

In addition, knowing how you'll use the printer means a better chance picking the right style up front — and avoiding costly nightmares later on.

	Inkjet	Laser
Price of printer	$100 - $800	black and white: $200 and up color: $500 and up
Cost of ink cartridges	tricolor: $10 - $40 single-color: $5 - $60	single-color: $50 - $150
Average print per cartridge	100 - 1,000 pages	up to 6,000 pages
Best choice if you …	need to print a little bit of everything want good quality photos	print large documents need speedy printing need low cost per page don't plan to print photos
Drawbacks	slow printing	also needs an image drum

If you decide to buy an inkjet printer, pick one that uses separate cartridges for each color ink — not combined color cartridges. That way you can replace only the color that runs dry first.

Deals and discounts: print for less

Eventually your inkjet cartridge will run dry and you know how expensive replacement cartridges are. In fact, some printer companies make more than two-thirds of their profit from selling ink — not printers.

Refill to reuse. Refilling an empty ink cartridge is a pretty messy job if you try doing it yourself. Even *Consumer Reports* says to avoid most of these DIY

Want to take your laptop traveling and still be able to print? Check out the new portable printers. They're tiny — most weigh just 2 to 5 pounds — but can print a full-size sheet of paper. Look for sales because they are high-priced.

kits. But you can take the empties to some office supply stores and drugstores for refilling. They'll handle the mess and save you money to boot.

Buy third party. Off-brand ink cartridges can cost about half the price of the name-brand model, and will do a fine job on basic printing. You may even get more pages per cartridge. But if you need top quality printing — and especially if you print color photos — pricier ink is the way to go. The images will be crisper and less likely to fade.

For information on how to save money by shopping online for computer accessories like printer cartridges, see page 244 in the *Internet deals & steals* chapter.

Add on more savings. Try these other money-saving tricks.

◆ Ignore your printer when it claims it's out of ink. Just keep on printing until you notice that the quality is going downhill. You'll waste up to 60 percent of the ink in the cartridge if you follow directions unnecessarily.

◆ Buy ink cartridges in bulk. Even the two-pack saves you money.

◆ Save your empty cartridges and return them to the manufacturer for a rebate on the price of new ones. Some companies will even include postage-paid shipping materials for this kind of recycling when you buy their printer or ink cartridges.

For information on more ways to save time and money when you print, see page 70 in the *Control panel: customize your PC* chapter.

Don't get tangled in cable confusion

You bought a new printer, but its cord won't fit into the special outlet on your computer — called a port — that your old printer used. Most likely your new printer uses one of the new types of cables and matching ports — either universal serial bus (USB) or FireWire, whereas your old printer plugged into your computer using a parallel cable.

Don't worry. Your new printer should hook in just fine. You'll simply need to find the right kind of port on your computer or buy an adapter for the new cord. Here's what you need to know about computer connections.

USB cords and ports come in several

flavors, but the most common is series A. You can recognize this port on your computer because it looks like a little rectangle-shaped slot. It works at two speeds — USB 1.1 and USB 2.0. Both types of cords will connect to the same ports in your computer, but USB 2.0 moves information much faster.

FireWire, also referred to as standard IEEE 1394, is great for connecting devices that need to transfer lots of data. People like this type of cable for jobs like moving video from a digital camcorder to a computer.

It's a lot faster than a USB 1.1 connection and just a little slower than USB 2.0. FireWire cable comes in several styles, but perhaps the most common type fits a port that is a fat rectangle with two corners clipped off.

Both cable types are plug and play and allow hot swapping, meaning you can plug in and use a new mouse, for instance, without having to turn off your computer. Your machine will instantly recognize the accessory. And in newer machines, USB ports are often on the front of your computer tower for easy access.

The most common style of USB cable

A common type of FireWire cable

Pick proper paper for perfect printing

For the absolute best quality printouts, you'd buy the brand-name paper and ink made to work with your brand of printer. But let's be honest — sometimes you just need a copy of that grocery list, and fabulous print quality is not important. Save money when you can.

Buy common grade. Plain copier paper works great in your inkjet printer. It's a bit cheaper than some other types of paper, but you won't notice any quality difference. Look for reams marked as 20# — this is the weight measurement of about 500 sheets of large-format paper, and indicates an average quality paper.

Reduce waste. Keep paper from jamming or crumpling in the printer. A botched print job means a repeated print job.

> Whenever you connect a printer or other piece of equipment to your computer, you'll also need a device driver. This is a piece of software that lets gadgets talk to each other. Adding it should be simple. For information on helping your peripherals communicate, see page 126 in the *Fast fixes you can do yourself* chapter.

◆ Store your paper flat so it doesn't get torn or wrinkled.

◆ Be sure all paper in the printer tray is the same weight.

◆ Before you load paper in the tray, fan the stack to keep sheets from sticking together.

Use specialty papers sparingly. Sometimes a special job calls for more expensive paper.

◆ Use glossy coated paper to print photos. You'll get better color and overall quality.

◆ Try a cotton rag paper if you want the best results from a high-end inkjet printer that uses pigment-based inks. But if your inkjet is more moderately priced, it probably uses dye-based inks and there's no benefit to using cotton rag paper.

◆ Smoother papers work best in laser printers, which use heat and toner to create images.

Fax for free — without a fax machine

You can easily double or triple the cost of a computer by loading it up with every available gadget or gizmo. But a fax machine is one extra piece of equipment you don't have to buy.

The Windows XP operating system has a built-in fax function. And since most computers built in the last five years come with a dial-up modem, you're probably already set to fax anything you can print.

Simply plug a phone cord into your modem's jack and a working phone jack in your wall. Even if you use a broadband connection for your daily Internet use, you can still connect your dial-up modem to the phone line. The two functions can coexist peacefully.

For information on how to turn on the fax feature in the Windows XP operating system, see page 329 in the *Chat for less — use the net* chapter.

If your computer does not have a built-in modem and if you connect to the Internet using a broadband connection like a cable modem, you still don't have to buy a fax machine. Instead, use one of the free or budget online fax services. Some let you send faxes, while others also let you receive faxes to your e-mail account.

eFax	www.efax.org
FaxAway	www.faxaway.com
FaxZero	www.faxzero.com

Scan your way to computer fun

A scanner lets you take anything on paper — documents, photos, even images on slides — and put them on your computer in digital form. Then you can store, share, or print them out. Decent-quality scanners aren't all that expensive, either. You can get a fine model for $100 to $200. It'll let you do some nifty things you may not have thought about.

Store old photos or slides.
If you have boxes of old slides or negatives you want to put into your computer, and then perhaps on CDs for storage, look for a scanner that's made for this specific job.

Make copies. Scan a document, store it on your computer, then print out a copy.

Send a fax. Although you don't need a scanner to do the sending, you'll need one if the item you want to fax is on paper — not already in your computer.

Make changes to text. Have a letter you want to make changes to, but you don't want to type it in again? A scanner with optical character recognition (OCR) software turns printed text into a digital document you can edit to your heart's content.

Save money and desk space with a multifunction unit that combines the tasks of a printer, scanner, copier, and fax machine in one nifty piece of equipment. It's a snap to hook up and you save money by buying only one item — not four. The quality of printing may not be quite as good as specialty printers, but then again it may be just fine for your needs.

For information on scanning photos, see page 354 in the *Make the most of your digital images* chapter.

When you're shopping for a new digital camera, be sure it's WIA compatible. That means it supports the Windows Image Acquisition (WIA) standard, so Windows XP will recognize the camera when you connect it with a USB cable. Then you can use all the great features of the camera right on your computer screen. Check the list of WIA-compatible cameras at **www.support.microsoft.com/kb/293168.**

Modems made easy

You need a modem to connect to the Internet and get e-mail, but you may not need to buy one. This piece of equipment takes the information that comes into your house through cables and translates it into a language your computer can understand. It can be either built inside your computer or external — a separate little box. Three types of modems match up with the three main Internet connections.

Telephone modem is standard equipment. Your computer probably has one of these inside. To be sure, check the back of your computer for a phone jack that looks like the ones on your wall. Don't confuse a phone jack with an ethernet port, which is a bit larger. If you see a phone jack and you plan to connect to the Internet through your phone line, you won't need to buy a modem.

DSL does double duty. A digital subscriber line (DSL) also connects to the Internet using your telephone line, but it's much faster than a regular phone connection. It's also a bit more expensive than dial-up service, and you'll need to rent or buy a separate DSL modem.

Cable gives you speed. Rent or buy a cable modem and you can get to the Internet using the same cables your TV signal uses. Prices are higher than a phone connection, but it's up to 500 times faster.

Experts say you should also have a router if you use a DSL or cable modem. Unlike dial-up connections, these two broadband connections are always on, and thus more vulnerable to hackers. A router is a small piece of equipment you hook up between the modem and your computer. It acts as an additional layer of security, essentially hiding your PC from potential intruders.

For more information on various ways to connect to the Internet, see page 195 in the *Internet: quick-start guide* chapter.

Speed up your computer in 1 easy step

Adding hard drive space is like moving another filing cabinet into your office — it gives your computer room to breathe freely and may help it find things faster. You could replace the old hard drive in your computer's tower with a bigger one or add a second internal hard drive. But these are jobs you might prefer to leave to the experts. An easier route is adding an external hard drive.

These can be small — about the size of a deck of playing cards — and they connect to your computer with a cable that fits either a USB or FireWire port. Check your computer's ports to see which you have available before you go to the store. You can buy a large, 500 gigabyte (GB) external hard drive for less than $100.

A typical flash drive

Flash drives: storage on the go

Your new PC doesn't have a floppy disk drive. How can you make backup copies of documents or move files from one machine to another? Use the tiny device with a big brain — a flash drive.

These little gadgets — also called jump drives, thumb drives, or pen drives — are portable storage units that let you copy files or photos from your computer using any USB port. You could buy one big enough to hold every single thing on your computer, but you probably don't need that. Instead, shop for a 4 gigabyte (GB) flash drive for $30 or less. Here are a few ways flash drives can make your computing life easier.

✦ Make a daily backup of important files. Just don't use a flash drive for long-term storage — they're not as reliable as CDs or DVDs.

✦ Move files from your computer to share with someone else. For instance, take a letter to your son's computer to print. Or load your digital photos on the flash drive, then take it to a store's photo kiosk for printing.

✦ Keep your sensitive files on a flash drive in your pocket instead of on your laptop — it's harder to steal.

For more information on backing up important files, see page 114 in the *Keep your PC problem-free* chapter.

Traveling with a medical condition may have gotten just a little bit safer. Before you hit the road, ask your doctor about loading your medical information onto a small flash drive. It can hold your health history, details from your last checkup, ultrasounds, and even images of your heart or other problem area. In case there's an emergency while you're out of town, just give the drive to your new doctor.

chapter 5

Home network options

❝I see no reason why anyone would want a computer in their home. **❞**

Kenneth Olsen, American engineer and 1977 co-founder
of Digital Equipment Corporation

Home sweet home network: easy and cheap

Once upon a time, you were special if you had a computer in your home. Now it's not uncommon for each person in a house to have their own machine. But setting everyone up with their own complete workstation could get expensive. Save money by creating a simple local area network (LAN).

A network is merely linking two or more computers together so they can communicate with each other — often with a printer, modem, or other devices included in the mix. Connecting computers into a network lets you:

◆ share a printer, fax, scanner, or other hardware, so you don't have to buy a separate one for each computer.

◆ share storage and swap files. Your computers can talk to each other, so you can easily move documents or photos from one computer to another, for example.

◆ share an Internet connection. You need only one modem and one router to serve your whole house. Each computer plugs into the router and it doles out access to the Internet.

Get wired. A network that uses cables to physically connect computers is called a wired network. In contrast to a wireless network, which uses radio waves to connect, a wired network is cheap, secure, and easy to set up. You'll need cables and a router, and each computer needs to have an ethernet port in the back. That's an opening that looks like a phone jack but slightly larger. The one drawback to a wired network is having to run the cables from room to room, or perhaps drill holes to hide them behind your walls.

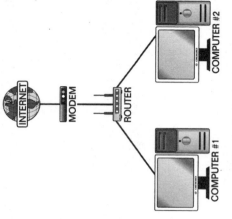

A typical wired network

A new solution to this problem is using powerline adapters, which free you from running cables through your house. Instead, you plug one little adapter box into an electrical outlet near your computer, and plug another box into an out-let near your router. Then run a short cable from each box to the device, and the boxes talk to each other through the electrical wiring in your house. You can probably buy the equipment for less than $200.

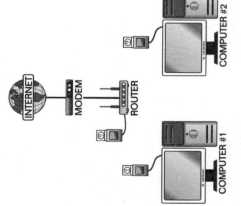

A wired network using powerline adapters

Call in the wizard. After you wire up your computers, run the Windows XP Network Setup Wizard on each computer in the network. This software helps you set up the connections through simple, step-by-step instructions. It applies the correct permissions and puts in code numbers where they belong so your computers can communicate. Running the wizard makes the process automatic, and it's the only reliable way to be sure your network has the right settings.

To run the wizard, click on START, then open the CONTROL PANEL. Be sure you are in Classic View and double-click on NETWORK SETUP WIZARD. Answer the questions and follow the steps.

Boost your wireless signal in 3 easy steps

When you want your computers to talk but you don't want to trip over cables, wireless is the way to go. A wireless network, also called Wi-Fi, uses radio signals to send information between your computers and other hardware. At the heart of a wireless network is a wireless router which can broadcast up to 300 feet in all directions. If the router is also hooked into your Internet connection and you're within this area, called a hotspot, your computer can tap into wireless Internet access. By setting up a wireless network, you can turn your entire home into a hotspot, letting you take your laptop to any room or even out on the porch to read e-mails.

The downside is that sometimes a weak Wi-Fi signal can disconnect you from your network just when you're in the middle

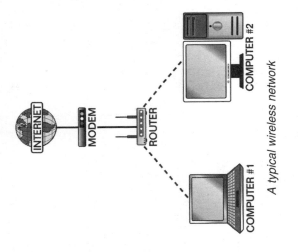

A typical wireless network

of an urgent task. Try these solutions to make your network more stable so you don't get tuned out unexpectedly.

Change channels. Wireless routers broadcast on channels, just like radio stations. The United States and Canada use channels 1, 6, and 11. If your neighbor is broadcasting on the same channel, the signals can interfere with each other. You may be able to stop the interference by changing the channel on your router.

Replace your phone. Many other gadgets, including microwave ovens, baby monitors, and cordless phones, broadcast into the same airspace. When these gizmos are close to your router they can cause interference. Try moving them farther away from each other. You can also change the channel on some cordless phones. For a long-term solution, replace your 2.4 GHz phone with a 5 GHz phone so there's no chance of interference.

Enhance your network. If you've tried these solutions and you're still getting kicked off the network, it may be because the farther you get from your router, the weaker your Wi-Fi signal is. An antenna or bridge might help. A new high-gain antenna for your router will focus the signal in one direction — where you need it most. A bridge, also called a repeater, acts as a middleman in your wireless "bucket brigade," taking your Wi-Fi signal and passing it along. This gives you a boosted network all the way to the far end of your house.

Setting up a wireless network requires you to type in the same password on each device. That password may be up to 64 random characters, so it's easy to make mistakes.

Here's how to make the process foolproof. Before you run the Network Setup Wizard the first time, insert a flash drive into your computer's USB port. If you let the wizard pick your password — the encryption key — it'll automatically save it on the flash drive. Then you can remove the flash drive and insert it into your router and the other computers on your network. No more mistakes.

Slam the door on Wi-Fi invaders

Ever notice your computer can "see" the wireless network your neighbor is running? Maybe you've even accidentally clicked into her network, thinking it was your own. That happens when people don't secure their wireless networks.

A Wi-Fi network can broadcast up to 300 feet from the router. Even if you like your neighbors, it's better to keep your network to yourself. Anyone who taps into your network could view and alter files on your computer. They can slow down your Internet connection, and they could even read your e-mails or intercept secret passwords. Worse, a stranger parked on your street with a laptop could use your network for illegal purposes.

Keep your Wi-Fi from advertising itself by changing the Service Set Identifier (SSID). This is a code the router sends out that tells its make and model. Keeping the default SSID makes it easier for hackers to break into your system. Changing the SSID is done differently on various routers, but it's typically performed using an online help system. You'll probably go to your router manufacturer's configuration Web page and make changes there. See your router's setup instructions for details.

For information on safely connecting to a wireless network in a public place, see page 19 in the *Everything laptop* chapter.

chapter 6

Get to know your XP desktop

"If GM had kept up with technology like the computer industry has, we would all be driving $25 cars that got 1,000 MPG.**"**

Bill Gates

Tidy up desktop clutter

Icons, those tiny pictures on your desktop, can simplify your life — but just like clutter in your house, icons on your desktop can get out of hand fast. An icon is just a doorway that opens windows, programs, folders, and files. Nearly every time you create a document or install a new program, Windows creates another icon. Soon enough, you'll have to do a little housekeeping.

1. Right-click on the desktop and choose ARRANGE ICONS BY from the shortcut menu that appears.

2. Click on SHOW DESKTOP ICONS to erase the check mark. All those icons should vanish. To bring them back, simply place a check mark next to SHOW DESKTOP ICONS again.

Example of a desktop icon

Here, you can also arrange your icons in neat, equally spaced groups (AUTO ARRANGE) by NAME or date (MODIFIED), and even schedule Windows to delete icons you haven't used in a while (RUN DESKTOP CLEANUP WIZARD). Now that's a cleaning service.

For information on creating shortcuts, see page 106 in the *Organize files & folders* chapter.

4 fast ways to delete files

Keeping your computer clean is a whole lot easier than keeping your house clean, especially when Microsoft gives you so many ways to delete old files. Each sends the item to the RECYCLE BIN, your computer's trash can.

✦ Single-click on the item you want to trash and press DELETE on your keyboard.

✦ Right-click on the item and choose DELETE from the short-cut menu that appears.

✦ Single-click on an item in a window, click on the window's FILE menu, and choose DELETE.

✦ Drag and drop the item into the RECYCLE BIN.

You can skip the RECYCLE BIN entirely and permanently zap a file from your computer's memory. Just press the SHIFT key while deleting an item. Unlike putting it in the RECYCLE BIN, which acts as a temporary holding tank, shift-deleting a file gets rid of it for good. Use the power wisely.

Recycle Bin icon

Rescue files from your Recycle Bin

Oops, you accidentally erased an important file! Don't panic. Windows makes it easy to recoup your losses. To rescue a deleted file, double-click on the RECYCLE BIN to open it. Then you can either:

◆ Right-click on the item you want to bring back and choose RESTORE from the shortcut menu.

◆ Single-click on the item and select RESTORE from the FILE menu.

◆ Single-click on the item and choose RESTORE SELECTED ITEM from the task pane on the left.

◆ Drag the item out of the RECYCLE BIN and back onto your desktop.

Restoring a file has a major advantage over dragging it to the desktop. RESTORE returns it to its original location on your computer, which saves you the trouble of moving it there yourself.

The RECYCLE BIN is a lot like the garbage can in your kitchen. You have to "take out the trash" manually by emptying the bin, just like you would at home. In your computer's case, that means one of three things:

◆ Right-click on the RECYCLE BIN and choose EMPTY RECYCLE BIN from the shortcut menu.

◆ Double-click on the bin to open it in a window. Then choose EMPTY THE RECYCLE BIN under RECYCLE BIN TASKS on the left.

◆ Click on a specific item inside the bin window and press DELETE on your keyboard.

Emptying the trash may seem like a hassle, but it's really a built-in safety feature. It makes rescuing files much easier if you accidentally delete them, because they aren't really gone.

Boost memory without spending a dime

Save your cash for retirement, not a new computer. You can get more hard drive memory, and more mileage out of an old computer, by shrinking the RECYCLE BIN.

By default, the RECYCLE BIN eats up a whopping 10 percent of your hard drive space. That steals 2 gigabytes (GB) of memory from a tiny 20 GB hard drive. The larger your drive, the more memory the bin gobbles up. The problem is, you may need this space, especially if you have an older computer with a small hard drive. Luckily, you can get more memory by changing the amount Windows sets aside for the RECYCLE BIN.

1. Right-click on the RECYCLE BIN on your desktop and choose PROPERTIES from the shortcut menu.

2. Drag the slider right or left to change the size of the bin.

Some experts recommend reducing the bin to only 1 or 2 percent of your hard drive. Keep in mind, the RECYCLE BIN automatically starts emptying itself when it hits its maximum capacity. Once it empties a file, you may not be able to retrieve it. If you enjoy the safety net the bin provides, you may want to set the capacity higher.

Act fast to bring back deleted files

Lottery tickets, wedding rings, checks — when people accidentally throw away important items, they end up digging through the dumpster. You may sympathize if you empty your RECYCLE BIN only to realize you've lost important files. Have no fear. As long as you don't save anything else to your computer, you can retrieve those files — without smelling like a dumpster.

As soon as you realize your mistake, hold everything. Don't download, install, run, or even save any programs or files to your hard drive. Instead, head to Web sites like these for free software to rescue those files.

OfficeRecovery.com	www.officerecovery.com
SnapFiles	www.snapfiles.com

Go to OfficeRecovery.com and click on FREEUNDELETE. Or visit SnapFiles' home page and navigate to HANDY PROGRAMS TO PUT ON A USB DRIVE, then click on RESTORATION.

Download and install the software on a USB flash drive or separate hard drive, if you have one, and run it from this location. Do not download or install it on your computer's hard drive. If you want to head off potential problems, download and install the software now, then burn it to a CD or DVD. This way, you'll have it handy should disaster strike.

Move Taskbar to meet your needs

The Taskbar doesn't have to sit at the bottom of your screen. You can move or even hide it while you work. Right-click on the Taskbar, then click on LOCK THE TASKBAR in the shortcut menu to remove the check mark beside it. Now you can drag the Taskbar to the top, left, or right of your screen.

To make it disappear like the lady in a vanishing act, right-click on the Taskbar and choose PROPERTIES from the shortcut menu. Under the TASKBAR tab, put a check mark next to AUTO-HIDE THE TASKBAR. Click on OK and watch the little blue strip magically melt away. Simply hover your cursor where it vanished to make it reappear.

Start button   *Quick Launch*   *Notification Area*

For information on how the Taskbar helps manage multiple windows, see page 86 in the *Navigating know-how* chapter.

Clean up your desktop with Quick Launch

Shortcuts on your desktop can get out of hand — fast. Luckily, the Taskbar offers a clutter-cutting solution. Quick Launch is a special toolbar you can add to the Taskbar, and it's a handy spot for the short-cuts you normally keep on your desktop.

First, unlock the Taskbar. Then right-click on it, point to TOOLBARS, and click on QUICK LAUNCH to put a check beside it.

✦ To add a shortcut icon, drag it from your START menu, desktop, or any open window and drop it into the Quick Launch area.

✦ Tidy up this toolbar by deleting shortcuts you never use. Right-click on a shortcut icon and choose DELETE from the menu that appears. Deleting the icon doesn't delete the file or program, only the shortcut that leads to it.

✦ Make those tiny icons bigger if you find them hard to see. Right-click on an empty area in the Quick Launch toolbar, point to VIEW, and click on LARGE ICONS.

✦ Enlarge the Quick Launch toolbar if some of your shortcuts are hidden. Grab the dotted "handle" and drag it to the right to expand Quick Launch, or to the left to shrink it.

Open Web sites and folders from Taskbar

Three special tools can keep the Web sites and documents you use regularly at your fingertips. Right-click on an empty spot on the Taskbar and point to TOOLBARS in the shortcut menu. Those with a check mark already appear on your Taskbar. To add a toolbar, like the following examples, click on one to place a check beside it. You can also turn any folder into a toolbar by dragging and dropping it onto the Taskbar.

✦ DESKTOP toolbar. This handy item lets you open things on the desktop from your Taskbar, no matter what windows you have open or what program you're in.

◆ LINKS toolbar. Try this for fast access to your favorite Web sites in Internet Explorer. You can also create links to programs, files, and folders by dragging their icon to the LINKS toolbar.

Shed light on hidden icons

You have hidden icons lurking on your Taskbar. Like magic, you can make them vanish and reappear with a wave of your mouse. The Notification Area on the Taskbar contains a tiny arrow pointing to the left. Click on it, and it expands to show you more icons for programs and tools.

Notification Area of Taskbar

Some of these will be used often, like the volume control. Others, like fax software, you may never use. Keep this area tidy by right-clicking on the Taskbar, selecting PROPERTIES, and putting a check mark next to HIDE INACTIVE ICONS. Now, the Notification Area will automatically hide an icon if you don't use it for awhile.

You can banish them manually, too. In this same dialog box, click on the CUSTOMIZE button and scroll through the list of programs and icons. Each item has a drop-down list. Here, you can choose to ALWAYS HIDE the icon or HIDE WHEN INACTIVE. You may want to see a few icons, like the volume control, all the time so you can open them quickly. Change these to ALWAYS SHOW.

For information on changing the volume, see page 342 in the Audio magic chapter and page 74 in the *Control panel: customize your PC* chapter.

Never miss another Daylight Saving switch

Every year, you have to reset all your clocks — the bedside alarm, the microwave, the stove, and the car, just for starters.

Your computer, however, is the one clock you may never have to set again.

Double-click on the time displayed on the Taskbar to open the DATE AND TIME PROPERTIES dialog box. Under the TIME ZONE tab, put a check mark next to AUTOMATICALLY ADJUST CLOCK FOR DAYLIGHT SAVING CHANGES.

If you get nostalgic for the old days when you had to set all your clocks by hand, Windows lets you do that, too. Select your time zone from the TIME ZONE tab. Under the DATE & TIME tab, click on the correct day and select the current month. Click inside the TIME box to type in the time.

Better yet, let Windows figure out the correct time for you.

Under the INTERNET TIME tab, put a check mark in the box beside AUTOMATICALLY SYNCHRONIZE WITH AN INTERNET TIME SERVER. Choose a server from the drop-down list and click on UPDATE NOW.

Simplify Start from the get-go

Your START menu may look so crowded it doesn't make sense. Bring order to the chaos and make your favorite files and programs easier to find. Click on the START button at the left end of your Taskbar.

Your START menu has separate areas for pinned items, recently used programs, Windows components and files, and the main program list.

Start whipping this menu into shape. Right-click on the START button and choose PROPERTIES from the shortcut menu. Under the START MENU tab, click CUSTOMIZE START MENU. From here you can:

Enlarge your icons. Click on the GENERAL tab and choose LARGE ICONS.

Click less, scroll more. Some items in the START menu, such as CONTROL PANEL, act like links. You have to click on them to open them, and then they open in a different window. Change this under the ADVANCED tab. Find the item you want to change in the START MENU ITEMS list and select DISPLAY AS A MENU.

For information on the Control panel, read stories in the *Control panel: customize your PC* chapter starting on page 60.

Clear the clutter. You can even delete these items using this list. Choose DON'T DISPLAY THIS ITEM.

Adjust number of programs. Maybe your list of recent programs is getting too long for comfort. Under the GENERAL tab, raise or lower the number of recent programs that appear in the START menu.

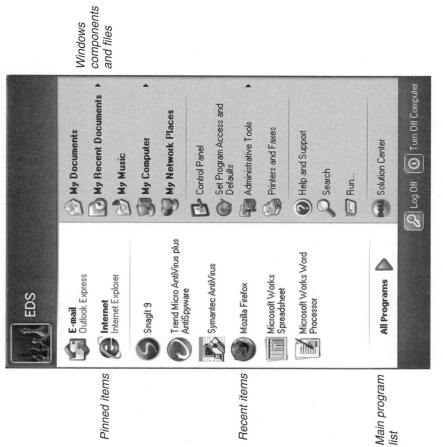

Pinned items

Recent items

Main program list

Windows components and files

Pin your favorite programs for easy finding

Think of the Pinned area of the START menu like a bulletin board. Here, you can tack up your favorite programs and get to them quickly, without rooting around in the ALL PROGRAMS list. Pinned items appear in the upper left part of the START menu.

✦ Pin up more applications by right-clicking on a program in the ALL PROGRAMS list and choosing PIN TO START MENU.

✦ Delete those you don't need by right-clicking on the pinned item and selecting UNPIN FROM START MENU.

Tame program list with a few quick clicks

Reign in those runaway programs by changing some simple settings in your START menu.

Restore order. Neat freaks rejoice. You can alphabetize the program list in a snap. Point at the ALL PROGRAMS menu to open it and right-click anywhere inside. Choose SORT BY NAME from the shortcut menu and — presto — get instant order.

Remove icons. Pare down a crowded list by right-clicking the icon and choosing DELETE or REMOVE FROM THIS LIST from the shortcut menu that appears.

Add your own. Find the icon of the item you want to add and drag it on top of the START button.

chapter 7

Control panel: customize your PC

❝I think it's fair to say that personal computers have become the most empowering tool we've ever created. They're tools of communication, they're tools of creativity, and they can be shaped by their user.❞

Bill Gates

Easy switch to Classic view

Microsoft likes to switch things up in Windows every once in awhile. It's not an effort to confuse you. It's an attempt to make Windows easier to use.

Take the Control Panel. In older operating systems, it looked like a long list of cryptic icons. The people at Microsoft realized new computer users might feel overwhelmed, so the new XP Control Panel houses the same information as before but is easier to use. To open it, click on the START button and choose CONTROL PANEL from the START menu. A window should open that looks a lot like the following example.

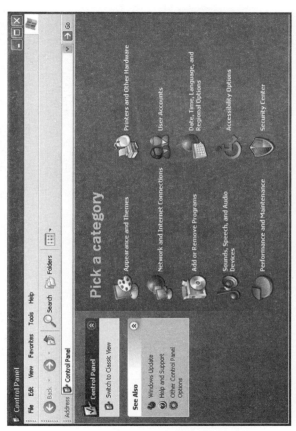

Control panel: Category view

In the Category View, Windows gives you 10 topics to choose from, along with some suggestions on the left side in the task pane. You can click directly on a job in the task pane or click on an icon.

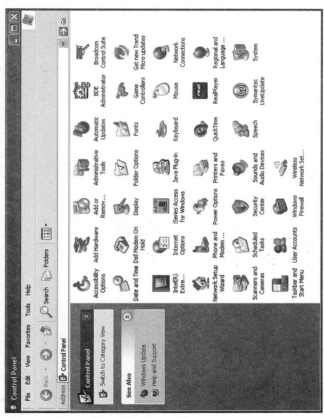

Control panel: Classic view

Maybe you're a creature of habit and dislike the fancy new look of the CONTROL PANEL. You can switch back to Classic view in the blink of an eye just by clicking on SWITCH TO CLASSIC VIEW in the task pane.

Even though the two views are organized differently, they house the same information and controls. Use this key to figure out how the Classic view programs are organized by Category.

Category name	Classic programs
Appearance and Themes	Display; Taskbar and Start Menu; Folder Options
Network and Internet Connections	Internet Options; Network Connections; Network Setup Wizard; Windows Firewall; Wireless Network Setup Wizard
Add or Remove Programs	Add or Remove Programs
Sounds, Speech, and Audio Devices	Sounds and Audio Devices; Speech
Performance and Maintenance	Administrative Tools; Scheduled Tasks; Power Options; System
Printers and Other Hardware	Add Hardware; Keyboard; Mouse; Game Controllers; Phone and Modem Options; Printers and Faxes; Scanners and Cameras
User Accounts	User Accounts
Date, Time, Language, and Regional Options	Date and Time; Regional and Language Options
Accessibility Options	Accessibility Options
Security Center	Automatic Updates; Security Center; Windows Firewall; Internet Options

Take a peek at Vista Control Panel

Vista isn't so different from XP, with a few notable exceptions. Click on the START button in Vista and select CONTROL PANEL. You'll notice an explanation below each icon in the CONTROL PANEL window. No more wandering around trying to find the setting you need. Vista takes away the mystery by telling you upfront which tasks and settings fall under each icon.

Some old XP categories got a name makeover to make them sound less cryptic. For instance, the old ACCESSIBILITY OPTIONS category is now known as EASE OF ACCESS. Similarly, APPEARANCE AND THEMES became APPEARANCE AND PERSONALIZATION.

You'll even see a couple of new categories. Microsoft has tried hard to make the CONTROL PANEL easier for you to figure out and move around in.

The old categories PRINTERS AND OTHER HARDWARE and SOUNDS, SPEECH, AND AUDIO DEVICES now live under one roof in the new Vista category HARDWARE AND SOUND.

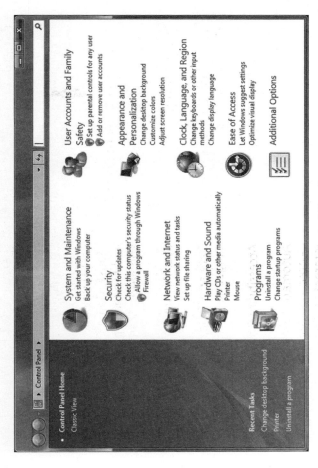

Vista Control Panel

If the changes confuse you more than the old CONTROL PANEL did, or if you yearn for the days of XP and Windows 98, just click on CLASSIC VIEW in the top left of the window.

Get creative and design your own desktop

Tired of staring at that boring green hill on your desktop? There's good news — Windows lets you pick your own background, whether it's a solid color that's easy on the eyes, a pre-loaded picture, or one of your own photos.

Just like the wallpaper behind your living room furniture, the wallpaper on your desktop acts as a decorative backdrop for everything you do. And like your living room wallpaper, you're bound to get tired of staring at it sooner or later. Thankfully, the desktop version is easier to change.

1. Click on APPEARANCE AND THEMES in the CONTROL PANEL.

2. Open the DISPLAY PROPERTIES dialog box by choosing CHANGE THE DESKTOP BACKGROUND under PICK A TASK.

3. Under the DESKTOP tab, scroll through the BACKGROUND list. As you click on each one, the tiny computer icon changes to show you what that wallpaper would look like.

4. When you find the right fit, simply click on the APPLY or OK button.

Maybe you're tired of wallpaper altogether and want to go with a nice, solid paint color. In that case, click on NONE in the BACKGROUND list. Then choose a desktop color under the COLOR drop-down menu, and voila — you have a calming place to rest your eyes.

Personal photos make the best backgrounds of all. Turn your favorite pictures of pets, grandkids, or faraway places into wallpaper.

Under the DESKTOP tab, click on the BROWSE button and mouse around your folders until you find the perfect photo. Any image can become wallpaper as long as the file ends with .bmp, .gif, .jpg, .png, .dib, .htm, or .html.

Create lively themes for Windows XP

XP only seems to give you two choices of themes — boring and more boring. It's a well-kept secret that you can hunt up more exciting ones, changing the look of everything from your desktop to your cursor.

The theme is the entire look of your computer — the size and shape of letters and cursors; color schemes of windows, menus, and dialog boxes; pictures used for icons; and the desktop wallpaper.

Make an instant switch. You can change the look of all these items at once by right-clicking on your desktop and choosing PROPERTIES. This will take you to the DISPLAY PROPERTIES dialog box. Select the THEMES tab and choose a new one from the THEME drop-down list.

The tiny computer icon lets you preview the new theme before you apply it. However, XP only comes loaded with two — not enough variety for a wild-and-crazy computer user like you. Luckily, you can satisfy your creative side with more themes on the Internet.

Surf for something special. Don't bother choosing MORE THEMES ONLINE from the drop-down list. This takes you to a now-defunct Web site, since Microsoft no longer sells themes for Windows XP. That's right — sells. Some cost money, while others are free. Instead, check these sites for interesting themes.

WinCustomize	www.wincustomize.com
customize.org	customize.org
Object Desktop	www.objectdesktop.com

Be sure to scan any downloads for viruses to help keep your computer safe.

For information on virus-free downloading from the Internet, see page 151 in the *Security matters* chapter.

Bigger icons for easy clicking

Those tiny icons can be hard to click on. If you're tired of opening one thing when you meant to open another, XP offers a way to make icons bigger everywhere in *Windows*.

First, you may need to change the scheme. Click on the APPEARANCE tab and select the WINDOWS CLASSIC STYLE scheme from the WINDOWS AND BUTTONS drop-down list. The regular XP scheme won't let you make the changes you're about to attempt.

Next, click on the ADVANCED button to open the ADVANCED APPEARANCE box. Choose ICON in the ITEM drop-down list and boost the SIZE number beside it.

You can make lots of neat changes here, like increasing the font size just on icons, menus, tool tips, or dialog boxes without changing it everywhere in the operating system. You can even choose different colors for each item.

Once you set everything the way you like it, you can save it as your own theme. Click on OK and close the ADVANCED APPEARANCE box. Back under the THEMES tab, click on SAVE AS and type the name of your new theme.

Guard against prying eyes

Lock your screen saver to keep strangers out while you're away. Password protecting it adds another layer of security to your computer. You can walk away knowing no one else can access your files or see what's on your screen while you are gone. Setting up this feature is a snap.

1. Open the DISPLAY PROPERTIES dialog box and click on the SCREEN SAVER tab.

2. Place a check mark in the box beside ON RESUME, DISPLAY WELCOME SCREEN.

From now on, every time you wake your computer out of screen saver mode, it will ask for your password before letting you back in.

> To wake your computer out of screen saver mode, bump the mouse. Clicking it or pressing a key might accidentally trigger a computer command.

You can pick a new screen saver under this tab, too. Choose one from the SCREEN SAVER drop-down list and watch the preview appear on the tiny computer icon above.

These come pre-loaded with XP, but you can also make your own. Create a slideshow from your favorite photos by selecting MY PICTURES SLIDESHOW from the SCREEN SAVER drop-down list. Next, click on the SETTINGS button.

Here, you can change how fast the photos change, how large they appear on-screen, and which photos the computer uses. Click on the BROWSE button to select a different folder of pictures on your hard drive.

Scrap screen saver to save money

Most monitors no longer need a screen saver to protect them. Now those moving images are mostly a decoration — an expensive decoration, since they can gobble up a surprising amount of electricity.

Old cathode ray tube (CRT) monitors that resemble televisions need screen savers to prevent phosphor burn. Otherwise, a still image could burn itself onto the screen if left up for too long. But those monitors are made of a different material than newer, liquid crystal display (LCD) monitors. These flat screens don't get phosphor burn.

Fun as they are, scrapping the screen saver may be a painless way to lower your utility bill. Using one can eat up more energy than not, particularly since energy-saving features in Windows may not work if the screen saver is running.

For information on saving energy with your computer, see page 137 in the *Smart shutdown* chapter.

Make things bigger in the blink of an eye

Tired of squinting at tiny icons and labels? It's time to take action by changing your screen resolution. Generally, lowering the resolution makes words and objects bigger on-screen, while raising it shrinks them.

To adjust it, open the DISPLAY PROPERTIES dialog box and click on the SETTINGS tab. Then grab the little lever under the heading SCREEN RESOLUTION and drag it left.

The preview area above shows you how words and windows will look with the new resolution. Keep adjusting it until you find the right balance between screen size and readability.

Sometimes this trick doesn't work very well on flat-screen, LCD monitors, such as laptops. Lowering the resolution may actually make objects and text look blurry. If that happens with your computer, try bumping up the resolution.

Cut colors to increase speed

Color depth is a fancy term for the number of colors your screen can show at one time. Photos and graphics look best at higher settings but all that color sucks up memory. And if you have an older computer, memory may be in short supply.

Freeing up more of it can considerably speed up computing. Setting your color depth on the highest number may give you great graphics but slow your computer to a crawl. Find the perfect balance of beauty and speed by choosing the right color depth for your computer.

Flip to the SETTINGS tab in the DISPLAY PROPERTIES dialog box, and click on the drop-down list under COLOR QUALITY. Set the color depth higher if you view lots of photos but reduce it to MEDIUM (16 bit) if you're trying to maximize speed.

While LOW (8 bit) — if your computer has that setting — may seem like a better choice for boosting performance, it will make photos look blotchy. The MEDIUM (16 bit) setting is a good compromise.

Tame hard-to-read type

XP offers a slick solution for blocky, hard-to-read words. ClearType sharpens the outlines of letters for easier reading, especially on LCD monitors such as flat-screens and laptops.

It's turned on by default in Windows Vista, but you have to switch it on manually in XP.

1. Open the DISPLAY PROPERTIES dialog box and click on the APPEARANCE tab.

2. Click on the EFFECTS button to open a new box.

3. Put a check mark in the box beside USE THE FOLLOWING METHOD TO SMOOTH EDGES OF SCREEN FONTS, then select CLEARTYPE from the drop-down list below.

Microsoft says you'll get the best results from ClearType by setting your color depth to HIGH (24-bit) or HIGHEST (32-bit).

Still having a hard time reading words on the screen? Try enlarging the letters. In the APPEARANCE tab, click on the drop-down list under FONT SIZE and choose LARGE FONTS or EXTRA LARGE FONTS. This changes the font size in the operating system but not within programs.

Spend less time and cash on printing

Two simple changes can save you time and money — speeding up your printer, while using less ink.

1. Choose PRINTERS AND OTHER HARDWARE in the CONTROL PANEL window.

2. Click on VIEW INSTALLED PRINTERS OR FAX PRINTERS under PICK A TASK.

3. Click once on the printer you want and choose SELECT PRINTING PREFERENCES in the task pane.

4. Flip to the PAPER/QUALITY tab in the PRINTING PREFERENCES dialog box. Select DRAFT in the QUALITY SETTINGS area and BLACK & WHITE in the COLOR area.

Draft-quality printing uses less ink and helps documents print faster, while choosing black and white instead of color will keep you from wasting expensive color ink on everyday print jobs.

Changing these settings through the CONTROL PANEL changes them for all the documents you print, but you can switch them back for individual print jobs.

For instance, maybe you need to print a batch of high-quality, colorful invitations. When you're ready, choose PRINT from the FILE menu while you have the document open. You'll get a print dialog box.

The Microsoft Trouble-shooter program can help solve most of your printing problems. Click on a blank area in the PRINTERS AND FAXES window, then choose TROUBLESHOOT PRINTING from the task pane on the left.

Click on PROPERTIES. Here you can specify color printing and high quality only for those invitations, and the changes you make here won't carry over to all your other print jobs.

Never lose another pointer

What's the point in having a pointer if you can never find it? One powerful dialog box offers all the options you need to make that little arrow easier to see.

In the CONTROL PANEL, click on PRINTERS AND OTHER HARD-WARE. Then click on the MOUSE icon below PICK A CONTROL PANEL ICON. This opens the all-important MOUSE PROPERTIES dialog box.

In the POINTERS tab, you can choose any imaginable combination of pointer size and color by picking something to CUSTOMIZE and selecting a SCHEME from the drop-down list. Certain schemes, like those marked EXTRA LARGE, will make the pointer easier to see on-screen.

But the real help comes from the POINTER OPTIONS tab. Try making these adjustments if you have trouble following or finding the pointer on your screen.

◆ Slow down the pointer speed under MOTION, so your eyes can follow it more easily as it moves.

◆ Put a check mark in the box beside DISPLAY POINTER TRAILS. This pins a "tail" to the moving pointer to help you track it. Adjust the trail's length to meet your needs.

◆ Check the box that reads SHOW LOCATION OF POINTER WHEN I PRESS THE CTRL KEY. Now, if that sneaky little pointer seems to disappear, you can scare it up by pressing the CTRL key on your keyboard.

For information on making your cursor easier to spot, see page 94 in the *Accessibility options work for you* chapter.

Minimize your mouse time

Spend less time chasing your mouse around with the Snap To feature. This nifty feature makes your cursor jump to the default button in every box, a boon if you have trouble steering your pointer to tiny buttons.

Click on the POINTER OPTIONS tab in the MOUSE PROPERTIES dialog box, then place a check mark next to AUTOMATICALLY MOVE POINTER TO THE DEFAULT BUTTON IN A DIALOG BOX.

This new setting may take some getting used to, but in the end, it can save you time and frustration.

Make your mouse fit for a lefty

Finally, something made for southpaws. It may be a right-handed world, but Windows gives lefties a hand by customizing the mouse for them. That's important, because instructions that tell you to right-click here or double-click there won't work if you're trying to mouse left-handed.

Wind your way to the MOUSE PROPERTIES dialog box from the CONTROL PANEL. Once there, click on the BUTTONS tab and put a check mark beside SWITCH PRIMARY AND SECONDARY BUTTONS. Click on OK, and you're ready for left-handed mousing action.

✦ You can also adjust how fast you have to click the mouse to produce the double-click effect that opens icons. For people with arthritis, slowing down the double-click speed can make mousing a lot less frustrating. Drag the lever under DOUBLE-CLICK SPEED to the left. Practice by double-clicking the folder icon to the right until you find the perfect speed.

✦ ClickLock, on the other hand, allows you to drag items or highlight text without holding down the mouse button. Instead, you click the mouse once to turn it on and again to switch it off. Click on the SETTINGS button in the

CLICKLOCK area to set how long you must hold down the mouse to turn on this feature.

Fine tune your settings with ease

Tweak UI literally helps you "tweak" XP to get it just the way you like it. This small but mighty program lets you skip the hassle of wrestling with Windows to fine-tune all sorts of settings, including the START button, Taskbar, and desktop.

You can download this free program from the Microsoft Web site at **www.microsoft.com**. Type **TWEAKUI** into the search field on the Web site and click on MICROSOFT POWERTOYS FOR WINDOWS XP in the results. Scroll down to TWEAK IU on the right side of the page.

You'll find more information about Internet basics, Freeware, and downloading and installing programs later in this book.

Fulfill your need for more speed

XP is packed with cool visual effects and lots of pretty graphics. Good thing, because you need something to stare at while waiting for the computer to start. In fact, all those nice visuals may be the reason your machine runs slowly. Try turning them off to speed things up.

Open the CONTROL PANEL, click on PERFORMANCE AND MAINTENANCE, and choose VISUAL EFFECTS. In the PERFORMANCE OPTIONS dialog box you can:

◆ do away with good looks and max out computing speed by choosing ADJUST FOR BEST PERFORMANCE.

◆ let Windows decide how to balance looks and speed by selecting LET WINDOWS CHOOSE WHAT'S BEST FOR MY COMPUTER.

◆ pick which visual effects you can do without and which ones you must have by clicking on CUSTOM.

Silence annoying computer sounds

Nothing gets on your nerves like the constant beeps, pings, and alarm sounds Windows makes — especially when you do something wrong. Luckily, you don't have to live with them. You can turn them off completely or swap them for softer, more pleasant tones.

Click on SOUNDS, SPEECH, AND AUDIO DEVICES in the CONTROL PANEL window. Next, click on the SOUND AND AUDIO DEVICES icon and then the SOUNDS tab in the dialog box that opens.

Under the SOUND SCHEME drop-down list, choose NO SOUNDS to turn off all the nagging noises XP makes. You can also leave some sounds on but turn off others. Click on an event in the PROGRAM EVENTS list and choose a SOUNDS option such as NONE from the drop-down list below. Or, if you prefer, assign it a more pleasant ping.

The VOLUME tab lets you control how loud or soft your music and warning noises are right from the Taskbar. Click to put a check mark next to PLACE VOLUME ICON IN THE TASKBAR. What's more, you can set different volumes for your CD player and computer alerts under the ADVANCED button.

Save custom settings with separate accounts

Now that you've set up *Windows* and the desktop just the way you like them, make sure those settings don't get lost. Give each person who uses your computer their own account to keep them from messing up all your custom changes.

User accounts help Windows identify and verify who you are when you start up the computer. That's important, since Microsoft created XP to allow more than one person to use it. Your spouse or grandkids might want access, too, and every single one of you will want to customize the desktop, folders, and volume a different way. User accounts make it happen.

When each person signs into their own computer account, the settings they change affect only their account — not yours. You keep your wallpaper, screen saver, pointer size, screen resolution, and all the other customizations you've spent hours making. This lets each person design their computer environment to suite them, without bothering anyone else.

You already have one account, otherwise you wouldn't be able to start up the computer. Still, it's a good idea to create one for each person.

1. From the CONTROL PANEL, select USER ACCOUNTS and choose CREATE A NEW ACCOUNT.

2. Type a name for the account, like the person's name. Don't include spaces. They cause trouble for some programs.

3. Decide how much power you want to give this person. Experts recommend you assign everyone a LIMITED account, not a COMPUTER ADMINISTRATOR account.

4. Click on the CREATE ACCOUNT button, and the new user is ready to go. Now, hand them this book and help them start computing.

Guard PC against hackers and viruses

Setting up separate accounts for everyone cloaks your computer in another level of safety. You can set up each account so only certain users — namely, you — have the power to download items from the Internet, empty the RECYCLE BIN, and otherwise mess with the heart of your computer. This adds another layer of protection against computer hackers, nasty viruses, and curious grandchildren. XP comes with four types of accounts.

Administrator. The big boss of the computer, Administrators can create, change, or delete any other account; install and remove programs and hardware; and have access to open, change, and delete all the files on a computer. Generally, XP gives the person who installs the operating system an Administrator account, but a computer can have more than one.

Limited. Think of Limited accounts as regular employees. They don't have as much freedom or power as Administrators, but it's enough to get most jobs done. Limited accounts can change their own account information, such as passwords, and use the programs and hardware the Administrator has installed on the computer. They can also create and manage their own files but not other users' files.

Guest. These accounts are made for just that — guests who visit you while on vacation and want to use your computer.

Logging them in under the Guest account saves you the hassle of creating a whole new account for someone who will only use the machine once or twice. They have powers similar to Limited accounts.

Unknown. You will only see an Unknown account if you upgraded to XP from an older operating system, such as Windows 2000.

Experts suggest everyone, including you, use a Limited account for regular computing and only use the Administrator account on rare occasions, like when you need to install new hardware or software. The reason is simple — security. If you accidentally catch a nasty computer virus while logged into a Limited account, only a few files will become infected. But if you catch the virus while logged on as an Administrator, every file and program in the computer can become infected and damaged.

Quick trick to move between accounts

You don't need to log off or restart your computer to go from a Limited account to an Administrative one. You only need to know the Administrator password. Windows XP allows you to move instantly between accounts with a feature called Fast User Switching.

Fast User Switching lets you keep one account running in the background while simultaneously working in another. It's handy if you follow the experts' advice and work from a Limited account most of the time and only use the Administrator account for special purposes.

Say you want to download a software update from the Internet, but the Limited account you're in won't let you. Simply switch to Administrator for a moment, long enough to start the download, then switch back to Limited and keep working. No closing your files or shutting down your computer.

First, turn on Fast User Switching. Open the CONTROL PANEL, select USER ACCOUNTS, and click on CHANGE THE WAY USERS LOG ON OR OFF. Place a check mark beside both USE THE WELCOME SCREEN and USE FAST USER SWITCHING, then click on the APPLY OPTIONS button.

The next time you need to switch accounts, click on the START button and choose LOG OFF. When the LOG OFF box appears, select SWITCH USER, then specify the account you want to open.

Stop prying eyes dead in their tracks

In the electronic Information Age, identity theft is more common than ever. Keep your personal files and financial information under lock and key by creating passwords for each user account.

Aside from guarding financial information saved on your computer, a good account password can keep all your other computer and

Internet passwords from falling into the wrong hands if your computer gets stolen.

For more information on picking a good password, see page 161 in the *Security matters* chapter.

Open USER ACCOUNTS from the CONTROL PANEL, select the account you want to protect, and choose the CREATE A PASSWORD option. Type in your super-secret password, and create a hint in case you forget it later.

The computer will give you the hint whenever you try to sign in with the wrong password, so make sure it's a tip that will help jog your memory.

Consider password protecting the Guest account, too. Windows won't let you turn off the Guest account completely because it uses the account for file sharing.

Leaving it without a password is like locking the rest of your home tight but leaving a ground-floor window wide open.

1. Click on the START button. Point to ALL PROGRAMS, then to ACCESSORIES. Select COMMAND PROMPT to open a new dialog box.

2. Type the words NET USER GUEST <PASSWORD>, but type the new Guest account password in place of PASSWORD.

For information on protecting your files and folders, see page 104 in the *Organize files & folders* chapter.

Memory-proof your passwords

The day may come when you can't remember your account password. Without it, you are completely locked out of your own computer. Don't wait until that day. Create a backup plan now with a Password Reset Disk.

This convenient tool allows you to create a new password if you get locked out of Windows and can't remember your old one — just pop the disk into your computer. XP does not create one automatically when you assign passwords and accounts, so you must do it manually.

Sometimes the Wizard saves your Password Reset file in the wrong place. Don't worry. Look for a file named USERKEY.PSW. Once you find it, drag it onto a floppy disk, flash drive, or blank CD to save it.

1. Log in to the account you want to create a Password Reset Disk for.

2. Insert a floppy disk into your computer's floppy drive, or a flash drive into the USB port.

3. Open the CONTROL PANEL and click on USER ACCOUNTS. Select PREVENT A FORGOTTEN PASSWORD in the task pane on the left. If you're logged in as an Administrator, you'll see all the available accounts. Choose the one you're creating the disk for, then click PREVENT A FORGOTTEN PASSWORD.

4. This launches the Forgotten Password Wizard. Read the instructions and click on the NEXT button.

5. Choose where you want to save the Password Reset file from the drop-down list — a floppy disk (drive A:) or the flash drive (sometimes listed as "Removable disk" or drive E:). Click on the NEXT button.

6. Type the account password in the blank field and click on NEXT. The computer will create and save the Reset file to your disk or flash drive.

7. Once it says PROGRESS 100% COMPLETE, click on NEXT. Read the final instructions on the last page and select FINISH.

8. Remove the disk or flash drive. Label it "Password Reset Disk" and the user account name, then store it in a safe place.

Put it somewhere you will remember. The disk won't help if you forget where you hid it.

Once you create a Password Reset Disk for an account, you'll never have to create another one, even if you change the password. Be sure to create a separate disk for each account.

What to do when you forget your password

Maybe you chose a tricky password to fool potential thieves. Or maybe you bumped your head and lost your memory. Whatever the case, that dreadful day is here — the day you forgot your account password. Never fear. These three tips are guaranteed to get you out of that jam.

Take a hint. Remember that handy hint you set up when you created your password? Now is the time to use it. Click on the question mark that appears next to the box where you usually type your password.

Dig up your Reset disk. OK, so you never got around to creating a hint. No problem. Find your Password Reset Disk and pop it into your computer.

Now, click on the green arrow button next to where you normally enter your password. A small bubble appears with this question — DID YOU FORGET YOUR PASSWORD? Click on the link labeled USE YOUR PASSWORD RESET DISK to open the Password Reset Wizard.

This program will walk you through the process of creating a new password for this account, which will log you on to the computer. Remember to set a new hint while you're at it.

You know you typed your password correctly, but the darn computer doesn't agree. Check to see if your CAPS LOCK key is on. Passwords are case-sensitive, so you must get both the spelling and the case right when you type them.

Depend on an Administrator. So you never created a hint or a reset disk. All is not lost. If you know the password for the administrator account, log on to it.

If not, find someone who does. The Administrator can change any account's password. The trouble is, once that happens you may no longer have access to some files from the old account.

Pick a picture that suits you

You aren't stuck with the account picture XP assigned you. Windows offers lots of pictures to choose from. You can even use one of your own.

◆ Open the START menu and click on the picture beside your account name at the top. This opens the USER ACCOUNTS window with a whole list of XP images. Select one and click on the CHANGE PICTURE button. The new image replaces the old one immediately.

◆ Don't see something you like? Click the link in this window that says BROWSE FOR MORE PICTURES. You can poke around your personal folders until you find one of your own photos to use. Select one and click on the OPEN button to replace the old image.

Shift, show, and hide Vista Sidebar

This new Vista feature is packed with gadgets and cool tools, if you know how to find it. The Sidebar is simply an area on the Vista desktop that houses "gadgets" — mini-programs like a calculator, weather reporter, and stock ticker that run right on your desktop.

You probably see the Sidebar as soon as you log on to Vista. If not, you can open it by clicking on the START button, then pointing to ALL PROGRAMS and choosing ACCESSORIES, then WINDOWS SIDEBAR.

Now you can set it to open automatically whenever you start Vista. Right-click on a blank spot in the Sidebar and select PROPERTIES. In the WINDOWS SIDEBAR PROPERTIES dialog box, put a check mark next to START SIDEBAR WHEN WINDOWS STARTS.

Here, you can also move it from the right to the left side of the desktop. Should the Sidebar ever wear out its welcome, simply close it.

♦ Right-click on a blank area on the Sidebar and choose CLOSE SIDEBAR from the shortcut menu that pops up. This basically hides the Sidebar so you no longer have to see it, but it's still running in the background.

♦ Go down to the Notification Area in the Taskbar and right-click on the Windows Sidebar icon. Then select EXIT from the short cut menu. This quits the Sidebar program completely, so it's not using up memory.

Vista Sidebar

Go crazy with Vista gadgets

Get the weather, stock performance, and even a daily Bible verse delivered directly to your Vista desktop. There's a whole world of gadgets for the Sidebar and adding them is a cinch. Vista comes loaded with some fun and useful gadgets, and you get to choose which ones you want.

Example of a Vista Gadget

Click on + at the top of the Sidebar to open the gadget gallery, a list of all the gadgets installed on your computer. To see a summary of each, select one and click on SHOW DETAILS in the lower left corner of the window. Double-click on a gadget to add it to the Sidebar.

You can find even more gadgets by clicking on GET MORE GADGETS ONLINE in the lower right corner of the gallery window. This spirits you to a Windows Web site where you can look over hundreds of handy gadgets, most of which are free. Download what you want, then double-click on the file on your hard drive to open it and add to your Sidebar.

With all these additions, the Sidebar may get a little crowded. Keep it clean by closing the gadgets you don't need. Hover your pointer over one and click on the X button that appears. You can also drag them off the Sidebar and plunk them down anywhere on your desktop.

A tiny wrench pops up when you hover over a gadget, too. Click on this button to customize your gadgets — for instance, to pick a city for a weather-watching gadget, or specific stocks for a stock ticker.

The Internet giant Yahoo! has created a version of Vista gadgets just for XP. They're called Yahoo! Widgets, and they're not only cute but super-handy. Surf over to the Web site **widgets.yahoo.com** to browse and download these free tools to your XP desktop. You can even build your own right on the site. Remember to scan all Internet downloads with anti-virus software.

chapter 8

Navigating know-how

"One machine can do the work of fifty ordinary men. No machine can do the work of one extraordinary man. **"**
Elbert Hubbard, The Roycroft Dictionary and Book of Epigrams, 1923

Find any file with My Computer

You know they're in there somewhere — those pictures you just saved to your computer. But where on earth did they go? Getting into your hard drive can feel like cracking a safe, unless you know the power of My Computer.

This humble icon is the doorway into your hard drive, where every file, folder, and photo you ever create lives. Click on the START button and select MY COMPUTER on the right-hand side. This opens a window that does just what it says — shows you the contents of your computer, including your:

✦ hard drive (drive C:)

✦ floppy drive, if you have one (drive A:)

◆ CD or DVD drive (usually drive D:)

◆ removable, external hard drive, such as a flash or zip drive (sometimes drive E:)

◆ digital camera or scanner, if you have one hooked up

◆ main document folder for each user account

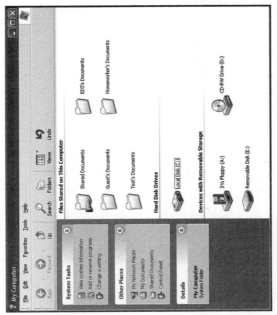

My Computer

Double-click on any of these icons to open them. For instance, open the hard drive, and the window changes to show you everything stored inside it.

XP packs folders within folders. Each time you double-click on an icon, you dig deeper into the layers, until finally you'll find the one folder, document, or photo you're looking for. So don't be afraid. Put on your archeologist's hat and start digging.

Tell windows how you want them to open

Every time you double-click on something inside a window, the new window opens inside the old one. Sure it keeps your desktop clean, but one of these days you'll need to open them separately. Thankfully, XP will let you.

Press the CTRL key on your keyboard while double-clicking on an item and — voila! — it opens in its very own window.

This works fine on a case-by-case basis, but, if you want this effect all the time, click on the TOOLS menu inside MY COMPUTER, and select FOLDER OPTIONS. In the GENERAL tab, mark OPEN EACH FOLDER IN ITS OWN WINDOW, then click on OK.

Cram enough stuff into a folder, and you won't be able to see it all in a regular-size window. You could click on the Maximize button to super-size it, but there's an easier solution. Double-click on the Title bar across the top of any window to make it full-screen, and again to shrink it back to normal.

Hide windows with one quick click

XP gives you a fast way to hide and organize windows before they overwhelm you. Every time you open one, a little button pops up on the Taskbar along the bottom of your desktop. Click on this button once to make the window disappear without closing it, and again to bring it back.

You can do this with any window — a folder, program, or Internet page — because they all show up as buttons on the Taskbar. This lets you see at a glance which windows are open without sifting through them all on-screen. It also makes hiding and restoring them super-simple. Plus, you can switch from one window to another by clicking its button.

Go crazy, however, and you could end up with a dozen open windows on your desktop. Taskbar can handle that, too. When it runs out of button space, it starts grouping windows based on what program they belong to.

Open three Internet windows and one MY COMPUTER folder, and you'll see two buttons appear — one for the three Web pages and one for MY COMPUTER. Clicking on the "grouped" button presents you with a list of condensed windows. Choose one to bring it forward.

Buttons on the Taskbar

Tidy up by tiling

See all your windows at once, without them looking like a hodge-podge. XP can rearrange your windows in nice, neat, side-by-side rows or layered like a cake. Tiling tricks make it simple.

◆ See all of your active (not minimized) windows on-screen at once. Right-click on a blank area of the Taskbar and choose either TILE WINDOWS VERTICALLY or TILE WINDOWS HORIZONTALLY from the menu that appears.

◆ Stack them like a layered cake by right-clicking on the desktop and selecting CASCADE WINDOWS from the shortcut menu.

◆ View two selected windows side-by-side. Click on the first window's button on your Taskbar. Then, press the CTRL key on your keyboard while you right-click on the second window. Another shortcut menu will pop up. Choose TILE VERTICALLY.

Flip through windows fast, instead of clumsily clicking to find the right one. On your keyboard, hold down the ALT key and press TAB to pull up a floating box of icons. Each icon represents one of the windows on your screen. Keep holding down the ALT key and pressing TAB until you highlight the icon you want. Release the keys and that window leaps to the front of the pack.

Cut to the chase with keyboard shortcuts

Quit mousing around. A couple of keystrokes can open menus and execute commands with far less hassle. The secret — underlined letters in the Menu bar and menus themselves.

Every window has a Menu bar near the top with options like FILE, EDIT, VIEW, and TOOLS. Clicking on one of these words opens a drop-down menu full of commands. Your options will change a bit depending on whether you're in a folder, program, or some other type of window.

You've probably noticed by now the underlined letters in both menu names and commands. It's secret code for a keyboard shortcut. Press the ALT key plus the underlined letter on your keyboard to carry out that command.

1. Press ALT plus F to open the FILE menu.

2. Under FILE, notice that the C in CLOSE is underlined, too. You can press ALT plus C to close that window, without having to go through the FILE menu.

This nifty trick works throughout the operating system and in lots of programs. Don't see any underlined letters? Press the ALT key once to make them appear, then again to quit the shortcut mode.

Timesaving Toolbar tips galore

Every window has a Toolbar, a strip near the top with buttons that help you navigate the guts of your computer. The average Toolbar comes furnished with a few basic buttons, like BACK, FORWARD, SEARCH, FOLDERS, and VIEW. However, you can customize your own Toolbars. Start by adding the icons you use most.

1. Right-click on an empty spot on the Toolbar and select CUSTOMIZE from the shortcut menu that appears.

2. Scroll through the list of icons on the left under AVAILABLE TOOLBAR BUTTONS.

3. Select one, click on the ADD button, and watch it move to the right pane under CURRENT TOOLBAR BUTTONS.

4. Click on the CLOSE button. Your newly customized Toolbar now displays your favorite buttons.

You can make lots of changes in this dialog box. Boost the size of Toolbar icons by choosing LARGE ICONS from the drop-down list of ICON OPTIONS.

Or end the guessing game over what each button does. Choose SHOW TEXT LABELS from the TEXT OPTIONS drop-down list.

Change the view to suit you

It may seem like every time you open a window, the items inside look different. One time they're icons, the next they're a confusing list. Tame the jumble by choosing a view and making it stick.

Click on the Toolbar button labeled VIEW, and take turns selecting from the drop-down list until you find a look you like. THUMBNAILS or TILES may be easier on your eyes.

Plus, these views give you the complete name of each icon, so you don't have to guess what it represents. You can switch views from the VIEW menu, too.

Next, tell XP to use this view for all your windows. Set up one window just the way you want it. In that window, open the TOOLS menu and choose FOLDER OPTIONS. Click on the VIEW tab in the dialog box and select APPLY TO ALL FOLDERS.

You can change other window behaviors here, too, but remember — anything you change will affect all your windows.

Surf drives and Web sites from one location

Open any Web site, folder, program, or document right from your window toolbar. Besides buttons, it features a LINKS Toolbar that lets you open specific documents, files, programs, and folders, as well as an ADDRESS bar that opens Internet sites directly from any window.

Address bar   *Links toolbar*

Link up. Right-click on an empty spot on the Toolbar and select LINKS from the shortcut menu. A tiny button will appear on the Toolbar labeled LINKS. Click the tiny black arrows to the right of the button to open your list of links.

You probably have a few things linked already — Web sites, programs, or files Microsoft thinks you can't do without. It's easy to delete them from the LINKS Toolbar, or to add more.

✦ Right-click on a linked item on the list and choose DELETE from the shortcut menu.

✦ Add your own by poking around MY COMPUTER to find the program, file, or folder you want to link. Then simply drag and drop its icon onto the LINKS Toolbar.

Browse. You can browse the Internet from any window. Right-click on an empty space on the Toolbar and choose ADDRESS BAR from the shortcut menu.

Type a Web address into the ADDRESS field, and you're off. You can also surf your hard drive with this handy feature. Click on the down arrow at the right end of the ADDRESS bar to see a list of all the drives and major folders. Select one to see its contents in the window.

90

Get the scoop on the size of your hard drive

Ever wondered how big your hard drive is, or how much memory is left? Find out with the task pane, an area that appears at the left side of every desktop window. It puts often-used commands, such as MAKE A NEW FOLDER, at your fingertips. The options you see will change depending on the window you're in.

The DETAILS section is one of the most useful features in the task pane. Open the MY COMPUTER window and click once on the hard drive icon. The DETAILS pane shifts to show you what size hard drive you have and how much unused memory is left.

The same happens when you click on a folder, file, or group of items. You'll see how many items are in the folder, how much memory they take up, and the last time you saved any changes to them.

Besides getting this basic information, you can also use the task pane to:

◆ jump to MY COMPUTER and other commonly used folders like MY DOCUMENTS or MY PICTURES from any open desktop window, thanks to the links under the OTHER PLACES pane.

◆ use the links under special panes such as FILE AND FOLDER TASKS for common activities without going through menus.

Outsmart the folder maze

You wish My Computer were easier to use. Trying to find the file or folder you need is like looking for the proverbial needle in a haystack. Relax. Windows Explorer takes you anywhere you need to go and helps you navigate the maze of computer files.

Click the FOLDERS button on any desktop window's TOOLBAR, and a folder tree, much like a family tree, will replace the task pane. It's a neat, streamlined way of seeing all the folders on your computer and how they relate to one another.

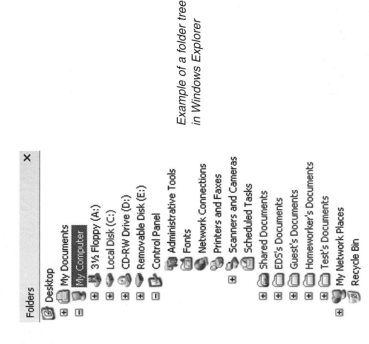

*Example of a folder tree
in Windows Explorer*

Folders that have items in them appear with a + next to them. Click on the + to expand the folder, then again to close it. Digging through files this way is faster than double-clicking your way through window icons, and you won't get lost as easily, either.

Notice when you select a folder in the Explorer bar, you can suddenly see its contents in the window pane on the right. Click on the FOLDERS toolbar button again to return to the task pane view.

Exploring with Vista windows

Vista windows are a different animal from those in XP. For starters, every window in Vista opens with Explorer showing in the left pane.

The task pane, Menu bar, and old Toolbar have been rolled into one super-duper Task Toolbar with some neat, new features. Take time to explore Vista windows.

chapter 9

Accessibility options work for you

❝Assistive technologies are built on the assumption that it's the people who have to adapt to the technology. We tried to reverse this assumption, and make the software adapt to people.❞

Krzysztof Gajos, developer of personalized computer interfaces that adapt to each user's vision and motor abilities

Handy help for typing troubles

Whether you suffer from arthritis or you're recovering from a stroke, keyboards pose special challenges if you have trouble typing. Thankfully, Microsoft XP comes with features to make typing easy.

First, click on the START button and choose CONTROL PANEL. Click on SWITCH TO CLASSIC VIEW in the window's task pane, then double-click on the ACCESSIBILITY OPTIONS icon. Flip to the KEYBOARD tab, and you'll see several check boxes.

STICKYKEYS. These are perfect for people who have a hard time pressing two or more keys at once. With this feature, you can execute tricky keyboard combinations such as CTRL + ALT + DEL by pressing the keys one at a time instead of simultaneously.

Simply press the first command key twice (in this case, CTRL) to turn on STICKYKEYS, then press the other keys singly. Click on the SETTINGS button to tweak how the feature works.

FILTERKEYS. Being heavy-handed with a keyboard can result in lots of repeating letters and misspelled words. Holding down a key for too long makes the letter repeat, while bumping a key makes it show up on-screen.

The FILTERKEYS option tells Windows to ignore quick keystrokes and to slow down the repeat rate.

Click on the SETTINGS button beside this feature to have Windows ignore repeated keystrokes altogether. In this new dialog box, click on the new SETTINGS button to access SLOWKEYS, a helpful feature that controls how long Windows waits to accept a key you pressed.

TOGGLEKEYS. This feature tells your computer to beep at you anytime you press the CAPS LOCK, NUM LOCK, or SCROLL LOCK. This way, you'll know if you accidentally press one of these keys.

Check out the DISPLAY tab while mousing around this dialog box. There, you can fatten-up your cursor so it's easier to see by dragging the WIDTH lever to the right under CURSOR OPTIONS. For information on making the pointer easier to spot, see page 71 in the *Control panel: customize your PC* chapter.

Get around without a mouse

Ditch the mouse and go completely keyboard. With MouseKeys, you can scoot your pointer around on-screen by pressing the number keys on your keyboard.

Key	Pointer action
2	down
4	left
6	up
8	right
5	left-click
-	right-click
+	double-click

Click on ACCESSIBILITY OPTIONS in the CONTROL PANEL, and flip to the MOUSE tab in the dialog box that opens. Put a check mark in the box next to USE MOUSEKEYS to turn on this feature.

Click on the SETTINGS button to adjust how fast the pointer moves, among other things. When you're done, click on the OK or APPLY button and start moving. Here's a quick cheat-sheet to which keyboard keys do what.

Type text with your mouse

On-Screen Keyboard (OSK) may be better than the real thing for people who can't type or have limited use of their hands. It lets you type text with your mouse or by hooking up a simple joystick.

To turn on OSK, click on the START button and point to ALL PROGRAMS. Next choose ACCESSORIES, then ACCESSIBILITY, and select ON-SCREEN KEYBOARD.

A small version of your keyboard will appear on the desktop. Unlike the real one, you can customize it. Notice the Menu bar across the top of OSK. The options here work like menus in a regular window.

95

- Click on KEYBOARD to change the layout. Selecting ENHANCED KEYBOARD, for instance, adds a numbers panel, arrow keys, and so on.

- Make letters larger or bolder if you have a hard time seeing the keys. Click on SETTINGS in the Menu bar and select FONT.

- Pick how you type by clicking a key or hovering over it. Select TYPING MODE under SETTINGS. If you use a joystick instead of a mouse, choose that option here.

> Special keyboard features are great, except when you turn them on without realizing it. And warning beeps don't help if you're hard of hearing. Before you get frustrated, take advantage of the visual warnings Windows offers. Under the GENERAL tab in the ACCESSIBILITY OPTIONS dialog box, you can decide whether you want Windows to make a sound or show you a warning message when you turn on a special feature.

Foolproof tool for special needs

One tool can set up your computer to accommodate any physical challenges you face. The Accessibility Wizard is a small program that asks questions about how large you want text and icons to appear and if you have difficulty using the keyboard or mouse.

Answer all its questions, and the program will set up the computer to suit your special needs, all from one simple place. Open the START menu and point to ALL PROGRAMS. Next, choose ACCESSORIES, then ACCESSIBILITY, and click on ACCESSIBILITY WIZARD.

Shine 'light' on tiny text

Just like the magnifying glass you use to read the newspaper, Windows comes with a magnifier for reading tiny print on-screen.

Click on the START button and point to ALL PROGRAMS. Choose ACCESSORIES, then ACCESSIBILITY, and click on MAGNIFIER.

This opens a small window on your screen which magnifies whatever your pointer or cursor touches. It also opens the all-important MAGNIFIER SETTINGS window, where you can boost the magnification from 2X, the default, up to 9X.

Explore the other options here, too. For instance, tell the program whether to follow your pointer or the text you're typing on-screen.

To enlarge the magnification area, hover your pointer along the border between the normal screen and magnified window.

When the pointer turns into a two-sided arrow, click and drag the edge of the window to make it bigger.

Now you can surf the Web, even if you can't see it. A new program developed at the University of Washington lets people with poor vision, and those who are blind, explore the Internet from any computer. Best of all, it's free, and there's no software to install.

Just head to the Web site **webanywhere.cs.washington.edu.** The software runs from the Web page. That means you can access it from a public library computer, a laptop in an airport, a friend's computer, or your own at home — any machine with a sound card.

Talk to your computer for easy computing

It's time to toss out your keyboard. Inexpensive software can turn your words into computer text and commands with 99-percent accuracy. No, it's not science fiction. It's the next step for people who can't move a mouse or use a keyboard.

Programs such as Dragon NaturallySpeaking are like electronic dictation takers. They turn your words into text or computer commands. They can even surf the Web for you. For about $100, you can buy the basic version of NaturallySpeaking, or the fancier

Preferred edition for $200. Both learn over time, improving the accuracy of their dictation.

Also, they recognize eight different accents, including British- and Spanish-accented English. Spanish, French, and other languages are also available. For more information, visit the Web site **www.nuance.com/naturallyspeaking.**

Keep in mind, dictation programs like this one might not be for you if you have speech problems, need confidentiality, or use a computer in a loud room. But for some people, it may be the perfect solution for going truly "hands free."

Voice recognition for Vista users

Unlike XP, the Vista operating system comes with speech recognition software. Give it a whirl before investing in separate software. You'll need a computer with a built-in microphone or an inexpensive, headset microphone.

Click on the START button and point to ALL PROGRAMS. Choose ACCESSORIES, then EASE OF ACCESS, and click on WINDOWS SPEECH RECOGNITION to get the program going.

Take the tutorial the first time you use it. It teaches you how to phrase your commands, and it will help the program learn your voice. Also, print out the reference card it gives you, because you'll need it later.

chapter 10

Organize files & folders

> **"** Computers are incredibly fast, accurate, and stupid; humans are incredibly slow, inaccurate and brilliant; together they are powerful beyond imagination. **"**
>
> Albert Einstein

Solve the mystery of missing documents

All good documents don't go to heaven, but if you're lucky they do end up in the My Documents folder. If you've forgotten where you stashed your last letter, this is the place to start looking. It houses all the documents, photos, even music you save. Most programs automatically save to this folder, unless you tell them otherwise. You don't have to store your stuff here, but it's a good idea. The My Documents folder:

+ keeps your files separate from programs, so you don't accidentally delete or move programs when working with files.

+ prevents files from cluttering your desktop.

◆ stores your stuff in one place making it easier to find.

◆ makes backups a snap because you only back up one folder.

Click on the START button and choose MY DOCUMENTS to open it, or click on MY DOCUMENTS in the task pane area of most folder windows.

Skip MY DOCUMENTS entirely and go straight to the files you use most. The START menu keeps a running list of the 15 files you opened most recently. Click on the START button, then on an item from the MY RECENT DOCUMENTS list to open it. Don't see the list? Tell Windows to show it. Right-click on the START button and select PROPERTIES. To the right of START MENU, click on CUSTOMIZE. Put a check mark next to LIST MY MOST RECENTLY OPENED DOCUMENTS under the ADVANCED tab.

Find hidden info on files

Each type of file has a different icon — photos look one way, while Word documents look another. But there's a better, more accurate way to tell which type of file you're looking at.

Every document, program, photo, and item in your computer has a file extension, usually a three-letter suffix at the end of its name, such as .doc. Think of them as surnames. The computer uses file extensions to tell what family an item belongs to. Files ending in .doc belong to the Microsoft Word family, while those ending in .htm belong to the Internet Explorer family. Knowing a file's family tells your computer which program it should use to open it.

Windows hides file extensions in an effort to keep things tidy. However, you need to know the extension if you want to change which program opens it. To see the extension:

◆ on all files, click on the TOOLS menu in any folder window, and choose FOLDER OPTIONS. Under the VIEW tab, uncheck

HIDE EXTENSIONS FOR KNOWN FILE TYPES, then click on the OK button.

◆ on particular types of files, flip to the FILE TYPES tab in the FOLDER OPTIONS dialog box. Choose the type of file you want to see extensions for. Next, click on the ADVANCED button and mark the ALWAYS SHOW EXTENSION check box.

◆ one time only on a single file, simply select that file and look in the DETAILS area in the window's task pane.

Rename to maintain order

My Documents, My Computer, My Pictures. Yeesh! If XP's elementary names get on your nerves, put your personal stamp on icons by renaming them.

Right-click on any folder or file — on your desktop, in another folder, or on the START menu — and select RENAME from the shortcut menu. Type the new name, click once outside the icon, and you're set.

Names can be up to 255 characters long, but try to keep them short. Work out a naming system in advance for the types of files and folders you create most often, and stick with it.

Create folders within folders to help organize your filing system. Right-click on an empty spot in the MY DOCUMENTS window, and choose NEW, then FOLDER from the shortcut menu. Type in the new folder's name as if you were renaming it.

No, it's not your eyesight. Some file names are green, while others are blue. Windows XP may automatically compress files that don't get used very often so they take up less space on your hard drive. Compressed files have blue names, while regular, uncompressed files have green. For more information on compressing files to free up memory, see page 118 in the *Keep your PC problem-free* chapter.

Fast, simple way to manage files

You may never see it, but it's there, and it's one of the most powerful tools on your computer. Every time you copy, cut, or paste anything, you use the clipboard. It's like a cork board where you pin words, images, and files while you move or copy them from one place to another. The clipboard lets you make a copy of almost anything — text, drawings, Web addresses — and put it somewhere else. There are so many ways to use this function, you won't believe it.

Cutting, copying, and pasting with computers is faster and less messy than with scissors and glue. In fact, it's the fastest and simplest way people of all ages can modify and improve their files.

> You can name files anything you want. Well, almost anything. Windows won't let you use these nine characters, \ / : * ? " < > |, in the file name.

Copy. This command makes a copy of the original text, image, or file for you to paste elsewhere, without moving the original. Select the icon or highlight the text you want to copy. Click on EDIT in the window's Menu bar and choose COPY in the drop-down menu that opens.

Cut. Unlike copying, cutting removes the highlighted text, image, or file from one location so you can paste it in a new place. Select what you want to cut, then choose CUT under the EDIT menu.

Paste. This takes whatever you copied or cut from the clipboard and tacks it in a new location — minus the glue. Open the folder or document where you want to put the item, and choose PASTE from the EDIT menu. Keep in mind, the clipboard can only hold one item at a time. When you copy or cut something else, it replaces the last item on the clipboard.

More ways to move files and folders

Cutting, copying, and pasting aren't your only options for managing files. You can move them around other ways, too.

- In folder windows, click once on the item you want to move, then click on MOVE THIS FILE in the task pane to choose a destination.

◆ Switch to the Explorer view in a folder window by clicking on the FOLDERS button in the toolbar. Here, you can drag and drop an item in the window on the right into the destination folder on the left, in the Explorer pane.

For more information on the Explorer view and how to navigate Windows Explorer, see page 91 in the *Navigating know-how* chapter.

◆ Open two windows — one showing the item you want to move, and the other showing the place you want to move it to. Then drag the item from one window and drop it into the other.

◆ Highlight text in a document, then drag and drop it from one location to another.

There's more than one way to skin a cat, or in this case, to copy, cut, and paste. Right-click on any highlighted text, image, or icon and choose either COPY, CUT, or PASTE from the shortcut menu that appears. Or try a keyboard shortcut. Highlight whatever you want to move, and press CTRL + C to copy, CTRL + X to cut, or CTRL + V to paste.

Save time moving multiple files

You feel the need, the need for speed. Satisfy it by moving lots of files at once instead of one at a time. Start by selecting, or highlighting, the items.

◆ To select all the files in a folder, or all the text in a document, press the keyboard combination CTRL + A.

◆ To highlight several items in a row, click on the first file to highlight it, then hold down the SHIFT key and click on the last file.

✦ To select scattered files that aren't in a row, simply press the CTRL key as you click on each one. When you finish, release the key. Each file you clicked should still be highlighted.

Once you select all the files you want to move, now's the time to cut, copy, paste, or drag them to their new destination.

Bring order to out-of-control folders

To tidy messy folders, in ICONS view, right-click on an empty spot inside any folder window and point to ARRANGE ICONS BY in the shortcut menu that appears. You'll get even more options to choose from, which vary depending on the type of folder you're in.

Select SHOW IN GROUPS for starters. It's great for folders loaded with lots of different types of files, such as MY DOCUMENTS or MY COMPUTER. Next, choose a category, such as SIZE (size of the file), NAME, or TYPE. Now, all your icons are organized by category under each group heading.

Protect your privacy

Add another layer of security to sensitive files, such as financial information. Protect the contents of any folder from prying eyes by making it private. Only you can access your private folders. No one who signs in under a different account can get to them.

It's a snap. Right-click on the folder you want to protect, and choose SHARING AND SECURITY. Under the SHARING tab, mark the check box labeled MAKE THIS FOLDER PRIVATE. Now this folder, and any folders nested inside it, are private. Consider keeping all your sensitive files in one folder, and save yourself the hassle of hunting through your hard drive marking scattered folders private.

Or, make all your folders and files private with one click. Open MY COMPUTER from the START menu, and double-click on the LOCAL DISK (C:). From here, open the DOCUMENTS AND SETTINGS folder and right-click on the folder with your user name on it. Make it private just as you would any other folder.

There's a small chance you won't see a SHARING tab in the FOLDER PROPERTIES dialog box. That's because hard drives can be formatted as either FAT32 or NTFS, but only NTFS-formatted drives let you privatize files. Find out for sure how yours is formatted. Right-click on MY COMPUTER and select PROPERTIES. Near the top of the dialog box, look for the phrase NTFS or FAT32.

Learn to share with others

The flip side of making some folders private is making others public. Share specific files and folders with other users on the same computer without jeopardizing the security of your private files.

◆ Drop individual documents, photos, folders, or other items right into the SHARED DOCUMENTS folder inside the MY COMPUTER window.

◆ Share specific folders throughout your computer by marking them public. Right-click on the folder you want to share and choose SHARING AND SECURITY. Under the SHARING tab, uncheck the box beside MAKE THIS FOLDER PRIVATE, then click on the OK button.

However you do it, the files you share can be viewed, changed, or deleted by anyone with access to your computer, so don't make them public unless you're sure you want to share.

For information on sharing files online, see page 226 in the *Secrets to safe surfing* chapter.

Spend less time mousing around folders

Shortcuts offer a quick way to open programs, files, and folders on your computer. Shortcut icons look like regular icons, except for a small arrow in their bottom left corner.

Regular icon

Shortcut icon

Double-click on a shortcut icon, and it opens the original item it represents. You can create a shortcut to almost anything in your computer, from nearly anywhere. However, most people keep shortcuts on the desktop for quick access.

To create your own, right-click on the original file, folder, or program. Then choose SEND TO and select a destination such as DESKTOP or MY DOCUMENTS. To plop a shortcut in a more specific spot, press the ALT key on your keyboard while dragging the item to the place you want to put a shortcut.

Shortcuts taking over? Right-click on the shortcut icon and choose DELETE from the menu, or drag it to the RECYCLE BIN. Deleting a shortcut only erases the quick path you created, not the original item.

For more information about adding shortcuts to the START menu or Taskbar, see page 55 in the *Get to know your XP desktop* chapter.

chapter 11

Find stuff on your computer

66 I do not fear computers. I fear lack of them. 99

Isaac Asimov
biochemist and popular science fiction writer

Locate lost files quickly

Cut the hours spent finding lost files by putting the Microsoft Search feature to work.

✦ To start a search in an already-open window, press F3 on your keyboard, the Windows key + F, or CTRL + E.

✦ To dig through a specific folder, such as MY DOCUMENTS or MY COMPUTER, right-click on its icon and choose SEARCH from the shortcut menu. This also launches a new search window.

✦ If you aren't sure which folder to look in, click on the START button and choose SEARCH from the START menu to look through them all.

Windows may ask you what type of file you're looking for. Then you can search by file name, type, or date, among others. The options change depending on which file type you choose. Click on the link USE ADVANCED SEARCH OPTIONS or MORE ADVANCED OPTIONS if you don't see the choices you want.

You may get better results with free search software. These programs run faster than Windows Search and take up less space on your hard drive. Try Everything at **www.voidtools.com** or Windows Search 4.0 at **www.microsoft.com**. In the search bar at the top of the page, type in `Windows Search 4.0`.

Say so long to cartoon characters

XP sends Rover, the courageous search dog, to "fetch" your files when using the Search feature. Fortunately, if you're a cat person, you can send Rover packing.

Open a Search window and click on CHANGE PREFERENCES just above Rover's head. Here, you can choose to go it alone WITHOUT AN ANIMATED SCREEN CHARACTER, or perform searches WITH A DIFFERENT CHARACTER. Pick the latter and Windows offers you more search companions, including Merlin the wizard. Flip through them by clicking on the NEXT or BACK buttons, then choose OK when you're satisfied. Have even more fun by clicking on the character. Select DO A TRICK in the menu that appears, and watch Merlin perform a magic trick or Rover fetch the paper.

Find stuff faster with a few clicks

You could make dinner, do the dishes, and wash a load of laundry all in the time it takes XP to perform a simple search — or so it seems. Speed things up with Indexing.

This feature tells Windows to create a catalog of most, if not all, of the files in your computer. Now when you search for something, Windows finds it with a quick check of the catalog, instead of digging through every item in your computer — a difference that can speed up searches dramatically.

Indexing also gives you more ways to search. You can look for a file by who created it or when it was last opened, saved, or printed, as well as many more options.

Open a Search window and click on CHANGE PREFERENCES. Next, click on WITH INDEXING SERVICE, and select YES, ENABLE INDEXING SERVICE. The first index takes a while to build. Turn it on right before bed and let it run overnight. After that, XP will update the index automatically whenever you aren't using the computer. The biggest downside — how much memory the catalog eats up. If you have a small hard drive or don't find yourself doing many searches, leave indexing turned off.

Vista makes searching simple and fast

Vista gives the Search feature a much-needed face lift. For starters, Search boxes are everywhere in Vista — on the START menu, at the top of every desktop window, and in many Microsoft programs. Turn on the natural language option to search using plain old English by typing phrases such as **MUSIC BY MOZART**. Open a folder window and choose FOLDER AND SEARCH OPTIONS from the ORGANIZE menu. Under the SEARCH tab, put a check mark next to USE NATURAL LANGUAGE SEARCH.

Tired of doing the same search again and again? Next time, save it and save yourself some hassle. After you perform a search, click on FILE in the results window and choose SAVE SEARCH. Name it as you would any new file, and save it someplace easy to reach, like the desktop. The next time you need to run the same search, simply double-click on its icon and press the SEARCH button in the left pane.

chapter 12

Keep your PC problem-free

❝From then on, when anything went wrong with a computer, we said it had bugs in it. ❞

in Time magazine article regarding the removal of a 2-inch-long moth from an experimental computer at Harvard, 1945

Grace Murray Hopper, computer scientist,

Free maintenance at your fingertips

Computers need checkups and tuneups, just like people and cars. Luckily, the XP operating system comes with its own doctors and mechanics. When your computer runs slowly or your hard drive crashes, don't panic. The helpful troubleshooting guide and system maintenance tips you'll find for free in XP will keep your computer in tiptop shape — without costly trips to the PC doctor. Click on the CONTROL PANEL icon in the START menu or the Quick Launch portion of the Taskbar. Then, click on PERFORMANCE AND MAINTENANCE. (If you don't see it, click on SWITCH TO CATEGORY VIEW in the window's task pane.) Here you can:

◆ Add zip to your computer's drive to make it run faster.

◆ Beef up memory by cleaning out junk.

◆ Squish files together to free up more hard drive space.

◆ Create backup copies of your files.

◆ Get new software for your computer, automatically.

The following stories explain how to make the most out of this free housekeeping. So before you call in a maintenance crew, check out these tips from the pros.

Get more memory instantly

Like a messy kid, Windows leaves crumbs and spills behind while doing everyday tasks. Tidying with Disk Cleanup will instantly free up more memory on your hard drive.

Start it up. In the CONTROL PANEL window, click on PERFORMANCE AND MAINTENANCE, then click on FREE UP SPACE ON YOUR HARD DISK to launch Disk Cleanup. If you have more than one hard drive, select the one you want to tidy. The computer will spit out a report telling you how much memory you'll save by letting Disk Cleanup trash unnecessary files.

Pick your targets. Place a check mark next to each type of file you're willing to delete, including TEMPORARY INTERNET FILES and RECYCLE BIN. Experts warn against emptying the DOWNLOADED PROGRAM FILES folder because it usually contains useful items.

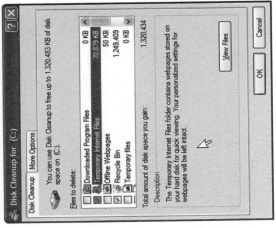

Disk Cleanup dialog box

111

Single-click on a group of files to see a summary in the DESCRIPTION area below, or click on the VIEW FILES button to choose exactly which ones you want to kiss goodbye.

Say goodbye to clutter. When you're ready, click on the OK button to permanently delete them. Remember, Disk Cleanup doesn't just send these files to the RECYCLE BIN. It permanently erases them from your computer's memory. Be sure you don't need them before taking the plunge.

Know when and when not to defrag

Defragging — it's a funny word for cleaning up your slow computer and helping it run at maximum proficiency again. Files are stored like a child's building blocks in the computer's memory. When you create new ones, and move or delete old ones, the computer shuffles the blocks. Eventually, things get messy. The blocks end up scattered around the memory in fragments, which can really slow down computing.

Defragmenting gets your drive in order by restacking all the blocks in nice, neat rows again. It's one of the surest ways to speed up your computer.

Windows keeps track of how much memory you have left on your hard drive. When you reach critically low levels, XP begins sending dire warnings about "low disk space." The fix — click on the warning message to run Disk Cleanup.

1. Close all of your programs and files. Disable your anti-virus software, turn off the screen saver, and empty the RECYCLE BIN.

2. Open the CONTROL PANEL and click on PERFORMANCE AND MAINTENANCE. In the new window, choose REARRANGE ITEMS ON YOUR HARD DISK TO MAKE PROGRAMS RUN FASTER.

3. Click once on the drive you want to defrag.

4. Click on the ANALYZE button. Windows checks the drive to see how the blocks are arranged, and decides whether they are messy enough yet to make rearranging them worthwhile.

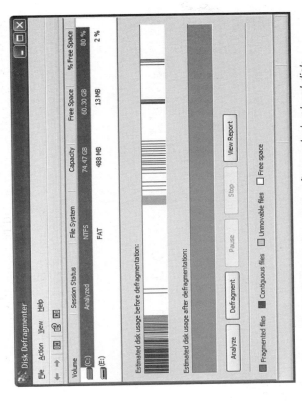

Disk Defragmenter screen after analyzing hard disk

Eventually, a box will pop up telling you whether or not you need to defrag. If so, click on the DEFRAGMENT button in the box and let the computer do its thing.

Defragging can take a long time — in some cases, all day, depending on how messy the drive was. You may want to start the process right before bedtime and let the Defragmenter run overnight. Don't use the computer while it's running. Saving changes to a file during this process will cause the Defragmenter to start all over again. If you just can't wait, click the PAUSE button first. You should never defrag:

◆ during a thunderstorm.

◆ if your hard drive has been acting "sick" lately.

◆ if your laptop is running on a battery. Plug it into a wall outlet, instead.

Enjoy an error-free PC

You've been getting pesky error messages all day. Is it time to call in the maintenance crew? No, because there's one already on your PC. Run the built-in Check Disk program that comes free with Windows XP for a tune-up that will keep your computer in tiptop condition. This tool finds and fixes problems with the hard drive caused by normal wear-and-tear, power surges and outages, voltage problems, and more.

1. Open the START menu and click on MY COMPUTER, then right-click on the hard drive icon.

2. Choose PROPERTIES from the shortcut menu.

3. Under the TOOLS tab, click on the CHECK NOW button.

4. This opens another dialog box. In it, place a check mark next to AUTOMATICALLY FIX FILE SYSTEM ERRORS if you want Windows to try to repair any problems it finds.

5. You can also put a check mark beside SCAN FOR AND ATTEMPT RECOVERY OF BAD SECTORS, and Windows will move files from any bad parts of the hard disk to a good area, as well as cordon off the damaged section so it doesn't store files there in the future.

6. Close all open files and programs, including anti-virus software and anything running in the Notification Area of the Taskbar. Otherwise, Check Disk won't work.

7. Click on START under CHECK DISK OPTIONS to launch Check Disk. Experts recommend scanning for problems every few months to keep your PC running smoothly.

Safeguard files against disaster

Hard drives eventually fail. It's a fact of life. Ask anyone who has spent hours on the phone with tech support or hundreds of dollars at the computer repair shop, and they'll tell you that backups are essential — unless you don't mind losing all of your photos, files, letters, and addresses without warning.

Now there's no more excuse for not creating a backup. XP comes with a tool that automatically copies the contents of your computer and stores them in a safe place.

Your Backup Wizard may balk at saving to a CD or DVD. Get around this hiccup by saving the backup to your desktop. Once completed, insert a blank disk. Open the MY COMPUTER window and drag-and-drop the backup file onto the CD/DVD icon. Or skip the backup process completely by dragging and dropping individual files and folders onto the disk for burning. Next, click on the tiny message that appears on your Taskbar. It reads, YOU HAVE FILES WAITING TO BE WRITTEN TO CD. In the new window, choose WRITE THESE FILES TO CD in the task pane on the left to launch the CD Writing Wizard.

Open the CONTROL PANEL and select PERFORMANCE AND MAINTENANCE, then click on BACK UP YOUR DATA. This launches the Backup Wizard, a tiny program that walks you through the process. You'll be faced with a few choices, but nothing you can't handle.

The What. The Wizard asks what you want to back up — the settings and contents of MY DOCUMENTS or the entire operating system (OS) and all of its programs. Chances are, you still have the software CDs that came with your OS and any programs you installed. If that's the case, you don't need to back them up.

The Where. Next, decide where you want to store these files — on a CD, floppy disk, external hard drive, or elsewhere. Choose that destination from the drop-down list in the Wizard's next screen.

If the destination doesn't appear in this list, click on the BROWSE button. You may get a message saying PLEASE INSERT A DISK INTO DRIVE A:. Just click on CANCEL, and a new window should open. Dig around in it until you find where you want to save your backup. Click on the SAVE button to return to the Wizard screen. The new location should appear under CHOOSE A PLACE TO SAVE YOUR BACKUP. Lastly, click on NEXT and then on FINISH to create your backup.

For more information on restoring backups after a crash, see page 135 in the *Fast fixes you can do yourself* chapter.

Stash backups online

The Internet has changed the way you do lots of things, including backing up important files. If you don't feel like wrestling with the XP Backup tool, Web sites offer another way to safeguard your information.

You can store data from multiple computers and devices in one safe location, plus access your backed-up information from any computer, anywhere. Some sites are mainly for storing files, while others let you share your files with family and friends, sort of like the SHARED folder on your computer. Some are free, although they may charge a fee for storing large amounts of information. Take a look at these storage services recommended by experts.

Windows Live SkyDrive	*skydrive.live.com*
MozyHome	*mozy.com*
Carbonite	*www.carbonite.com*
Box.net	*www.box.net*

Keep computer up-to-date automatically

Avoid crashes, viruses, and frustrating error messages. Simply set up regular "patches" to be downloaded from Microsoft or different manufacturers' Web sites. These patches often cover newly discovered "holes" in XP security, so keeping them up-to-date can go a long way in protecting your PC from viruses and hackers. Having updated software can also help your PC run faster.

Open the CONTROL PANEL and choose PERFORMANCE AND MAINTENANCE. Click on the SYSTEM icon in the bottom of the window, and flip to the AUTOMATIC UPDATES tab. Here, you have several choices about how and when you get updates.

Automatic. Microsoft really wants you to choose this option, because it offers the most protection from viruses, hackers, and malicious software. Your computer will connect to the Microsoft Web site on its own and download any available updates, without ever pestering you.

This works best if your computer is always connected to the Internet through DSL or cable Internet service. You can pick the day and time for these downloads here, too. Since computers run slower while they're installing updates, pick a time like the middle of night.

Delayed. The second choice, DOWNLOAD UPDATES FOR ME, BUT LET ME CHOOSE WHEN TO INSTALL THEM, allows the computer to connect to Microsoft and get updates, but makes it ask you before installing them.

The third choice goes a step further. NOTIFY ME BUT DON'T AUTOMATICALLY DOWNLOAD OR INSTALL THEM does exactly what it says. The computer checks Microsoft for updates and tells you if any are available, but doesn't do anything about them on its own. Instead, a yellow shield with an ! in the center will appear in the Notification Area of your Taskbar. Click on it to download and install your updates.

Off. Choose TURN OFF AUTOMATIC UPDATES, and your computer won't check for updates. It's a bad option if you want to stay protected from the latest bugs and hackers.

Pick your favorite option from this list, and click on the OK button. Be warned — the computer will only notify an Administrator, not someone using a Limited account, that updates are available. So if you choose one of the delayed options, log in as an Administrator often to check for updates.

For information on keeping anti-virus and other software up-to-date, see page 154 in the *Security matters* chapter and page 171 in the *Straight talk about software* chapter.

Enlarge your hard drive for free

Photos and other files can eat up lots of memory. You need more room, but you don't want to splurge on a bigger, better hard drive, right? Now you don't have to. You can create more room on your old one without spending money or getting rid of files.

Compression is the key. Windows XP comes with a tool that squeezes files together so they take up less space on your hard drive. When you open a compressed file, XP expands it to normal size, then shrinks it again when you close it.

Only hard drives formatted a certain way, called NTFS, can compress files. Those formatted using FAT32 cannot. Check yours by opening MY COMPUTER and right-clicking on the hard drive icon. Choose PROPERTIES from the shortcut memory, and flip to the GENERAL tab. If you see the letters NTFS in the FILE SYSTEM area, congratulations. If you see FAT32, you won't be able to take advantage of file compression.

With NTFS compression, you can squish individual files, entire folders, or even your whole hard disk, although if you're worried about slowing down your computer, stick to compressing folders. First, close all open programs and files. Windows can't compress open items.

All at once. To compress your entire hard drive, open MY COMPUTER, right-click on the hard drive icon, and select PROPERTIES. Under the GENERAL tab in the dialog box, place a check mark next to COMPRESS DRIVE TO SAVE DISK SPACE and click on OK.

One at a time. To compress a file or folder, right-click on it and choose PROPERTIES. Under the GENERAL tab, click on the ADVANCED button and put a check mark beside COMPRESS CONTENTS TO SAVE DISK SPACE.

Click on the OK button in this dialog box and the next two that pop up. From now on, the names of compressed files appear in blue, while uncompressed file names are black.

A few more things to remember:

◆ When you copy a regular file and place it in a compressed folder, the computer automatically compresses the file.

◆ On the other hand, when you move that regular file into a compressed folder by dragging and dropping it, the computer leaves it uncompressed.

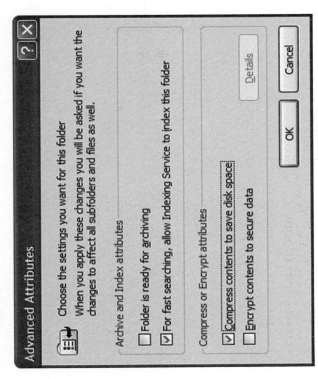

Compressing a single folder

chapter 13

Fast fixes you can do yourself

"Want to make your computer go really fast? Throw it out a window.**"**

Author unknown

Help for hairy PC problems

You're never lost with Windows Help. That's the idea, anyway. Navigating the Help features can get a little sticky, but this guide will help you clear up the confusion.

Open the Help section by navigating to START, then HELP AND SUPPORT. You'll notice several major sections of the Help window, but different computer manufacturers sometimes add slightly different headings.

◆ Common problems, such as security, printing, and Windows basics, are typically covered on the left-hand side of the screen. When you click on one of these topics, you'll open up a more specific list of subtopics. Keep clicking and you may find your problem.

◆ Links to online help tools lead you to REMOTE ASSISTANCE, Customer Support, and other aids.

◆ Utilities, such as SYSTEM RESTORE, WINDOWS UPDATE, and the hardware/software compatibility checker, can be lifesavers.

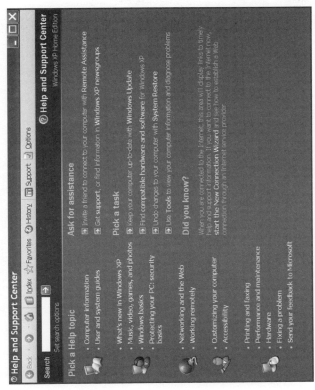

Windows Help and Support Center

If you don't see the topic you need on the main page, you have two other great tools.

Search box. Type a word or phrase into the SEARCH box that relates to the topic you need help with, then click on the green arrow. You'll get three categories of results — click on the category name to see details.

◆ SUGGESTED TOPICS are articles Microsoft developers believe will answer your question.

◆ FULL-TEXT SEARCH MATCHES are articles that contain the words you included in your search.

◆ MICROSOFT KNOWLEDGE BASE contains links to Internet articles and discussion groups that may address your problem. It's only available if your computer is online.

If at first you don't find help, try and try again by altering your search. Click on the SET SEARCH OPTIONS link under the SEARCH box to place limits on your search. You can choose to search only within a certain category of documents, search for an exact phrase rather than separate words, or see more or fewer results.

Index. This handy tool shows you what words and phrases Microsoft uses to describe topics. Click on the INDEX button on the toolbar to open it, and an alphabetical list of Windows Help topics appears.

In the TYPE IN THE KEYWORD TO FIND box, you can enter the first few letters of the item you need help with. Windows scrolls through the INDEX list of terms looking for a match. If you see one that's close, double-click on the link under the main topic heading to open that Help page.

Expert aid a click away

Get help from a real, live pro without ever leaving your home with remote help. You don't even need to have a technician visit. Instead, she can see and control your computer through the Internet, diagnosing problems and helping you fix them on the spot.

Reputable remote services are safe to use, because even though the helper runs your computer using her mouse and keyboard, you can watch your screen, see what's being done, and stop the session if you get nervous about it. Your tech-savvy friend can help, or you can hire an expert to work on your computer problems. But you need software to make this work.

Remote Assistance. This software is part of the *Windows XP* package. The easiest way to invite your friend to help is to send an invitation using WINDOWS MESSENGER. Access it through START, click on ALL PROGRAMS, and then WINDOWS MESSENGER.

Click on the ACTIONS tab and choose ASK FOR REMOTE ASSISTANCE. Then you can send an invitation to your friend, who must agree to help before the remote session can begin. The two of you can talk on the phone while he helps, or you can continue chatting through WINDOWS MESSENGER. You'll disconnect the session when you're done.

CrossLoop. But what if all your friends are computer-challenged? Then you can locate an expert and download free software for remote access at **www.crossloop.com**. As with Remote Assistance, you give up control of your computer only when you're comfortable with the person helping you. There's a list of experts on the CrossLoop Web site — along with their ratings by others who have received help — and you agree to a certain price for help.

GeekGhost. This online service uses its own software to access your computer through the Internet. Sign up at **www.geekghost.com**. You'll pay a flat fee — around $90 — to have an expert's help. If he can't fix it, there's no charge.

Is your monitor flashing a strange menu or message? That happens when the monitor is working fine, but it's not receiving a signal from the computer tower. Then you'll know the problem is with either your video card or the cable connection. If you've already checked the cables, then look to the video card to solve the problem.

Solve the mystery of blank screens

Getting a blank screen when you turn on your computer can feel as bone-chilling as a murder mystery. But you can pinpoint the culprit quickly and painlessly. A blank screen usually means your monitor is on the fritz.

Try these easy troubleshooting tips to find common problems and probable solutions.

Check power to your computer. Are you sure your computer is turned on? Is it plugged in? If you're using a power strip, is that plugged in and turned on? Make sure the power strip is still working.

Check power to your monitor. Is the monitor's "on" button lit up? If not, check the connection between the power cord and the wall, and between the power cord and the monitor. A bad AC adapter can also keep your monitor from getting power.

Check the cable between your monitor and PC. Is the cable connected properly at both ends? There may be a bad connection if the cable has a bent or missing pin in the end. If one is bent, use needle-nose pliers to gently straighten it.

But if a pin is missing — or if you break off one while trying to straighten it — you'll need to buy a new cable. Even if the pins look fine, try another cable to see if that solves the problem.

Monitor cable connector's bent pin

Connect a spare monitor. Before you spend money on a new monitor, try this. Borrow a monitor from your neighbor and connect it to your PC. If that monitor works, then it's probably time for you to buy a new one.

For more information on how monitor settings and screen resolution can affect the way images look on your monitor, see page 30 in the *Hardware hazards* chapter and page 68 in the *Control panel: customize your PC* chapter.

Take control of a stubborn computer

You are facing a complete computer meltdown. Your programs are frozen. The cursor won't move. You can't even pull up a menu. Should you simply unplug everything and put your machine out of its misery? The answer is no — at least not at first.

Experts say pulling the plug should be your very last resort. It's a drastic measure that bypasses many of your system's built-in safeguards — a little like stopping a car by driving into a wall.

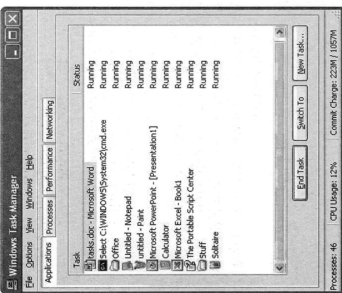

*Windows Task
Manager dialog box*

What you really want to do is open WINDOWS TASK MANAGER,
a display that gives a realtime look at what exactly is going on in
your system — what applications and processes are running, how
much memory is being used, the state of your network connection,
and other helpful bits of information. From here, there's a good
chance you can identify the source of your trouble.

1. Press these three keys simultaneously: CTRL + ALT + DEL.

2. Inside WINDOWS TASK MANAGER, click on the
   APPLICATIONS tab.

3. Single-click on any application name with a status of
   NOT RESPONDING.

4. Click on the END TASK button.

5. If you get a dialog box telling you THIS PROGRAM IS NOT
   RESPONDING, click on the END NOW button.

6. Close WINDOWS TASK MANAGER and get back to business.

125

Make sure you've given your computer plenty of time to perform whatever tasks you've initiated before forcing a quit through WINDOWS TASK MANAGER.

Whip your printer into tiptop shape

Streaked photos and hard-to-read printouts are a sign it's time for some printer maintenance. Try these money-saving maintenance measures for the best-quality printing. You don't even have to get your hands dirty — use the tools available in your printer software.

First, check the ink levels in your printer. If they're not low, you probably need to clean the print nozzles.

1. Navigate to CONTROL PANEL, then PRINTERS AND OTHER HARDWARE, and PRINTERS AND FAXES.

2. Right-click on your printer's name.

3. Click on PROPERTIES, and a dialog box opens.

4. Depending on your brand of printer, you should see a service, maintenance, or utilities tab or button.

5. Look for an option like CLEAN THE PRINT CARTRIDGES, also called nozzle cleaning. This process uses up lots of ink, so do it only when you're having problems.

Another common printer maintenance task is aligning the print cartridge. You need to do this after you install a new print cartridge. It's also helpful if there are vertical lines on your printouts that appear wavy, or if letters don't line up correctly on the left-hand side of the page.

Update your drivers with Device Manager

There are at least 10 different ways for every piece of hardware in your computer to break. Consider drivers one of them. This software lets hardware gadgets "talk" to your computer, and vice versa. Unfortunately, a faulty or outdated driver can gum up the works and bring your machine grinding to a halt. You can save money, and solve most driver problems yourself, with a small but mighty tool called DEVICE MANAGER.

Any piece of hardware, like a printer, made before Windows XP came out may not be able to talk to your computer. If a device won't work from the first time you plug it in, chances are you need to update the driver.

Right-click on MY COMPUTER and choose PROPERTIES from the shortcut menu. Flip to the HARDWARE tab in the SYSTEM PROPERTIES dialog box, and click on the DEVICE MANAGER button. Here, you'll see a list of every piece of hardware inside or connected to your computer.

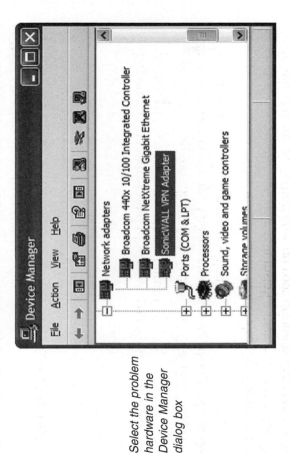

Select the problem hardware in the Device Manager dialog box

If you don't see a device you know is there, change the view. Devices that are not "plug and play" don't automatically appear on the list. To see them, click on VIEW in the menu bar and select SHOW HIDDEN DEVICES.

Click on the + signs to expand the list, and double-click on the trouble-making device to open its PROPERTIES box. Flip to the DRIVER tab and click on the UPDATE DRIVER button. Windows will leap into action, using the Update Device Driver Wizard to walk you through the process.

If Windows can't find a better driver, you'll have to do a little detective work. Click on the GENERAL tab to find out which company made the device, then get on the Internet and head to their Web site. Once there, check the Support or Downloads area for an XP-compatible driver for your hardware. Still no luck? Try the Web sites **www.driverguide.com** or **www.driverfiles.net**. Now it's time to install the new software. You may have to restart your computer when you are finished.

1. Download the driver, then return to the DRIVER tab and click on the UPDATE DRIVER button again.

2. Select INSTALL FROM A LIST OR SPECIFIC LOCATION (ADVANCED) since you know where you saved the new driver, and click on the NEXT button.

3. Choose SEARCH FOR THE BEST DRIVER IN THESE LOCATIONS, and put a check mark next to INCLUDE THIS LOCATION IN THE SEARCH. (If the new driver was on a disk, you would check the SEARCH REMOVABLE MEDIA box.)

4. Click on the BROWSE button and hunt around in the FIND YOUR DRIVER box to select the new driver.

Sometimes, updating a driver can actually foul up hardware that used to work just fine. On the same DRIVER tab where you see the UPDATE DRIVER button, you'll also find the ROLL BACK DRIVER button. Click on this to uninstall the new driver and revert to the old, better-working one.

Turn back the clock on computer problems

Wouldn't a computer time machine be wonderful? You could travel back to the moment just before you downloaded the software that crashed your hard drive, and stop yourself before you click on OK.

System Restore, a tool included in *Windows XP*, is not time travel, but it can literally reverse troublesome changes to your computer as if they never happened. It takes snapshots of the system files and settings on your computer at regular intervals, storing them in a safe place on your hard drive. Typically, it's done once a day, and then again when you install or remove a program or driver.

System Restore can get you out of several types of jams — even when other tools don't work.

Program conflicts. Not all program updates or patches mesh well with the software that's already on your computer. If you do an install and have problems, you can try uninstalling the offending new software. But if that doesn't work, use System Restore to return your PC to the way it was before the update.

Driver update problems. A driver update may slow down or crash your computer. Use the Driver Rollback feature in the Device Manager to put things right, or use System Restore to switch back to the old, working driver.

Software incompatibilities. When several family members share a computer, it's likely there will be lots of software installed. That can slow the PC or make it crash for no good reason. Use System Restore to return the computer to an earlier, faster version — before all the crud crept in. But don't count on System Restore to fix everything on your PC.

◆ It doesn't save copies of your personal files, including photos, images, e-mail messages, and any files in MY DOCUMENTS, RECYCLE BIN, or FAVORITES. That means you still need to back up your important files regularly.

◆ It can't protect your computer from viruses, worms, or other malware. If your computer gets infected with one of these nasty items, it likely has infected restored versions of files, as well.

You can do a System Restore if your computer is in either Safe Mode or regular mode. You'll need to log in to XP as Administrator, log off other users, and close all files and programs.

1. Navigate to START → ALL PROGRAMS → ACCESSORIES → SYSTEM TOOLS. Click on SYSTEM RESTORE.

2. The WELCOME TO SYSTEM RESTORE window will open. Place a check mark in the box next to RESTORE MY COMPUTER TO AN EARLIER TIME. Click on NEXT.

3. On the calendar in the left-hand pane, select the most recent date the computer worked and click on it. The right-hand pane shows all activity that day.

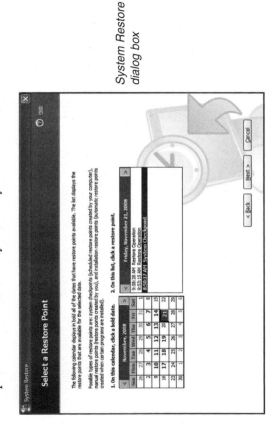

System Restore dialog box

4. Find a SYSTEM CHECKPOINT from the list and click on it to highlight it. Click on NEXT.

5. The CONFIRM RESTORE POINT SELECTION window will open. Click on NEXT to confirm the SYSTEM RESTORE.

The restore takes a few minutes, and your computer will restart during the process. If you accidentally restore to the wrong date, you can undo the change. Just launch SYSTEM RESTORE again and choose UNDO MY LAST RESTORATION.

Safety net saves you during serious crashes

Computer crashes can be frustrating, but they aren't the end of the world. The Safe Mode feature helps you fix problems, even when your PC won't boot normally. It loads only the programs and drivers absolutely necessary for basic computer functions. Turning off all nonessentials could allow your computer to boot up if it couldn't before. To enter Safe Mode:

1. Press the power button to turn on the computer, then immediately start pressing the F8 key along the top of your keyboard. If the Windows logo appears onscreen, you pushed F8 too late. Shut down and try again.

2. Keep trying until you get a message reading PLEASE SELECT THE OPERATING SYSTEM TO START. Instead, press F8 again to enter the special ADVANCED OPTIONS MENU.

3. Use the up and down arrow keys on your keyboard to highlight the first SAFE MODE option. Press ENTER.

4. Next, choose your operating system (Microsoft Windows XP) and press ENTER.

5. Click on YES in the dialog box that appears to start up in Safe Mode.

Right away, you'll notice your desktop icons don't look the same. Remember, Safe Mode gives you a bare-bones version of the operating system (OS).

Why not poke around a little. If your computer seems to be working fine, you can assume the basic OS software is not causing your woes. Instead, the likely culprit is one of the programs or drivers turned off during Safe Mode.

Think carefully about what changes you made the last time you used the computer. Maybe you installed a new scanner or other hardware, or installed new software. A new driver, patch, or update could also be to blame. The same goes for any settings you changed recently.

Once you finger a few suspects, use the appropriate XP tool to fix the glitch. You can still access XP's important fix-it features in Safe Mode. Restart the computer in regular mode after each fix to see if you've solved the problem.

XP tools	What they do
Help and Support Center	Open this window to search the Help topics for advice or to run troubleshooting utilities.
Device Manager	Remove a faulty driver or undo a dubious driver update.
Add or Remove Programs	Uninstall new programs if you think they're behind the recent trouble.
Settings	Messing with certain system settings can throw a wrench in the works. Change them back and see if things return to normal after you reboot.
System Restore	If nothing else works, take your computer back to the last day you know it worked normally. Be warned — you can't undo a System Restore performed in Safe Mode.
Backup Utility	Make a backup of important files, just in case your PC is still acting squirrelly when you reboot into normal mode.

Fix-it feature gets Vista running again

Windows Vista comes with a grab bag of tools that used to be available only to computer repair geeks. Thanks to Vista's free Startup Repair feature, when your computer won't start you may be able to save hundreds of dollars by fixing it yourself.

Startup Repair is a special recovery mode, similar to Safe Mode, that runs from your Windows Vista installation disc. Since it's on your DVD, you can pop it in and fix problems even when Windows Vista won't start up. Here's how.

1. Insert the Vista disc.

2. Restart your computer and boot up Windows from the installation disc instead of your hard disk.

3. The Vista installation screen appears. Select language settings and click on NEXT, if needed.

4. Click on REPAIR YOUR COMPUTER.

5. Click on your hard drive's copy of Windows on the screen.

> You probably got a Vista installation disc when you bought your computer. If not, your computer maker may have included a restoration disc. If you've backed up your files recently, use the disc to restore your computer to its default settings. This erases your data — so don't forget to reload those files from your backup source to your hard drive. If you don't have a recent backup, call your computer maker about getting a Vista installation disk. Then, you can fix Vista without losing data.

Click on STARTUP REPAIR to fix files that could be causing the hiccup. You may have to run it more than once to fix them all. If that doesn't work, try the WINDOWS MEMORY DIAGNOSTIC TOOL.

This attempts to find and repair problems with RAM, or memory. If your problems persist, try SYSTEM RESTORE. This takes the operating system back in time to a point where it ran fine. STARTUP REPAIR and its buddies won't fix hardware failures, like a dead hard drive or incompatible hardware.

Escape the Blue Screen of Death

This menace has a reputation as the biggest, baddest, ugliest error message you can ever get. Yet, behind the hoopla, the blue screen of death (BSOD) isn't so scary after all.

133

You'll know it when you see it — a gibberish-looking message against a solid blue background. This geek-speak is telling you Windows hit a road bump. A damaged driver, incompatible hardware, or an ailing hard drive, for instance, made the operating system (OS) stop responding or become unstable. In turn, Windows drops everything to protect the OS from damage.

XP may automatically restart when a blue screen of death strikes, leaving you no time to write down the error message. You can turn off this feature before it hits. Right click on MY COMPUTER and choose PROPERTIES. Under the ADVANCED tab, find STARTUP AND RECOVERY and click on the SETTINGS button. Remove the check mark next to AUTOMATICALLY RESTART.

Grab a pencil. Write down what the message says, even if it doesn't make sense. Get all the numbers and letters, especially those following the word STOP.

Take action. Go online for instant help. Type the STOP error information into Google (**www.google.com**), the Microsoft Knowledge Base (**support.microsoft.com/search**), or Smart Computing's Tech Support Center (**www.smartcomputing.com/techsupport**).

Retrace your steps. If your search yields more than one possible reason for the BSOD, think about what changes you recently made to your computer. These are likely culprits. Roll back updated drivers or remove and reinstall hardware and software, then restart and see if the BSOD strikes again. Can't restart normally? Enter Safe Mode and make changes from there.

Simple trick makes computer glitches disappear

Restarting your computer can solve many head-scratching problems. All you have to do is press the CTRL, ALT, and DELETE keys simultaneously. Restart your computer if any of these happen.

- The cursor stops responding.

- Your keyboard only beeps when you press a button.

- The power goes out unexpectedly.

- Everything on your screen "freezes up" and stops responding.

- You see a blue screen of death with a FATAL EXCEPTION error message instead of the word STOP.

Rescue lost files from oblivion

Backup files will have you dancing for joy, if you ever need them. Call on the Wizard to help you get started.

1. Insert the disc, flash drive, or other media that contains your backup files. Next, open the CONTROL PANEL and click on PERFORMANCE AND MAINTENANCE, then on BACK UP YOUR DATA to launch the Backup Or Restore Wizard. Click on NEXT, and select RESTORE FILES AND SETTINGS.

2. Under ITEMS TO RESTORE, choose the place where you saved your backups — a disc, flash drive, or hard drive. Don't see it listed? Click on the BROWSE button above. In the OPEN BACKUP FILE box, click on BROWSE again and mouse around until you find the files.

3. Select the files to resurrect under ITEMS TO RESTORE on the main Wizard screen. Here, click on the + signs to see the folders inside folders. You can restore the whole backup or choose a few specific files or folders. Double-click on a folder name on the left to see which files it contains on the right. To restore an entire folder, put a check mark beside it on the left.

If you have trouble convincing the Wizard to restore files from a CD or flash drive, just drag a copy of the backup file onto your desktop and restore it from there.

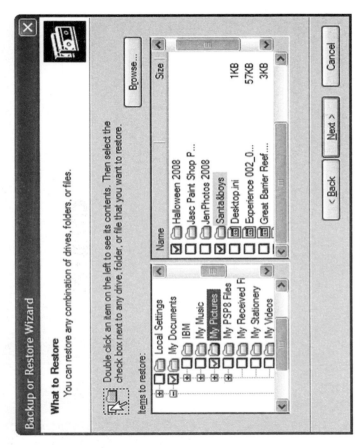

Choose files and folders to restore from backup

To restore a few files in that folder, place check marks next to their names on the right.

4. Pick a place to save them. On the *Wizard's* final screen, click on the ADVANCED button to choose where to put these files. ORIGINAL LOCATION returns them to their original folders on your hard drive. If you want to store them somewhere else, select ALTERNATE LOCATION or SINGLE FOLDER.

Be careful not to overwrite good files with their old backup versions. On the next HOW TO RESTORE screen, tell the computer how to handle the files currently on your hard drive when it restores the backup versions.

For more information on backing up important files, see page 114 in the *Keep your PC problem-free* chapter.

chapter 14

Smart shutdown

"The attention span of a computer is only as long as its electrical cord."

Author unknown

Power down to save energy

Some people say to leave your computer running to make it last, since repeatedly turning it off and on could wear out its hard drive, as well as other components. But others say to turn off your PC when you're not using it to save energy.

Most computer experts say it's fine to turn off your computer to save energy. That won't shorten your PC's life span, as people once thought.

Nowadays, computers are built to be turned on and off around 40,000 times. At that rate, even if you turn your machine off twice a day, it would take about 55 years to wear out. Surely, you'll want a new computer before then.

For the wisest energy savings, consider turning off your monitor if you won't use it for 20 minutes or more, and turning off both the computer and monitor if you won't use them for two hours or more.

Aside from the power draw, a computer produces heat when it's running, making your home air conditioner work harder to keep things cool. And turn off your computer's power strip when the machine is off to stop this small waste of energy.

Unfortunately, you don't like waiting for your computer to reboot. Your PC probably has two energy-saving settings to cut down on power use without giving up convenience.

Vista wins out over Windows XP When it comes to saving energy in hibernate mode. Some applications and peripheral devices can override the hibernate mode in Windows XP and continue to run. But that won't happen in Vista. Instead, they're warned by the operating system to save their work, then the computer puts itself into full hibernate mode — everything turns off.

Hibernate. The hibernate option saves an image of the open files and folders on your desktop, then turns off your PC. When you turn the power on again, your desktop will look just as it did — with all files and folders open. The computer comes back on more quickly from hibernating than from a regular shutdown.

Standby. The standby mode, which some people call "sleep" mode, turns off power to the PC's peripheral devices, monitor, and even some hard drive functions. But power still goes to the computer's memory to save your open files.

When you're ready to use your computer again, just move the mouse a bit or press a key, and it will quickly come back to life. You can select when to have your PC put itself in hibernation or standby mode.

1. From the START menu, click on CONTROL PANEL. Then click on PERFORMANCE AND MAINTENANCE and double-click on POWER OPTIONS.

2. Open the HIBERNATE tab and be sure the ENABLE HIBERNATION check box is checked. Click on APPLY.

3. Switch to the POWER SCHEMES tab. See the SETTINGS FOR HOME/OFFICE DESK POWER SCHEME section at the bottom of the box. On the SYSTEM STANDBY drop-down menu, you can make a choice ranging from AFTER 1 MINUTE to NEVER.

4. Then, on the SYSTEM HIBERNATES drop-down menu, you can select a choice ranging from any time longer than what you chose for SYSTEM STANDBY up to AFTER 6 HOURS or NEVER.

5. Click on APPLY, then OK to exit.

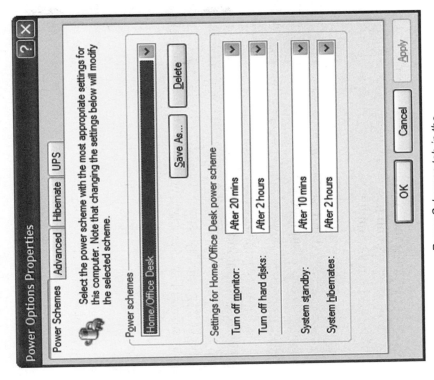

Power Schemes tab in the
Power Options Properties dialog box

For information on conserving energy when using a laptop computer, see page 18 in the *Everything laptop* chapter.

2 ways to shut down fast

Sometimes, you just can't wait. You have two options to shut down your PC quickly with Windows XP.

Prepare a shortcut. You can plan ahead and create a desktop icon for fast shutdown.

1. Right-click anywhere on your desktop. Select NEW and then SHORTCUT.

2. Type `shutdown -s -t 00`. Be sure to type this exactly as illustrated, with spaces, hyphens, and zeros.

3. Click on NEXT and give your shortcut a name, like Quick Shutdown.

4. Click on FINISH. Your new shortcut will appear as an icon on your desktop.

Next time you're in a hurry, double-click the shortcut icon and your computer will safely shut itself off.

Use your keyboard. You don't need a shortcut to power down your computer using just the keyboard — no mousing required.

Windows key

Press the Windows key, which looks like a flag with four squares, at the bottom of the keyboard. Then press the U key, and the TURN OFF COMPUTER window will open. Type S for standby or U to turn it off. You also have the option of typing R for restart.

On some systems, you may need to press the S key twice to toggle between SHUTDOWN and STANDBY, then press ENTER.

chapter 15

Operating system upgrades

❝Man is still the most extraordinary computer of all.❞

John F. Kennedy

Can your computer handle Vista?

Windows Vista is a different animal from XP. It demands more power, speed, and memory. If you're getting a new computer that comes with Vista, you have nothing to worry about, but if you're considering an upgrade, your old computer may not be able to handle it. To run the Home Basic version of Vista, your computer must meet these requirements. You'll need even more of everything to run the Home Premium or higher versions.

✦ 800-megahertz processor

✦ 512 megabytes of RAM

✦ 20-gigabyte hard drive with 15 gigabytes of available space

✦ Super VGA (800 X 600) resolution monitor

- DirectX 9-class graphics card
- DVD drive
- Internet access

Make Microsoft do the checking for you. Download the Vista Upgrade Advisor from the Internet at **www.microsoft.com/windows vista/getready/upgradeadvisor.** *Plug in all the printers, scanners, faxes, CD burners, and other gadgets you use with your computer, then run the Advisor program. It will scan your computer and equipment and spit out a report telling you whether your computer can handle Vista and which gadgets, programs, and drivers won't work with the new operating system.*

Vista upgrade: 5 tricks that lend a hand

You can load Vista one of two ways — an upgrade or a clean install. If your computer uses:

- Windows XP Home edition, you can simply upgrade.
- Windows 98, 2000, or XP Professional, you must do a clean install.

Upgrading is cheaper since you don't have to buy the full version of Vista. Plus, it allows you to keep all your old settings, like your desktop wallpaper. On the downside, it carries over gunk and clutter that can clog your computer, sort of like plaque buildup in your arteries, causing glitches and making things run slower. You're also more likely to have trouble with your non-Microsoft programs if you simply upgrade your operating system. A clean install wipes out everything, so you start with a blank slate and, hopefully, a faster system. That's why many experts suggest doing a clean install, no matter what.

Whatever you choose, you'll follow some of the same basic steps to prepare your computer. Some tips are simply expert suggestions; others are must-do's. Either way, they'll make the process smooth and worry-free.

Take notes. Write down the user names and passwords for favorite Web sites, in case they don't carry over.

Blast viruses. Make sure your anti-virus program is up-to-date, then scan your computer for viruses before installing the new operating system.

Back up your stuff. Creating backup copies of all your files and programs is a good idea if you're upgrading, but it's a must if you do a clean install. Copy the files on your hard drive to a DVD, external hard drive, or network server.

For information on backing up files, see pages 114 and 116 in the *Keep your PC problem-free* chapter.

Windows Vista can also help you move or back up files with the Easy Transfer Wizard. Just pop in the Vista disc and click TRANSFER FILES AND SETTINGS FROM ANOTHER COMPUTER. The wizard software will walk you through the transfer process. Experts recommend creating another backup separate from the wizard, just in case something goes wrong.

Fix problem programs. Before you start the actual Vista installation process, uninstall your anti-virus software, and turn off non-Microsoft firewalls, Internet ad-blocking software, and programs that automatically start when you turn on your computer. Then either fix or remove any program the Vista Upgrade Advisor told you was incompatible.

Unplug gadgets. Disconnect everything you don't need to run your computer, including scanners, printers, fax machines, and game controllers.

Teach old software new OS tricks

You upgraded to Vista, and now half your old programs or gadgets won't work. Don't panic. You can fix them faster than you can say Microsoft.

Check for updates. Go to the Web site of the company that made your gadget or program. Head for the Support section and look for software updates. You might find a patch for your program or new driver for your printer that enables them to work with Vista.

Seize power. When you set up your user account in Vista, you can give yourself Administrator or Standard status. Being an Administrator gives you special power over your computer, like opening stubborn programs. Log in as an Administrator and follow these simple steps.

1. Right-click the program in the START menu and select PROPERTIES from the pop-up menu. This opens the shortcut's PROPERTIES dialog box.

2. Click the OPEN FILE LOCATION button under the SHORTCUT tab. A new window will open.

3. Right-click the troublesome program and select PROPERTIES from the pop-up menu. This opens the program's PROPERTIES dialog box.

4. Click on the COMPATIBILITY tab. Put a check mark beside RUN THIS PROGRAM AS AN ADMINISTRATOR.

Fool flaky programs. Some old software just can't figure out what kind of animal Windows Vista is. If the other methods don't work, try this.

1. Go back to the program's PROPERTIES dialog box and click on the COMPATIBILITY tab.

2. Put a check mark beside RUN THIS PROGRAM IN COMPATIBILITY MODE FOR.

3. Select the operating system that the program used to work in from the drop-down list.

From now on, the program should start right up. However, don't try this trick with anti-virus software, backup programs, CD-burning software, or any hard drive utilities.

chapter 16

Security matters

> **"**There are over 10,000 known computer viruses. Over 200 new viruses are being discovered every month.**"**
>
> University of Houston

Keep hackers from snatching your data

Malicious hackers and their hacker programs are always on the hunt for the personal information you store on your computer. Protect your privacy with a personal firewall. This virtual safety barrier stands between your computer and other computers on the Internet.

You can get software firewalls that run on your computer and hardware firewalls that protect a group of computers. A firewall checks every incoming Internet transmission and only allows the ones that have been invited — either by you or by programs from your computer. The rest simply get blocked. This helps prevent computer criminals from invading your computer when you're connected to the Internet.

Fire up a free firewall. Windows XP comes with a software firewall already installed that can stop hackers and identity thieves cold. But it only works if it is turned on. Turn it off and it's like leaving your front door wide open. Here's how to check whether yours is running right now.

1. Click on the START button.

2. Click on CONTROL PANEL to open the CONTROL PANEL dialog box.

3. Check the left pane on the CONTROL PANEL window. If it says SWITCH TO CATEGORY VIEW, click on the text. If it says SWITCH TO CLASSIC VIEW, move on to the next step.

4. Click on the SECURITY CENTER icon to open the WINDOWS SECURITY CENTER dialog box.

5. Check to see if the word ON appears in green next to FIREWALL. If so, your firewall is already protecting you. Click the red X to close this dialog box and skip the remaining steps.

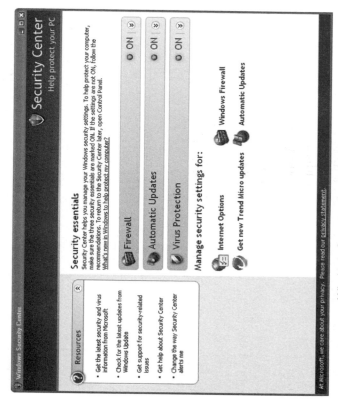

Windows Security Center dialog box

6. If the word OFF appears instead, move your cursor to the WINDOWS FIREWALL icon below MANAGE SECURITY SETTINGS FOR:. Click on the icon to open the WINDOWS FIREWALL dialog box.

7. Click the ON radio button, click OK, then close this dialog box.

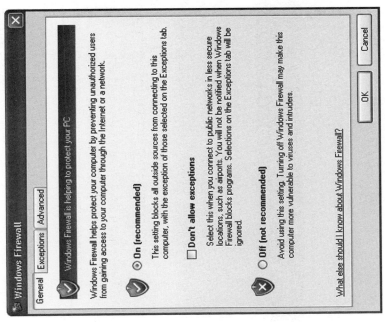

Windows Firewall dialog box

8. The word ON should now appear in green next to FIREWALL. Close the SECURITY CENTER.

Don't leave it all to the wall. Be aware that there are some thingsthe Windows XP firewall can't do.

◆ It can't stop you from opening a dangerous e-mail attachment or downloading a corrupt file.

◆ It can't protect you from a virus or malicious software that is already on your computer.

147

◆ It only monitors and blocks inbound traffic. Therefore it can't prevent a virus on your computer from sending out data or performing harmful outbound actions.

Alternatives may fit the bill. There are other firewall options that might suit your needs better. These are free, as well, and offer a few things Windows firewall doesn't — like blocking unauthorized outbound information. Just remember, if you install one of them, you need to disable the Windows XP firewall. Do that by selecting OFF in the WINDOWS FIREWALL dialog box as explained earlier.

| ZoneAlarm | www.zonelabs.com |
| Comodo Firewall Pro | www.comodogroup.com |

Stop bogus security alerts

You installed a new firewall yourself and disabled the Windows built-in firewall. But because Windows doesn't recognize this program, it thinks it doesn't exist. Now you keep getting warnings that you have no firewall protection. This is a severe case of hyperactive security alerts, but it can be cured.

First check your third-party firewall to make sure it is running and that all the options are set properly. When you are absolutely sure your firewall is protecting your computer, follow this process.

1. Click on the START button.

2. Click on CONTROL PANEL.

3. Check the left pane on the CONTROL PANEL window. Make sure you are in category view as explained earlier.

4. Click on the SECURITY CENTER icon to open the WINDOWS SECURITY CENTER dialog box.

5. Underneath the red area with the words FIREWALL and OFF, find the RECOMMENDATIONS button. Click on it.

6. Click on the checkbox next to: I HAVE A FIREWALL SOLUTION THAT I'LL MONITOR MYSELF. You'll also see a reminder that this means Windows won't monitor the status of your firewall.

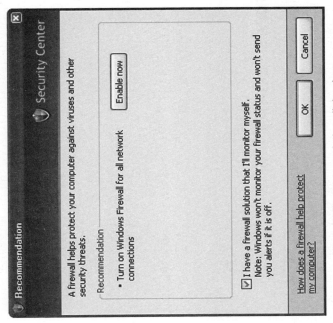

Firewall Recommendation dialog box

7. Click OK and close this dialog box. The WINDOWS SECURITY CENTER dialog box should now show you a yellow area with the words FIREWALL and NOT MONITORED.

Firewall exceptions: risky or required?

Sometimes a firewall can work too well. If it's preventing your software from functioning properly, you may need to take a brick out of it. For example, some software periodically contacts the Internet to download an update or security patch. If your firewall blocks this program, you're not getting important improvements. There are two ways you can allow specific programs through your firewall.

Unblock on the fly. When a program tries to access the Internet for the first time, your firewall may ask whether you want to allow this. You can choose to keep the blocking in place, or to unblock. If you choose to unblock it, you won't get this choice again.

Remove a brick yourself. If you know you want a certain program to have outside access, you can set this up yourself as an exception.

1. Navigate to the WINDOWS FIREWALL dialog box as explained earlier.

2. Click on the EXCEPTIONS tab.

3. Click on ADD PROGRAM.

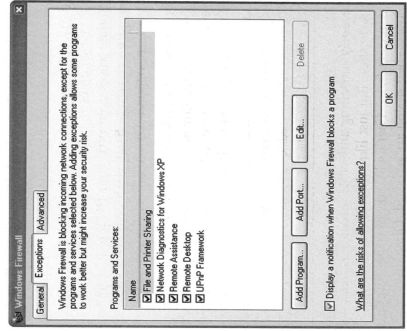

Exceptions tab in the Windows Firewall dialog box

4. When the list of programs appears, scroll to the one you want to to add. Click on the program name and then click on OK.

5. Close the WINDOWS FIREWALL dialog box and the CONTROL PANEL.

Microsoft says, allowing an exception is "like poking a hole through the firewall." That's why you should only unblock a program you recognize and when you decide it's absolutely necessary for it to work correctly.

Don't let a virus plague your computer

You can try running — even to space — but you can't hide from computer viruses. They are so widespread that some have even been found on laptops aboard the International Space Station. These wicked little software programs really can make your computer sick. They slow down your computer, damage files, delete information, cause programs to suddenly shut down, or even wipe out a hard drive. Viruses called worms make copies of themselves, then e-mail these copies to other computers using your e-mail account. Some viruses even turn your PC into a "zombie" — a kind of computer slave to a hacker, who can then delete or steal your information, or send out e-mails as if he were you.

Viruses can sneak in by lurking inside e-mail attachments and seemingly harmless file downloads or they may simply spread to your computer from the Internet. So never connect to the Web, or use e-mail or a chat program without anti-virus software running.

For more information on e-mail viruses, see page 300 in the *E-mail essentials* chapter and to learn about downloading safely from the Internet, see page 165 in the *Straight talk about software* chapter.

Vaccinate early. Installing anti-virus software is like giving your computer a flu shot. But just like with the flu, once you're sick, the prevention doesn't help. That's why you must install the anti-virus software now — before you are infected. Once they are on your computer, many viruses can keep your anti-virus software from installing successfully.

Pick your protection. Windows XP does not come with built-in virus protection, so you're going to have to be proactive here and get some security yourself.

✦ You can either pay for an anti-virus program or use a free download. Just be aware that some free programs may not come with free technical support and may not update themselves as quickly as the paid versions.

For more information on sources of free software, see page 246 in the *Internet deals & steals* chapter.

✦ You can choose to install a bundle of security programs — called a security suite — that includes anti-virus software.

✦ Be particular about your anti-virus program. Don't install just any old software and especially don't install any you see in an Internet pop-up ad. Rogue security software ads can actually take you to Web sites that secretly install viruses. So pick from known winners like these. The last two are free.

Norton AntiVirus	www.symantec.com
McAfee VirusScan Plus	www.mcafee.com
Trend Micro AntiVirus	www.trendmicro.com
AVG Anti-Virus Free Edition	free.avg.com
avast! antivirus	www.avast.com

Over time, the list of top-rated programs may change, so be sure to read software reviews online to help you choose the best anti-virus software.

Practice virus vigilance. For added protection, follow these tips for avoiding virus infections on your computer.

◆ Scan your entire computer at least once a week. You can quarantine, repair, or remove infected files so they no longer threaten your computer.

◆ Review the options and settings in your anti-virus software. Turn on the option to automatically scan incoming and outgoing e-mails, chats, and files for viruses.

◆ Don't open any e-mail attachment you were not already expecting — even if it appears to come from a friend or family member. Instead, check with the sender to make sure that person really sent it. Remember, viruses and hackers can send e-mails, too.

◆ Scan any e-mail or e-mail attachment you're unsure about.

◆ Only download files from reputable sites. Files from questionable sites or from pop-ups may be more likely to slip you a virus.

Beware the dreaded hoax. Pranksters love to send out e-mails about viruses that don't exist. Either they want to see how many well-meaning people will forward these e-mails or they just want to cause as much distress as possible. These hoaxes may tempt some to disregard information about truly dangerous viruses or even trick people into deleting files that are a vital part of Windows — so don't automatically forward them. As if all that weren't bad enough, some viruses start out as hoaxes, but later become true viruses. Separate fact from fiction at these Web sites.

F-Secure	*www.f-secure.com/virus-info/hoax/*
McAfee Threat Library	*vil.nai.com/vil/default.aspx*
Snopes.com	*www.snopes.com*

Boost your protection with updates

Just like human viruses, computer viruses become resistant. What's more, tougher, newer computer viruses — and meaner versions of old viruses — are born every week. To stay protected against new threats, you must keep your computer's "vaccinations" up-to-date.

Your anti-virus software includes a database of virus definitions, so when it scans your computer it can recognize viruses wherever they hide. As new viruses are created or updated, your anti-virus software maker publishes definitions for these new viruses on their Web site. These new definitions are meant to act as a booster shot for your machine. But you must download them so they can be added to the database on your computer. Otherwise, your virus scanner won't recognize new viruses and your computer will stay in constant danger.

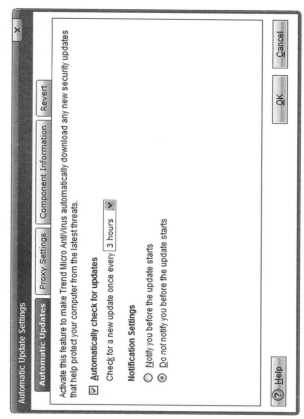

Automatically check for security updates

To make sure you always have the very latest virus definitions, visit the Options or Settings area in your anti-virus software. Turn on the option to automatically check for updates and automatically download and install them. If your software doesn't include these settings, check for an UPDATE option in your product menu or visit the product's Web site at least once every week to check for and download new updates.

Stop a virus cold

Your computer is behaving strangely and you suspect it may have managed to catch a virus in spite of your anti-virus software. But don't panic.

Check for symptoms. Strange happenings like these should raise a red flag.

✦ Your computer or your Internet connection runs slower than usual.

✦ Someone says you sent them an e-mail with an attachment when you did not.

✦ Your computer restarts on its own.

✦ You spot a file with two extensions instead of one — perhaps including .jpg, .exe, .gif, or .vbs.

✦ Your anti-virus program is disabled and its icon vanishes from the bottom of your screen.

✦ Files or programs disappear.

✦ You cannot start Task Manager.

Vanquish a virus. If you think you have a virus, take steps to corner and exterminate it right away.

1. Check for the very latest updates for your anti-virus software. Download and install them.

2. Close down all programs except your anti-virus software.

3. Run a scan of your entire computer.

4. If your software finds no infected files, visit the manufacturer's Web site to check for warnings or news about new viruses.

Cure a super virus

The worst has finally happened. Your computer has a super bug that your anti-virus software can't wipe out. But don't worry. You may find a free download that will exterminate that bug once and for all. Just remember, because they only target a small group of super viruses, neither of these options can or should replace your anti-virus software.

Visit your vendor. Go to the Web site of your anti-virus software maker. If you know which virus you have, they may offer a specific software tool to counteract it. Some vendors may even offer an all-in-one download for multiple viruses.

Let Microsoft lend a hand. The Malicious Software Removal Tool is a free Windows download for computers running Windows Vista and Windows XP and is designed to fix a group of particularly notorious viruses. Turn on Windows Automatic Updates and the tool is updated every month to cope with new threats.

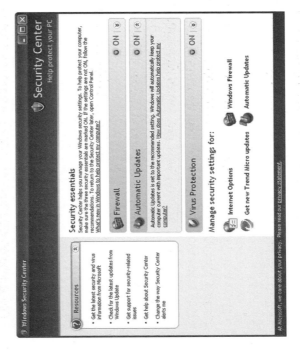

Automatic Updates option in the Windows Security Center dialog box

However, this software only works if your computer is already infected. Visit the Microsoft Web site at **www.microsoft.com** to learn more.

For more information on the Windows Automatic Updates feature, see page 116 in the *Keep your PC problem-free* chapter.

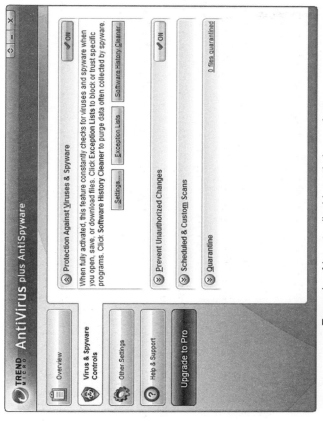

Example of how to disable anti-virus software

Quick fix for a foiled install

Your new software simply won't install. You followed all the instructions — except you didn't disable your anti-virus software. Don't be afraid of this very important step. You're only shutting it down for the few minutes it may take to install the software, then you'll turn it back on. While different anti-virus programs will ask you to handle this in different ways, here's an example of how it might work.

1. Open a main window for your anti-virus software.

2. Click on whatever choice you have for SETTINGS, CONTROL, or OPTIONS.

3. You should see an option that allows you to control your anti-virus protection.

4. Change the ON to OFF by clicking on it.

5. Close the window.

Now you can install your software. Just remember to turn your protection back on when you're through.

Escape the spyware nightmare

It's not a page out of a science fiction novel. It's a fact of modern life that some software exists purely to gather information from your computer and transmit it to others. It's called spyware. Some software — also known as adware — collects information for marketers to use, such as which Web sites you visit. An even worse kind is the dreaded keylogger. This records everything you type on your keyboard and transmits a record of those keystrokes to a hacker who can then easily get credit card numbers or other personal information.

But spyware has to get on your computer — usually without your knowledge or permission — before it can commit its crimes. This can happen in at least three ways.

◆ It may be hidden in a free software download. In that case, you may have given it permission just by agreeing to the end-user license agreement.

◆ It may be installed by a Web site you visit.

◆ It can break into your PC when you click on a link in a pop-up advertisement or unsolicited e-mail.

Read the signs. Symptoms like these may mean you're a victim of spyware.

◆ Your Internet home page mysteriously changes to a new Web site.

◆ Your Internet browser takes you to sites you never chose.

◆ You spot a strange, new toolbar in your browser.

◆ You find puzzling new icons on your desktop.

◆ Your computer or your Internet connection is suddenly slower than the after-Christmas returns line.

Stop those snoopers. One of the smartest ways to nip this problem in the bud is to install a spyware program that prevents and removes spyware. In fact, experts recommend having two spyware blockers. Use the best product as your main spyware blocker and set it to protect your computer all the time. Use the other to perform manual scans of your computer every week. It may catch a piece of spyware that your regular blocker missed. Read software reviews from sites such as **www.pcmag.com** to find the best ones. Good examples of free blockers are:

> Windows Vista includes Windows Defender, an anti-spyware and anti-malware program that is an optional download for Windows XP.

Spybot - Search & Destroy	*www.spybot.net*
Ad-Aware Free	*www.lavasoftusa.com*
Windows Defender	*www.microsoft.com*

Regularly check for patches and software updates for your spyware blocker as well as your firewall, browser, anti-virus software, and, of course, your Windows operating system. Here are more tips and tricks for snuffing out the spyware threat.

◆ Install a firewall that notifies you anytime a new program tries to send out information from your computer. Comodo Firewall Pro and ZoneAlarm Firewall can do this, but the built-in Windows XP firewall does not.

◆ Only download software from reputable sites.

◆ Always read the entire end-user license agreement before installing software. Otherwise, you may grant permission for spyware to report back to its masters.

◆ Consider using an Internet browser other than Internet Explorer. Read reviews at sites such as www.cnet.com to determine which browser is currently considered most secure.

◆ Never click on a link in a pop-up ad or unsolicited e-mail. Especially don't click on those links if they offer you a spyware blocker. These links are more likely to install the very spyware you're trying to avoid.

Cure a serious spyware infection. If spyware checkers cannot solve your problem, you may have to take drastic measures. Back up your documents, Internet bookmarks, pictures, and any other information you don't want to lose, and reformat your hard drive, reinstall Windows, and reinstall your firewall, spyware blocker, anti-virus, and other software programs.

For more information on making backups of your files, see page 114 in the *Keep your PC problem-free* chapter.

Double security can triple your trouble

In the world of vacations, friendships, and — we'd like to convince ourselves — chocolate truffles, more is better. In the world of computer security programs, this is definitely not the case. Install multiple anti-virus programs or firewalls on a single computer and you're just asking for trouble.

Many anti-virus programs could easily be labeled "does not play well with others." That means two different programs on the same computer will conflict — blocking some legitimate software, or creating gaps in your digital security perimeter that let viruses through. Using two firewalls may cause similar troubles.

You may even find problems when you get your spyware blocker from one software maker, your anti-virus software from another, and your firewall from a third. Programs from different vendors aren't always compatible. What's more, buying programs separately may cost more than purchasing them as a group.

If you buy all your security software in a single bundle — also known as a security suite — you get programs designed to work well together. You'll also spend less time on updates since they will all update at once. To determine which suite is your best bet, read online reviews from reputable Web sites such as **www.cnet.com** or **www.pcmag.com.**

Build a better password

Passwords help keep your personal information under lock and keyboard — but only if you make them tough enough and use them wisely. Otherwise, hackers can guess your password or use password-cracking software to figure it out. So make a thief-puzzling password and keep it safe.

Make it tough. Use these rules to build a tough-as-nails password.

✦ Don't use easy-to-guess passwords such as your birthday, address, last four digits of your social security number, or the names of friends, family, or pets.

✦ Don't use any word you can look up in a dictionary.

✦ Use combinations of upper and lower case letters, numbers, and special characters like &, $, and #.

✦ Include at least a few numbers and upper case letters in the middle of the password.

✦ If permitted, make each password at least eight characters long.

✦ Use a memory trick to help create a more protected password. For example, you might choose the password Ycbg41$A because each letter in the password represents one word in the sentence, "You can't buy gas for 1 dollar anymore."

And if you'd like help in making a more powerful password, get it for free from Web sites like these.

Password Bird	www.passwordbird.com
Strong Password Generator	www.strongpasswordgenerator.com
Gibson Research Corporation	www.grc.com/passwords.htm

You can also test the security of an old password and learn ways to beef it up by visiting **www.passwordmeter.com**.

Keep it safe. Of course, even the best passwords won't help you if you don't protect them.

◆ Don't use the same password in multiple places. The more places you use a password, the more trouble you'll be in if some hacker finds it.

◆ Change or update your passwords from time to time.

Manage password overload

Passwords are like rabbits. You start out with a couple, but they quickly multiply until you have far too many to remember. Don't make a mistake that could hand over your passwords to hackers. Instead, find out the safest ways to keep track of your passwords and keep them at your fingertips.

Never be a password pushover. First, don't tempt fate. Don't store a list of passwords on your computer. Also, don't click YES when Windows or your Internet browser offers to keep track of your password for you. Hackers find it all too easy to snatch from these lists.

Tame passwords with paper. In a high-tech world, low-tech can be the best way to go. Write down your passwords in a notebook or address book and hide them in a very unlikely place in a room where there are no computers. That linen closet in the upstairs hallway or a drawer in your kitchen will do just fine. Don't leave your password list beside your computer or put it in a desk drawer near your computer because that's where dishonest people will look first. And if you have passwords attached to your computer by tape or sticky notes, remove those right away.

Hire a manager. Of course, a hidden password list isn't the most convenient answer and you'll have to break out your eraser every time you update something. Fortunately, you still have one more option — password managers. This type of software stores and encrypts your passwords so they are easier for you to use but tougher for hackers to snatch. Some also include a password generator to help you create hacker-resistant passwords, as well as the ability to log you into Web sites automatically. But perhaps the best part about using a password manager is that you only need to remember one password — the one that gets you into the manager software itself.

If you'd like to try a password manager, read reviews on reputable sites like **www.pcmag.com** to find out which ones are the best. Many experts recommend Roboform, which is free if you only store 10 passwords. To get more features and larger storage, pay around $30 for the Pro version. Visit **www.roboform.com** for more information.

Passpack is an example of an online manager — nothing to download or install. They offer a free version allowing storage of up to 100 passwords. See the full list of features at **www.passpack.com.**

Worried about identity theft? A new study has surprising info on the most common source of this crime. According to the 2006 Federal Trade Commission report on identity theft, computer hacking and online scams accounted for only 2 percent of thefts reported. But among those who knew how their personal information was stolen, 16 percent said they knew the thief personally.

chapter 17

Straight talk about software

> **"**Software: These programs give instruction to the CPU, which processes billions of tiny facts called bytes, and within a fraction of a second it sends you an error message that requires you to call the customer-support hot line and be placed on hold for approximately the life-span of a caribou. **"**
>
> Dave Barry

Revive a stuck software installation

Your CD just sits and spins but no installation program appears. Many software installation CDs run automatically once you insert the CD in the drive, but some won't — so here's what to do next.

1. Click on START.

2. Click on CONTROL PANEL.

3. Click on ADD OR REMOVE PROGRAMS.

4. Make sure the CD is in the drive and then click on the ADD NEW PROGRAMS button.

5. Click on the CD OR FLOPPY button.

6. Click on NEXT.

Windows should seek out the file that will start your installation and trigger the installation process. If the installation still doesn't work, try these suggestions:

◆ Check whether you're logged in as Administrator. Most software will only install on the Administrator account. So restart the computer, log in as Administrator, and then try to install the software.

◆ Visit the Web site for the software maker and confirm that this program is compatible with your version of Windows. If the Web site does not provide this information, visit **www.microsoft.com** to see their list of programs compatible with Windows XP.

◆ Close every program you have open. Sometimes one program won't install until all the other programs are closed. If the program's instructions suggest you shut down your anti-virus program temporarily, do that, too. When everything is shut down, try to install the software.

For more information on temporarily disabling your anti-virus software, see page 157 in the *Security matters* chapter.

5 secrets to safer software downloads

It wasn't long ago that the best software only came on CDs, but now many people download their new software right off the Web. This may sound scary — especially if you've heard about hackers who hide spyware or viruses inside a download. But doing harm to your computer is harder than you think if you follow a few simple rules.

◆ Search the *Web* to find out if the program you want to download has been reported as a source of viruses or spyware. Such programs can trigger trouble on your computer or help identify thieves steal your personal information. Before you click a download button, be sure the program has a squeaky clean reputation.

✦ Make sure the Web site is legitimate before you download any software. Only download free software from Web sites you trust — never from links in pop-up ads and spam.

✦ Watch out for messages or links for "software you must have to view this site." Sometimes just clicking on the link to download can open the door for spyware and viruses. If the required software is QuickTime or another widely used plug-in, don't click the link provided. It may lead to an impostor site. Instead, restart your browser and go to the home page of the software you need.

✦ Read any licensing agreements or terms of use thoroughly before clicking on the I AGREE button when downloading or installing software. Some licensing agreements include permission to allow marketing spyware on your machine.

✦ Scan the file with your anti-virus and spyware checkers before you click on a newly downloaded file — if it wasn't already scanned during the download.

For more information on free software, see page 246 in the *Internet deals & steals* chapter.

Beware risky ActiveX alerts

During a software download or installation, you may see a message saying an ActiveX control or add-on is required.

 This website wants to install the following

Example of a partial ActiveX warning that appears below toolbars in your browser window

The problem is some ActiveX controls carry viruses and trouble-some programs that can infect your system. So what should you do? The answer is surprisingly simple. Only allow the ActiveX control to be installed if you are sure you can trust the source. or publisher, it comes from. If you don't know the source, don't install the control.

In spite of minor glitches like these, many downloads go smoothly and easily. What's more, most downloads are self-executing, like a wind-up toy that has already been wound up for you.

Just double-click on a file's icon to start the installation of your program. If double-clicking doesn't work after a couple of tries, check the software maker's Web site for installation instructions.

For more information on ActiveX, see page 223 in the *Secrets to safe surfing* chapter.

Get rid of unwanted junk programs

Did your computer come with a bunch of software you don't know what to do with? Here's what you really need and how to get rid of what you don't.

Separate the wheat from the chaff. All you really need are the programs you use and security software, such as your firewall, anti-virus program, and spyware blocker. With many computers, you may also get extra trial software, along with boatloads of offers and ads.

At first, it's just annoying, but all this extra software takes up space on your hard drive, and it may even interfere with your computer's performance — like turning a sports car into a golf cart. Before you put your delete button into overdrive, you should know two things.

◆ You can't delete just any old file because some seemingly use-less files may be important to Windows or other programs you use every day.

◆ A simple delete of a file or folder usually won't get rid of an entire software program. The trick is to know what you can delete and how to make sure it goes away completely.

Unfortunately, software tends to install itself in several different places on your hard drive instead of just contenting itself with a single directory. That's why deleting one file or directory won't remove the program. Don't delete a program — uninstall it.

Before you uninstall any program you've paid for or registered, make sure you have the discs or file needed to reinstall the program in case you need it later.

> The best programs to delete are programs you never use, trial versions of programs you don't want, and duplicate copies of any program with more than one version currently on your hard drive.

Improve your odds of success. You have two ways to get rid of a program. Many programs have an uninstall utility to remove the program for you. You just have to know where to look. Try checking the program's directory for an uninstall.exe file. If you don't find one, click on START and then click on ALL PROGRAMS. Hover your mouse pointer over the program's name to see if you find an uninstaller in the program's list of choices.

If the program doesn't have an uninstaller, Windows offers a utility that removes programs. Here's how to use it.

1. Click on START.

2. Click on CONTROL PANEL.

3. Click on ADD OR REMOVE PROGRAMS.

4. Find the program you want to remove and click on its name.

5. Click on the REMOVE button.

6. Click on YES to get rid of the program when asked, "Are you sure you want to remove?"

7. A dialog box will ask you to wait while it configures the program. When the dialog box vanishes, click on the close button for the program listing box and the CONTROL PANEL. The program has been deleted.

Short-circuit removal problems. Sometimes you'll hit a speed bump in the program removal road. Ease over them with these tips.

◆ If you see a message that warns against deleting "shared files" — because removing them may keep other programs from functioning — choose not to delete the files.

◆ If you get a message that the file can't be deleted because it is in use, choose not to delete that file.

◆ If you see a message that the uninstall can't proceed because Windows can't find something, visit the software maker's Web site. Find the support section and look for removal instructions or a file that will help you uninstall the program.

Removing programs in Windows Vista is similar to removing programs in Windows XP — with a few minor changes. To remove a program in Windows Vista, click on START ➔ CONTROL PANEL ➔ UNINSTALL A PROGRAM. Next, double-click on the program you want to remove. Because Windows Vista doesn't offer a REMOVE button like Windows XP does, the uninstall process begins immediately. According to Consumer Reports, many trial programs can be safely removed from Vista if you never plan to buy the full version of the program. These include Napster, games from Wild Tangent, financial programs, and Microsoft Office.

Rev up a slow startup

It's the strangest thing. You're sure your PC didn't run this sluggishly when you first got it. Perhaps your computer is slow because too many programs are starting up when Windows starts up.

Windows has always had a habit of starting up a few of its own programs whenever your computer booted up. That was true the first day you turned it on. But then, like everyone who owns a computer, you began adding new programs to your machine.

Anytime you install a new program, that program may ask to be started up every time Windows starts. The program doesn't need your help to do this. It just inserts a shortcut into your Windows Startup folder.

Any program tagged this way will invisibly start up every time Windows starts — and you may never even notice. That's why your computer may start up more and more slowly as time goes by.

On top of that, programs tagged in the Startup folder may slow down your PC's overall performance. They can do this because they constantly use part of your computer's memory and computing powers. That means less memory and computer brainpower to run Windows and the programs you start yourself.

The more programs and utilities in your Windows Startup folder, the more slowly everything may run. Fortunately, this can be surprisingly easy to fix. Here's how.

1. Click on START.

2. Click on ALL PROGRAMS.

3. Right-click on STARTUP.

4. Click on OPEN.

5. Review the programs listed in the Startup folder. Check for duplicates and programs you no longer use.

6. To stop a program from being started every time Windows starts, right-click on the program's icon and click on DELETE. This will not remove the program from your computer, but its shortcut should vanish from your Startup folder.

Now the program won't start up automatically anymore, but don't be surprised if your PC boots up more quickly and runs faster.

If you want help cleaning out your Startup folder and don't mind paying a small fee, experts recommend Startup Cop Pro 3. You can download this program for about $8 from **www.pcmag.com**. Keep in mind, prices can change, and you never know when a better program may come along. Read reviews and check prices before you choose a Startup cleaner.

Get more from programs you already have

You may not be getting all the software you paid for if you never check for recent software updates.

While software makers may save the really big changes for their next major software release, you could still be missing plenty of important extras right now.

If you update your software frequently, you'll get the newest features and improvements as soon as they are available. You'll also get the latest security patches. But who wants to visit the Web site for each of their programs every day just to check for updates.

Instead, check whether your software can automatically update itself for you. You'll usually find a setting for this in the options area for your software. Otherwise, check the product menu for an entry that says Update.

If you can't update automatically, you'll have to check your software maker's Web site for updates. To tell whether the version of software you have is the same as what's on the Web site, click on MY COMPUTER and find the folder and icon for your program. Typically, this will be on the LOCAL DISK (C:) in the PROGRAM FILES folder. Right-click on the icon, click on PROPERTIES, and then click on the VERSION tab.

chapter 18

Top tips for popular programs

"One of the effects of living with electric information is that we live habitually in a state of information overload. There's always more than you can cope with."

Marshall McLuhan, author of *Understanding Media*

Discover a world of Windows freebies

You get a lot of freebies with Windows, and you may be surprised at how many things they can help you do. You'll learn more about many of them later in the chapter.

Windows Media Player plays sound files like MP3s and movie files and comes with Windows XP and Vista. For more information, see page 332 in the *Audio magic* chapter. If one of your files won't play, try the free VLC media player from **www.videolan.org.**

Windows Movie Maker edits movies you make with your digital camera or other recorders. This comes with Windows XP and Vista. For more information, see page 347 in the *Video tips & tricks* chapter. You can also edit videos for free using the service at **www.jumpcut.com.**

Windows Explorer accesses the Internet. This comes with Windows XP and Vista. For more information, read stories starting on page 204 in the *Browsers: your key to the Internet* chapter.

Notepad and WordPad both come with Windows XP and Vista. Use Notepad to open, create, and make changes to plain, unformatted text documents. Use WordPad to create and format documents and even include graphics. For more word processing power and features, try the free EditPad Lite program — or buy Microsoft Works or the pricier Microsoft Word.

Paint offers an electronic way to paint or draw pictures. It can also do a few graphic editing or photo editing tasks. This comes with Windows XP and Vista.

Outlook Express sends and receives e-mails and any files attached to them. It comes with Windows XP. For more information, see page 294 in the *E-mail essentials* chapter. You can also choose free e-mail programs, like Thunderbird, or handle e-mail online for free with Hotmail, Yahoo!, Excite, or Google's Gmail.

Windows Photo Gallery repairs flaws in photos, organizes photos on your computer, and prepares photos to be shared with others. This comes with Windows Vista.

Windows Calendar keeps you organized by helping you schedule events, sending you reminders, and letting you share your schedule with friends and family. This comes with Windows Vista.

Windows DVD Maker helps burn videos to a DVD disk. If you have a DVD burner, you can use this to take your camcorder or digital camera movies and write them to a DVD. This comes with Windows Vista.

For more information on how to create desktop shortcuts that will open these programs, see page 106 in the *Organize files & folders* chapter.

173

Not only can your computer help you get things done, it can also help you relax. It might even help you entertain your kids or grandkids for free. That's because Windows comes with an assortment of games — like Solitaire — that won't cost you a penny. These include FreeCell, Hearts, Minesweeper, Pinball, and Spider Solitaire. If these aren't right for you, download free games from the Internet from reputable sites like **www.download.com** — or try free games online at sites like **www.kongregate.com**. You can also buy computer games in stores or online.

6 easy ways to learn a new program

The programs that come built-in with Windows XP are fairly basic. You can probably learn them just by experimenting. If you're having trouble or trying to learn a more complex program, you may need some extra time and help. Fortunately, you have plenty of options to guide you.

◆ Look at your menu options to learn where things are. Even if you're not sure what they do yet, this can come in handy later.

◆ Check the paper manuals, PDF manuals, manuals on CD, or online help that came with your software. These can turn hard tasks into easy ones.

◆ Check for wizards and tutorials in the menu options. They may coach you along or actually walk you through a task.

◆ Check for video tutorials in your software or online.

◆ Start with the easy and important stuff. For example, learn how to open, create, and save a new document or file.

◆ Look for built-in tools, like templates, that help you jump ahead by doing some of the work for you.

Paint may not be the best photo editor, but it could be just what you need if you're having computer problems. That's because Paint can take a picture of your screen — a screen shot — so you can show a technical support expert exactly what's wrong. To make this screen shot, press the PRINTSCREEN key near the top of your keyboard. Then open Paint and press CONTROL + V. When your screen shot appears, click on FILE, then SAVE AS. Click on the SAVE AS TYPE drop-down box and choose .jpg. Type a name for the file and click on SAVE.

Perfect digital photos every time

Now you can take perfect pictures, even if the light is wrong or the picture is off-center. Thanks to photo editing software, you can turn bad pictures into good ones — often for free.

The Microsoft Paint program that comes with Windows is not a bad place to start. Paint can help resize a picture, snip off or crop photo edges, flip or rotate an image, and compress an image file so it takes up less space on your hard disk. Paint can also help you make quick color sketches or create simple artwork as if you were painting. But you'll need something more powerful to help organize your photos and camouflage picture flaws.

Genuine photo editing software can do a lot, yet it doesn't have to cost a lot. Besides doing any photo editing task Microsoft Paint can do, here are just a few of the extra things these programs can do.

◆ get rid of red-eyes

◆ remove little flaws and scratches

◆ turn too-dark or washed out pictures into perfectly lit photos

If you've been looking for a program that can help you get more from the pictures you take, this software is for you. All you have to do is find the right program. When shopping around for your photo editor, keep the following things in mind.

Sharing tools. Look for tools to help control the file size, image size, and image resolution so it's easier to e-mail or transfer photos to share with others.

Technical support. Help screens, FAQs, and a place to e-mail or phone questions will come in handy.

Organizing features. These are important features to help you organize your images, such as showing thumbnails, multiple search options for images, or ways to store pictures in groups.

Wizards and tutorials. Wizards can coach you through a task. But your best bet is to find wizards and tutorials that explain why you'd want to use each tool, as well as how to use it. As a result, you'll probably learn how to make the program meet your needs far faster than you normally would.

Technical requirements. Make sure the program is made for your version of Windows and your computer has enough memory, disk space, and so on for the program to work smoothly and quickly.

Import and export formats. Notice the three-letter extension at the end of your file name, like .jpg. That's a file format. The more formats a program supports, the better.

Templates for simple projects. If you like turning your photos into greeting cards or other documents, make sure the software offers templates to help you do that.

Before you choose a program, read reviews of photo editing programs at sites like **www.cnet.com** or **www.pcmag.com**. These help you find today's best bets. Good examples of free photo editors include these.

The Gimp	www.gimp.org
Windows Live Photo Gallery	get.live.com
Picasa	picasa.google.com
Windows Photo Gallery	comes with Windows Vista

Programs you buy may offer even more than freebies, so don't rule them out. These are a few good choices.

| Adobe PhotoShop Elements | www.adobe.com |
| Paint Shop Pro | store.corel.com |

For more information on photos and digital images, see page 352 in the *Make the most of your digital images* chapter.

Create and edit documents for free

Forget Microsoft Word and its eye-popping price tag. The built-in text editors in Windows — Notepad and WordPad — may help you do everything you need to do. Each program offers you a different set of abilities.

In both Notepad and WordPad, you can set margins and add headers and footers. But in WordPad, you can also change the font for the entire document or portions of it, as well as insert bullets and graphics and align paragraphs left or right.

Wordpad is your best bet if you need formatting in your document. However, Notepad may be safer than Wordpad if you're exchanging documents with someone who has a Macintosh. You can also use Notepad to edit documents that must remain plain text with no formatting, such as HTML documents or Web pages. You won't know if WordPad and Notepad can do everything you need until you try them. You'll find both programs in ACCESSORIES.

Get eye-popping documents in a flash

Typing up formal letters to businesses and government agencies used to be challenging. But now you can whip up a business letter that looks like it came from the desk of a corporate executive. What's more, you can do it faster and more easily than ever before with templates.

You don't have to be a graphic artist or professional publisher to make professional letters and other documents. Now some word processors can do the difficult parts for you. Take Microsoft Word, for example. Click on the right sequence of keys and you'll see this.

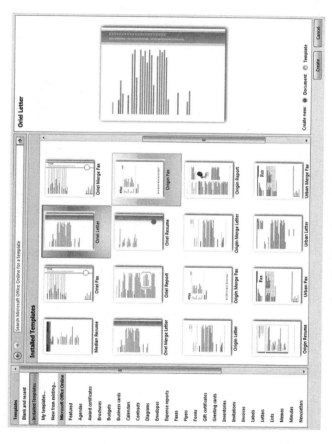

Installed templates dialog box

These are templates for business letters, resumes, fax sheets, and reports. A template produces a pre-formatted document where you need only fill in the blanks or make minor changes to get the document you need. Around 30 of these templates come installed in Word. But Word also offers downloadable templates for many other kinds of documents, such as greeting cards, calendars, brochures, budgets, and more. To use a pre-installed template:

1. Open Microsoft Office, then Microsoft Office Word, and click on the MICROSOFT OFFICE button at the top left of the page.

Microsoft Office button

2. Click on NEW. This opens the menu containing the templates.

3. Click on INSTALLED TEMPLATES to use a pre-installed template. When you find what you need, click on its picture.

4. Look for the DOCUMENT and TEMPLATE options at the bottom of the dialog box. If they're present, make sure DOCUMENT is selected and click on CREATE.

5. When your document appears, make your changes.

6. Click on SAVE AS and choose WORD DOCUMENT in the SAVE AS TYPE. If you have instructed Windows to show file extensions, you'll see that the document has a .docx extension.

Be careful when saving a document you've created with a template. If you see a .dotx extension, you're about to save your document as a template. To prevent that, click on CANCEL and save your document by choosing WORD DOCUMENT.

Design party invitations, newsletters, and more

You can make beautiful custom cards, stationery, and invitations — even if your hands or eyes aren't what they used to be. You can also make professional looking newsletters, business cards, and more with amazing ease.

Remember, Microsoft Word doesn't just come with pre-installed templates. It also comes with options to download many more templates of almost every kind of document you can imagine. With these, you can make your own award certificates, invitations, newsletters, and more. It's easy.

1. Open Microsoft Office Word. Click on the MICROSOFT OFFICE button at the top left of the page and click on NEW.

2. If you don't see what you need in INSTALLED TEMPLATES or MY TEMPLATES, click on MICROSOFT OFFICE ONLINE to find a template to download.

3. Look through the list of categories to find what you want and then click on that category. If a list of subcategories appears, click on the one you want. If no list appears, simply go on to the next step.

4. Click on the picture of the template you want and click on DOWNLOAD. Follow the prompts.

When you get ready to use the templates you added or downloaded earlier, don't go to the INSTALLED TEMPLATES folder — try this.

1. Click on the MICROSOFT OFFICE button and click on NEW.

2. Click on MY TEMPLATES.

3. Click on the icon for the template you want.

4. Look for the DOCUMENT AND TEMPLATE options under CREATE NEW on the right. If they're present, make sure DOCUMENT is selected and click on OK.

5. When the document appears, make your changes.

Jazz up your documents with WordArt

Your newsletter headline seems sleepy, and your flyers aren't very lively. With WordArt you have hundreds of different ways of depicting text. Let's say you want to make the headline "Big News" really sing. Here's how.

1. Open Microsoft Office Word and click on the INSERT tab near the top of the screen.

2. Click on WORDART.

3. Choose your favorite WordArt picture to pick the style for "Big News." Click on the picture.

4. When the dialog box appears, overtype YOUR TEXT HERE with Big News or whatever text you'd like.

5. Click on OK and your headline will look something like this.

WordArt example

6. Press the ENTER key and start the next line of your one-of-a-kind newsletter.

WordArt isn't the only way to decorate your document. Click on the PAGE LAYOUT tab at the top of your screen and you'll discover several other options.

◆ PAGE BACKGROUND lets you choose various background colors or patterns for your document.

◆ PAGE BORDERS lets you pick your favorite border to surround your page of text.

◆ BORDERS lets you choose from various borders to surround a paragraph or table.

◆ THEMES are coordinated packages of headline fonts, text fonts, and graphic effects. You can use them to make your document look more professional.

Add first-class artwork to Word documents

Another way to liven up letters, flyers, and newsletters is with clip art. These ready-made illustrations of items, scenes, and people can make your documents snazzy, more professional, or simply more friendly. You have zillions to choose from, and they're easy to add to a page. Use this process to paste a copy of any clip art into your document.

1. Position your cursor where you want the clip art to go.

2. Click on the INSERT tab.

3. Click on the CLIP ART button.

4. When the CLIP ART pane appears, click in the SEARCH FOR box and type in a search term.

5. Click on the arrow in the SEARCH IN drop-down box and on the checkboxes for the collections you want to search.

6. Click on the arrow in the RESULTS SHOULD BE drop-down and click on the CLIP ART checkbox to select it. Make sure none of the other checkboxes is filled.

7. Click on GO.

8. Click on the clip art picture you want to insert, and it will appear in the document.

9. Click on the close button for the CLIP ART pane.

Dear family and friends,

A very Merry Christmas to you and yours from all of us in the Wright family. It's been a great year for us and we're excited to share all our news with you.

As you know, we're always very involved with all the exciting activities going on at our church and this year has been no exception. In fact, in January, we

Example of clip art in a Christmas letter

To make the text wrap the way it does in the picture, try this.

1. Right-click on your clip art.

2. Click on TEXT WRAPPING and click on MORE LAYOUT OPTIONS.

3. Click on the radio button for SQUARE.

4. Move your cursor down and click on the radio button for RIGHT ONLY.

5. Click on OK.

For more information on clip art, see page 273 in the *Use the Internet for fun & learning* chapter.

Save time with Word's select secrets

Selecting text can help you do amazing things in Microsoft Word — and now you can do this task more easily than ever before. Try these easy shortcuts and you may soon be selecting text with pinpoint accuracy and blazing speed.

To select	Do this
A single word	Double-click on the word or click in front of the word, hold down the left mouse button, and drag the pointer over the word.
	Move the cursor in front of the text. Then hold down the SHIFT key and press the right arrow key until all the text is selected.
Sentence	Single-click in the sentence and press the control (CTRL) key on your keyboard at the same time.
Line of text	Single-click at the beginning of the line and then press the SHIFT and END keys at the same time.
	To select part of a line, single-click inside the line. Press the SHIFT and HOME keys to select all the text between your cursor and the beginning of the line. Press the SHIFT and END keys to select all the text between your cursor and the end of the line.
Paragraph	Triple-click anywhere in the paragraph.
	Single-click at the beginning of the paragraph, hold down the left mouse button, and drag the mouse pointer to end of the paragraph.

To select	Do this
Random block of text	Single-click at the beginning of the text you want to select, hold down the SHIFT key, then single-click a second time where you want the selection to end.
	Place your cursor at the beginning of the text you want to select. Hold down the SHIFT key and use the arrow keys to add or subtract text to your selection until it's exactly what you want.
Multiple pages	Single-click at the point where the selection should start. Scroll to the area where the selection should end, hold down the SHIFT key, and single-click after the last word you want to select.
Entire document	Press the CTRL key and the A key at the same time.
	Move your cursor to the left margin of the document outside the text and triple-click.

Preserve your family history

It's time to write your memoir and you won't believe how simple, swift, and satisfying it is to leave this precious gift to your descendants.

You can even make your memoirs look like a famous person's autobiography by adding headers, footers, page numbers, and dates in Microsoft Word.

Start with a classy header. Before you begin, choose the text you'd like to see in the header, perhaps the title of your memoirs. Here's how you can do it.

1. Open your document and click on the INSERT tab near the top of the screen.

2. Click on the HEADER icon and scroll down to find a header style you like.

3. To include the title of your memoirs, pick a header style that includes TYPE THE DOCUMENT TITLE and click on it.

4. Click inside the area that says TYPE THE DOCUMENT TITLE and type your title.

5. When done, click on CLOSE HEADER AND FOOTER.

Get organized with page numbers. To add a footer with a page number:

1. Click on the INSERT tab.

2. Click on the FOOTER icon and scroll down to find a footer that includes page numbers.

3. Pick your favorite and click on it.

4. When you're done, click on CLOSE HEADER AND FOOTER.

Now you have a professional-looking document with attractive headers and page numbers — the perfect place for your wonderful memories.

Establish a timeline. When your great-great grandchildren read your memoirs years from now, they'll want to know when your stories were written, so add the date between your chapter header and text.

1. Click the space in the document where you'd like the date to go.

2. Click on the INSERT tab.

3. Click on DATE & TIME.

4. Click on the date format you prefer.

5. Make sure UPDATE AUTOMATICALLY is not checked and click on OK.

Now that you know how to add headers, footers, page numbers, and dates to your memoirs, you can use them in other documents, too. Use a header to add a letterhead to letters; the footer to add page numbers; and go to INSERT, then click on DATE & TIME to add the date — and the time, if you want — to your documents.

You need to type the symbol for cents or yen, but you certainly won't find those items on your keyboard. So try this instead. Click on START → ALL PROGRAMS → ACCESSORIES → SYSTEM TOOLS → CHARACTER MAP. Click on the symbol you want. Click on SELECT, then COPY. Open the program and document where you want the symbol to appear and click where the symbol should go. Press CONTROL + V on your keyboard or use the PASTE command in your program's menu to paste in the symbol.

Hire a free typo exterminator

Imagine a document where your most common typos and spelling mistakes magically correct themselves, even as you type them. In just a few minutes, you can train Microsoft Word to do this for you with Autocorrect. This feature recognizes and corrects the most common typos and spelling mistakes. It comes pre-loaded with a list of corrections to make, such as changing "teh" to "the." You can also add your own words and corrections, too.

1. Click on the MICROSOFT OFFICE button in the left corner.

2. Click on WORD OPTIONS at the bottom of the box, then click on PROOFING.

3. Click on the AUTOCORRECT OPTIONS button.

4. When the AUTOCORRECT tab appears, find the REPLACE TEXT AS YOU TYPE checkbox and make sure it's checked.

5. Click inside the REPLACE box to type in the error you've been making. For example, if you forget to put the apostrophe in "there's," type **theres**.

6. Click inside the WITH box and type in the corrected version. For example, you would type **there's.**

7. Click on ADD to include your entry in the list.

Autocorrect only catches the spelling errors and typos in its list. Always follow up with the spelling checker for other errors. To find this feature, go to the REVIEW tab at the top of the screen and click on SPELLING & GRAMMAR.

Easy way to undo your 'deletes'

It's easy to retrieve a paragraph you deleted by mistake in Microsoft Word. Look for the narrow QUICK ACCESS TOOLBAR just above your document and find the button with an arrow pointing counterclockwise. It might remind you of a U-turn sign. This is the UNDO TYPING button.

The Undo Typing and Redo Typing buttons

Click on this button once to undo the last thing you did in Word, and you'll have your paragraph back. If you deleted your paragraph and then did other things, don't worry. Just click on the little arrow next to your UNDO TYPING button and move your cursor down the list to the place where you deleted the paragraph. Click on that line and you'll undo everything you did since deleting the paragraph.

And here's a bonus tip. If you ever need to reverse your undo action, click on the button next to your UNDO TYPING button. This is your REDO TYPING button, and it restores anything you undo.

For more information about the clipboard, which temporarily stores copied or cut text, see page 102 in the *Organize files & folders* chapter.

Save big bucks on printer paper

Make your pack of printer paper last longer. It's surprisingly easy. Just make sure you never have a last page with only a few lines on it. You can do this with Microsoft Word's Shrink One Page option. Shrink One Page adjusts the spacing and size of your text just enough to make your document one page smaller.

But you must add it to the QUICK ACCESS TOOLBAR to use it. To do this, click on the MICROSOFT OFFICE button in the upper left corner. Then click on the WORD OPTIONS button, then CUSTOMIZE. Click on the arrow in the CHOOSE COMMANDS FROM drop-down box. Click on PRINT PREVIEW TAB, then SHRINK ONE PAGE. Next, click on ADD and OK.

Shrinking can foul up complex formatting. Look your pages over before you print or save, and hit the UNDO TYPING button if you don't like what you see.

Never miss another appointment — or birthday

Let your computer help you remember birthdays, appointments, and even tasks on your to-do list with calendar and reminder programs. Calendar programs offer you hard-to-beat benefits like these.

Update appointments with ease. Enter or change the time and day of appointments, events, and tasks. You can set events to repeat daily, weekly, or monthly. Many also offer a to-do list.

Set reminder alarms. You can set an alarm a few minutes or hours before any appointment, task, or event deadline. Some can trigger reminder e-mail messages or send messages to a cell phone or personal digital assistant.

Coordinate schedules. Share calendars so you and family members or colleagues can see each other's calendars to help coordinate schedules or events. Many allow you to send notifications to other family members or colleagues.

Some calendar programs run on your computer, while others are Web-based services. Some programs may look like calendar programs, but they are slightly different. For example, "reminder" programs may not offer all the features of a calendar program but always offer reminder messages, which may be all you need. Similarly, some calendar programs are add-ins for an e-mail program rather than stand-alone software.

It always pays to read software reviews from **www.pcmag.com** and other reliable sources to help choose the best program. But here are examples of free programs recommended by people in the know.

Program	Source	Program type
Google Calendar	*Calendar.google.com*	online service
Yahoo! Calendar	*Calendar.yahoo.com*	online service
Cozi Central	*www.cozi.com*	PC software and online service
Sunbird	*www.mozilla.org*	PC software
Windows Calendar	*comes with Windows Vista*	PC software
Lightning	*www.mozilla.org*	add-on for Thunderbird e-mail
Sandy	*www.iwantsandy.com*	reminder online

Make friends with databases and spreadsheets

Databases and spreadsheets are great for businesses, but they can also help you stay organized at home and perform tricky calculations with ease.

Let spreadsheets crunch the numbers. To set up a budget and track your expenses, you could write down your planned budget, scribble your expenses in a nearby column, and then subtract to find out whether you met your budget. But if you had a spreadsheet, you could enter your planned budget in one column, expenses in the next column — and create a column to automatically calculate whether you met your total budget goal and goals for each category. You could even calculate averages, totals, and differences for each month.

Of course, budgeting isn't all spreadsheets can do. Spreadsheets can perform complicated calculations and crunch any kind of numbers quickly and efficiently. You could use a spreadsheet to help compare prices among grocery stores, balance your checkbook, solve number puzzles, or even calculate statistics for your favorite sports team.

And you can even turn all those numbers into graphs and charts to quickly see how well you're meeting your budget or whether prices are consistently higher at one supermarket than they are at another.

Organize your life with a database. If you have a lot of information about something — such as your family tree, recipes, or items in a collection — a database can help you organize, search, update, sort, and manage it better. For example, if you had a database of recipes and someone gave you a big bag of home-grown zucchini, you could quickly search your database for recipes that have zucchini as an ingredient.

Databases organize your information into records so you can get more bang for your information buck. For example, each record in a genealogy database could be dedicated to a different person. Or if you had a database on your CD collection, each record might contain information about a different CD.

Some database programs even come with templates for different kinds of databases, so you don't have to build that one from scratch.

If you don't find what you need, additional templates may also be available at the database maker's Web site. You may find templates for compiling a home inventory, cataloging your photos, and more.

To find a good database or spreadsheet, read software reviews at **www.cnet.com**, computer magazines, and other reliable sources. Look for easy-to-use programs with templates.

You may find freebies like the database and spreadsheet included in the openoffice office suite available at **www.openoffice.org**. Or you can create free spreadsheets online at **docs.google.com**.

If you've already paid for Microsoft Works, try the database and spreadsheet included there. You can also consider for-pay choices, such as the Microsoft Excel spreadsheet and the Microsoft Access database. Just be sure your computer and operating system meet the program's technical requirements.

Read PDFs for free

PDF stands for portable document format. That "portability" means documents from Microsoft Word and other expensive programs can be turned into PDF format so you can read them without buying those programs.

Of course, that also means you'll need a program that can read PDFs, but you don't have to pay for Adobe's pricey Acrobat program to do it.

Acrobat is meant for people who want to create PDFs, as well as read them. Adobe also makes a free program called Acrobat reader for people who just want to read PDFs.

You can download Adobe Reader from **www.adobe.com** or **www.download.com** and never pay a penny. If you want to do more, another free program called Foxit Reader lets you read PDFs, as well as highlight text and make notes in them. You can download the program at **www.foxitsoftware.com**.

Why you don't need pricey desktop publishing software

You want to create a booklet of recipes to pass on to your children, but you dread paying the high price of desktop publishing software. Fortunately, if you already have a word processing program, you may not need expensive software.

Some word processors now perform many tasks you might expect from desktop publishing software. For example, Microsoft Word has templates for everything from brochures to books.

You can even insert graphics and pictures into Word documents — and do simple page layouts. You may find you can create any document you need without ever paying the price of desktop publishing software.

If you're still wondering whether you need desktop publishing software, here are a few things to consider.

Offset printing. If you plan to print your own booklet or have the Kinko's or Staples print shop spiral-bind it for you, you probably don't need a desktop publishing program. But if you need something called "offset printing," you may need a high-end commercial printer. These printers are very different from Kinko's and usually require special features only available in desktop publishing programs.

Complex graphics and text. If you need a high-end graphics layout with a complex mix of graphic and text items on each page — like the kind you see in magazines or color catalogs — you probably need desktop publishing software. Good examples include Adobe InDesign and QuarkXPress.

You don't have Microsoft Office but people keep sending you Microsoft Word documents, PowerPoint presentations, and Excel spreadsheets. So how can you read these documents without paying a high price for Microsoft Office? Just visit **www.microsoft.com**. Look for their download area. There you'll find free viewer programs that let you read Microsoft Word documents, PowerPoint presentations, Excel spreadsheets, and even Microsoft Visio documents.

Take control of your finances and save money

Tracking your budget and taxes can be easier, speedier, and more accurate than ever before. You may even spot ways to save money. Here's what financial software can do for you.

◆ Helps you pay bills online or automate bill paying. However, you must determine whether online bill paying will be cheaper using the service provided by the software or using the service your bank provides.

◆ Puts all your financial information in a single place so you can get a complete picture of your finances, debts, bills, and payment schedules. This may uncover opportunities for saving that would otherwise be tough to find.

◆ Downloads financial information from your banks and other financial institutions so you enter fewer of your payments and expenses by hand. This can help avoid costly typos and math errors.

◆ Exports your financial information to tax software or provides other tools and information to help with preparing your taxes.

◆ Balances your checkbook electronically by comparing your records to your banks records.

◆ Helps you do most or all of your banking online.

◆ Assists you in planning a budget and tracking your spending in all sorts of categories. Just seeing how these numbers play out each month may help you find new ways to save money and keep you motivated to stick with your budget.

◆ Writes and prints your checks.

◆ Shows graphs and charts that tell you where your money is, where it has been, where it's going, and how your finances are doing. This may make it easier to spot drains on your finances and new ways to save money. Some versions of the software may also help you with retirement planning and investing.

Before you do anything else, read reviews of financial software from sites like **www.cnet.com**. Not only do reviews help you determine which product is best, they also help you find out which ones most closely match your particular needs.

When reading reviews or using a trial version of the software, check for features like these.

◆ easy installation

◆ ability to accept the file formats your bank and other financial institutions use

◆ simple to learn and use

◆ charts and graphs of your expenses so you can tell where the money goes

◆ help building a budget using your expenses and income

◆ compatible with your version of Windows and tech requirements that don't demand more than your computer has

Some programs come in a basic version and other versions offer features for investors or small businesses. Be sure you read reviews about the version that matches your needs. Good examples of programs you can buy include these.

Money	*www.microsoft.com/money*
Quicken	*quicken.intuit.com*

Internet: quick-start guide

❝While it took the radio 38 years, and the television a short 13 years, it took the World Wide Web only 4 years to reach 50 million users. **❞**

PC.com

Easy ways to connect to the Net

There's more than one way to access the Internet, but which one works best for you? Consider the pros and cons of each, then pick a provider, and learn how to get hooked up.

Choose a connection. Each type of Internet service comes with good and bad points. If you want to save money, you may have to sacrifice some speed. Sometimes, your options are limited by what's available in your area.

◆ Dial-up. One of the first gateways to the Internet was through your phone line — and dial-up service is still an option. It is the slowest option, but also the cheapest. Because your computer's modem has to actually dial in to the Internet, you can experience busy signals and dropped connections. If you're not careful, you can also experience unexpected phone charges. Make sure you have a local access number. Otherwise, you'll pay long-distance charges every time you go online.

◆ DSL (Digital Subscriber Line). This type of broadband Internet connection uses the same cables as those used for your telephone, but at higher data rates. That means it's faster than dial-up. It also costs more than dial-up and requires an extra piece of equipment — a modem — but the advantage is that you're always up and running. Although it shares the cables with your phone, DSL does not hog your phone line. You can still use your phone or fax machine while surfing the Web. One drawback is that the farther you live from your DSL service provider's facilities, the slower your Internet speed.

◆ Cable. Just as DSL uses a phone line, cable Internet access, another type of broadband connection, uses cable lines. You need a cable modem, but you don't need to subscribe to cable TV. This option is usually the fastest, but it's also more expensive than both dial-up and DSL. Sharing local bandwidth with other subscribers may affect your service. In other words, too many subscribers could lead to slower and less dependable Internet access.

◆ Satellite. This may be your only option for high-speed Internet service if you live in a rural area without access to DSL or cable. While much faster than dial-up, satellite does not have as much speed as DSL or cable — yet it costs more. Just as with satellite TV, your service can be affected by the elements, like wind and rain.

Pick a provider. No matter which type of Internet service you go with, you also need to choose an Internet service provider, or ISP. Here are some factors you should consider.

- ✦ Price
- ✦ Reliability
- ✦ Length of contract and penalties for breaking it early
- ✦ Technical support

Look for an ISP that offers a trial period, so you can make sure it's right for you before committing to a long-term contract. Many companies offer low introductory prices, but you'll still need to pay installation fees. For your first ISP, you may want to go with a larger, better-known company. As you become more familiar with the Internet, you can shop for other providers.

Summon a wizard. With Windows XP, setting up your Internet connection is a breeze. Just use the New Connection Wizard. This program walks you through what could otherwise be a confusing process. To get to the wizard, choose START, then ALL PROGRAMS → ACCESSORIES → COMMUNICATIONS → NEW CONNECTION WIZARD. If you are undecided about an ISP, the wizard even steers you toward one — MSN. If your ISP gave you a startup CD, you can insert the disc and follow its instructions.

> Not every Internet service provider is on the up and up. Here's one common scam. You might receive a check in the mail and think, "Great. Free money." But if you cash it, you may be trapped into a long-term contract for Internet service, including big penalties for cancellation or early termination. To protect yourself, read all the fine print carefully to make sure you know what you're agreeing to.

When your hook-up is on the blink

Sometimes the best solution is also the simplest. That's the case with Internet connection problems. If you have a sluggish Internet connection or lose your connection entirely, just try unplugging your high-speed modem. If you have a router, you'll need to

197

unplug that, too. Wait a few minutes, then plug everything back in and test your connection. This simple trick can save you a lengthy technical support call. You may want to turn off your computer as well, but it's not always necessary.

If unplugging doesn't work, look for possible culprits. Maybe you recently changed your settings or added or subtracted software from your computer. Try reversing what you just did and you may get your connection back. If you have a dial-up connection, check your phone line for static or other line noise, and make sure call waiting is disabled.

Not ready for a PC? You can still enjoy surfing the Internet and sending e-mail from your television. A device called MSN TV 2 Internet & Media Player, which comes with a remote and wireless keyboard, may be a good alternative for computer beginners. The system costs about $200, but you can buy a refurbished unit for less. You'll also have to pay a monthly fee for MSN TV service. Look for the system in some stores or call 1-866-901-4882 to order. You can also order online at **www.msntv.com**.

Speedy surfing may slow you down

Like a shady politician's career, a computer can be stalled by its past. Instead of scandals or dubious decisions, your computer has to overcome a backlog of information. Luckily, you can elect to fix this problem.

Every time you visit a Web site, your computer creates a temporary Internet file in something called the "cache." These files, located on your hard disk, help speed up browsing when you return to that same page. Rather than wait for the Web site's server to respond again, your computer simply retrieves the data from these files. Surfing the Internet becomes a snap. But there is a downside. All these temporary files accumulate and take up space on your hard drive. That means there's less space for other things, which can slow down your computer.

Clear the cache. Every once in a while, make some room by deleting your temporary files. To do that, open Internet Explorer. Under the TOOLS menu, select INTERNET OPTIONS. In the GENERAL tab, click the DELETE button under BROWSING HISTORY. Next to TEMPORARY INTERNET FILES, click DELETE FILES.

Shrink the space. You can also limit how much disk space goes toward temporary Internet files. Just open Internet Explorer, and go to INTERNET OPTIONS under the TOOLS menu. In the GENERAL tab, under BROWSING HISTORY, click SETTINGS. Set the disk space for temporary Internet files to somewhere between 100 and 500 MB. A lower limit means your computer will rotate old files out as soon as the allotted space becomes filled. A higher number means speedier browsing, but less room for other files and possibly a slower computer.

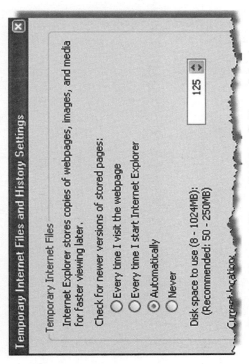

Temporary Internet Files and History Settings dialog box

Get a slow connection up to speed

The Internet should be a superhighway, but a slow connection can make it seem more like a one-lane dirt road. Here's how to merge back into the fast lane.

If you have a dial-up connection, that could be your problem. It's simply much slower than broadband Internet access. You might want to consider upgrading to a faster service, like DSL or cable. Tweaking some settings may also help. From your desktop, click on START → CONTROL PANEL → NETWORK AND INTERNET CONNECTIONS → NETWORK CONNECTIONS. This opens the NETWORK CONNECTIONS dialog box. Right-click your connection, then click PROPERTIES. Under the GENERAL tab, make sure the device listed is your correct modem. Then click CONFIGURE, and uncheck the ENABLE MODEM COMPRESSION box.

Perhaps you already have a broadband connection, in which case, you should examine your network connections. Maneuver to the NETWORK CONNECTIONS dialog box as previously described. Right-click on your connection, then click STATUS to make sure it's running at optimal speed. You can also click REPAIR. This closes and re-establishes your connection.

When times get really desperate, you can also speed things up by disabling graphics you would normally see on Web pages. Open Internet Explorer. Under the TOOLS menu, click INTERNET OPTIONS. Go to the ADVANCED tab, and scroll down to MULTIMEDIA. Uncheck the box next to SHOW PICTURES. When you restart Internet Explorer, you'll see blank spaces instead of graphics. This will speed up browsing, but will severely limit your surfing experience.

For information about computer security issues that might result in a slower Internet connection, like viruses, worms, trojans, malware, spyware, or adware, read stories in the *Security matters* chapter starting on page 145.

Focus in on hard-to-read Web pages

Thanks to the Internet, a world of information lies at your fingertips. Too bad you can't always read it. Here's how to get the most out of Web pages without squinting like Mr. Magoo.

If the text on a Web site is too small in Internet Explorer (IE), do this. Under the VIEW menu, go to TEXT SIZE, then choose LARGEST. You should be able to read the words now.

You may run into other problems, such as odd fonts or styles, like bold or italics, that make text hard to read. Or maybe the text and background colors blend together. To fix these, click on TOOLS → INTERNET OPTIONS. In the GENERAL tab, click ACCESSIBILITY. Click the box next to each of these three options, then click OK.

◆ Ignore colors specified on webpages

◆ Ignore font styles specified on webpages

◆ Ignore font sizes specified on webpages

Smart printing tricks

That Web page looks fine on your computer — but awful when you try to print it. Follow these suggestions for printing better-looking Web pages.

Click on the easy fix. Web designers often include a printer-friendly version of their pages. Look for TEXT ONLY or PRINT FORMAT options on the Web page you want to print.

Printer icon in IE7

Go wide. Under the printer icon, choose PRINT PREVIEW. This allows you to view your Web page as it will print. Notice the PRINT PREVIEW toolbar. Choose Landscape, or horizontal, mode instead of the vertical Portrait mode to keep your page from being cut off on the sides. The third icon from the left is Landscape.

Print Preview toolbar

Think small. Another way to squeeze all the information you need onto one piece of paper is Internet Explorer 7's new SHRINK TO

FIT option. This default setting in PRINT PREVIEW automatically adjusts the width of the Web page to fit on your paper.

Size it up. IE7 also lets you boost the size of text on a page, with a feature called "Print scaling." In PRINT PREVIEW, click on the SHRINK TO FIT drop-down menu. Select a zoom percentage from the list or scroll down to CUSTOM and enter your own. One neat thing about this feature is you can increase the size of just part of a page. Simply select the section of text you want to enlarge before going to PRINT PREVIEW.

Banish the background. A Web page's fancy background may look nice, but it also wastes a lot of ink. Under IE's TOOLS menu, go to INTERNET OPTIONS and click the ADVANCED tab. Scroll down to the PRINTING section and uncheck the box next to PRINT BACKGROUND COLORS AND IMAGES.

Shrink To Fit
30%
50%
60%
70%
80%
85%
90%
95%
100%
125%
150%
200%
Custom

Custom zoom

Cut paper waste

The average Internet user prints 28 pages a day — and a whopping 115 billion sheets of paper are used each year for personal computers. How many of those are wasted pages, with just a line or two of useless text?

Range it in. If you're printing something with multiple pages, scroll through each one in PRINT PREVIEW. Maybe you don't need the last page of a six-page document. Go to FILE → PRINT, then click the PAGES button under PAGE RANGE and enter **1–5**. You can even enter single pages rather than a range.

Narrow it down. Better yet, print only the portions of pages you want. Simply highlight the text you want to print, then go to FILE → PRINT and click the button next to SELECTION under PAGE RANGE.

Get outside help. Look for these software programs that help you save paper.

◆ GreenPrint automatically detects unnecessary pages and eliminates them from your printout. Download the program for free at **www.printgreener.com**. A faster version is available for $29.

◆ FinePrint lets you tweak your printouts to delete extra pages, print multiple pages on one sheet, and combine several print jobs into one. Available at **www.fineprint.com**, this program is powerful, but costs $49.95. They claim you can cut paper, ink, and printer costs by at least 30 percent.

Copyright alert: are you guilty?

Copying that yummy chocolate souffle recipe off a Web page and sending it to 20 of your closest friends may seem harmless enough, but technically, you just broke the law. Now don't panic. Chances are slim to none that anyone will hunt you down and prosecute, but everyone who surfs should know that copyright laws are alive and well on the Internet.

Just like books or music, Web page content can be copyrighted. In fact, everything you view on the net is copyrighted. You may see © or the word COPYRIGHT followed by the year the work was first published and the copyright owner's name. For example, © 2008 FC&A PUBLISHING. This is the first thing you must look for before you copy anything off the Internet. But even without this notice, Web pages are protected.

If you're like most everyday Internet users, you don't have to worry about copyright laws, because the information you print is for your own use. If, however, you have other plans for the copyrighted material — like making money from it or distributing it to others — you need to follow "fair use" guidelines. These guidelines are complex and often difficult to interpret, but generally, the more original material you take and use, the less likely it is fair use. Remember, if in doubt, you can always contact the copyright owner for permission to use Web page content.

chapter 20

Browsers: your key to the Internet

❝May, in spite of all distractions generated by technology, all of you succeed in turning information into knowledge, knowledge into understanding, and understanding into wisdom. ❞

Edsger W. Dijkstra, celebrated computer programming scientist

Explore options beyond Internet Explorer

Your new computer most likely came with Windows — and Internet Explorer 7 (IE7). But that doesn't mean you're stuck with Internet Explorer. Find out what other Web browsers are available and what to look for in a browser.

Browse for a browser. In order to view all the wonderful things on the Web, you need a Web browser. This software application allows you to display and interact with text, pictures, video, and other content found on Web pages. Think of a browser as your computer's eyes and ears when it comes to the Internet.

Used by nearly 75 percent of Web surfers, Internet Explorer is by far the most popular browser. But it's not necessarily the best. Because it's the most common, it's also the most commonly targeted when it comes to security issues. Just using a different browser may reduce your risk of falling prey to viruses or malicious software. If you do choose to use Internet Explorer, make sure you have the latest version. While older versions are much less secure, IE7 has addressed many of the browser's past problems.

Here's a quick look at some other common browsers, including notable highlights and where to download them for free.

Browser	Highlight	Download
Firefox	Considered best all-around browser	www.mozilla.com
Opera	Fastest browser	www.opera.com
Camino	Best browser for Macs	www.caminobrowser.org
Safari	Better for Macs than Windows	www.apple.com/safari
Google Chrome	New option for Windows	www.google.com/chrome

When comparing browsers, you may want to consider some of the following features. Many will be explained in later chapters.

◆ built-in security
◆ pop-up ad blocking
◆ tabbed browsing
◆ a download manager
◆ advanced bookmarking features
◆ a password manager
◆ a form filler
◆ an RSS reader

While you should use the browser that suits you best, most of the Internet stories in this book will use Internet Explorer 7 as an example — simply because it's the most common browser.

Give your browser a boost with plug-ins

Sometimes your browser needs a little help. That's where plug-ins come in. Also called add-ons, plug-ins are programs that interact with your browser to help it perform a specific function, like playing a video. There are dozens of browser plug-ins you can use to surf the Web. Here are the four you really need — and they're free.

Adobe Reader. This plug-in lets you view, print, and search within Portable Document Format (PDF) files, the standard way to send electronic documents.

QuickTime. Want to see the latest blockbuster movie trailer online? Then download this plug-in, which lets you enjoy the most common audio, graphic, and video formats on the Web. You can listen to music, catch up on the news, or watch a TV show from your computer.

Shockwave Player. If you like to play games, take this plug-in seriously. You'll experience the best the Web has to offer. This glitch-free software also lets you follow more serious pursuits, like online learning applications.

Google Toolbar. Add this toolbar to your browser for easy access to the famous Google search engine, plus other features like pop-up blocking, spell checking, and a map tool that automatically links Web addresses to maps.

For one-stop shopping for these essential plug-ins, go to **www.download.com** and enter the plug-in name in the search field.

If you have Internet Explorer 7, another add-on you should consider is IE7Pro, which gives your browser lots of extras and features to make it friendlier, more useful, more secure, and more customizable.

For quick access to more add-ons — which are not always free — click on the TOOLS menu in Internet Explorer, then choose MANAGE ADD-ONS → FIND MORE ADD-ONS.

For information on browser filters and security plug-ins, see page 220 in the *Secrets to safe surfing* chapter.

Surf smarter with tabs

You enjoy moving back and forth between Web sites, but don't like the clutter of several open browser windows on your desktop or Taskbar. Now you can surf the Web with tabbed browsing, a new feature in Internet Explorer 7. It lets you flip between multiple Web sites in a single browser window. When using tabbed browsing, you'll see a row of tabs under your toolbars and above the actual Web page. Each one shows the name of the site you're viewing. You automatically have one tab open when you start up IE7.

Start new. There are two ways to open a new empty tab.

◆ Click the smaller empty tab located to the right of the current tab.

◆ Press CTRL + T.

New tab button

Once you've got a new tab open, simply type a new Web address into the Address bar and press RETURN. The new site will open under that tab in your current browser window. But what if you're doing a search and you don't want to lose the main search page while you explore one of the sites the search engine found? Here are two ways to automatically open a linked Web page in a new tab.

207

◆ Hold the CTRL key down while you click on an active link on a Web page.

◆ Right-click an active link on a Web page, then choose OPEN IN NEW TAB.

Jump. Once you have multiple tabs open, probably the easiest way to move from one tab to the other is to click on the appropriate tab. But there are other options.

◆ To cycle forward through your row of tabs, press CTRL + TAB.

◆ To cycle backward, press CTRL + SHIFT + TAB.

◆ To tab by number hold CTRL while you type the number. For example, go to the second tab by pressing CTRL + 2.

◆ To get a list of all open tabs, click on the down arrow to the left of the first tab. Scroll through the list and click on the one you want.

View thumbnails. A neat way to see all your open tabs at once is through a feature called Quick Tabs. Just click on the button with four small squares in it. Or press CTRL + Q. You'll see all your tabs in thumbnail form. Go to the tab you want by clicking on its thumbnail. You can also close tabs here by clicking on the X in the upper-right corner of the thumbnail.

The Quick Tabs button appears when multiple tabs are open

Save a group of tabs. Just as you can save your favorite Web sites, you can save a group of tabs. Click on FAVORITES in your menu toolbar then choose ADD TAB GROUP TO FAVORITES. Give the group of tabs a name, then click on ADD. You'll find your tab group among your Favorites, and each Web page will open in a separate tab.

Bump up to bigger toolbar buttons

Good things come in small packages — but sometimes bigger is better. If you need the toolbar buttons in Internet Explorer 7 to be bigger, there's an easy way to do that. Just right-click anywhere in the toolbar area. Then click on USE LARGE ICONS. You'll see the HOME, PRINT, BACK, and other buttons grow before your grateful eyes.

Changing the size of the icons is just one way to customize your browser's toolbars. Here are some other ways to tailor your toolbar to fit your needs.

Look for the label. Maybe your icons are plenty big, but you forget what they mean. After right-clicking in the toolbar area, click on CUSTOMIZE COMMAND BAR, then choose SHOW ALL TEXT LABELS. This should make things clearer.

Play hide and seek. Reduce the clutter on your screen by hiding toolbars you rarely use, while keeping often-used toolbars easy to see. Again, right-click anywhere in the toolbar area, then check or uncheck whichever toolbars you want.

Rearrange the furniture. You can re-size toolbars and arrange them however you like. Just click on and hold the dotted vertical line to the left of the toolbar and drag it where you want it. When you're satisfied with your setup, you can right-click in the toolbar area and choose LOCK THE TOOLBARS.

Mix and match. For an even more customized toolbar, you can decide which buttons to feature. Here's how.

1. Right-click in the toolbar area, and choose CUSTOMIZE COMMAND BAR.

2. Click on ADD OR REMOVE COMMANDS.

3. This brings up the CUSTOMIZE TOOLBAR dialog box. The area on the left shows available toolbar buttons, and the one on the right shows the buttons currently on your toolbar.

4. To add a button to your toolbar, select it from the box on the left and click on ADD. The button will appear in the right-hand box.

5. To remove a button from your toolbar, select it from the box on the right and click on REMOVE. It will be whisked away to the box on the left.

Move into a new home page

Your home is your castle, where you feel most comfortable. Your Internet home page should be the same. Don't feel obligated to stick with the default home page set by your Internet provider. Get your surfing session off to a good start by setting your own home page. Here's how to switch from your default home page to something more personal.

1. Go to the Web page you want as your home page, then click on the arrow to the right of the HOME icon on your toolbar.

2. Click on ADD OR CHANGE HOME PAGE.

3. Choose USE THIS WEBPAGE AS YOUR ONLY HOME PAGE.

4. Click on YES.

FCA Publishing

Home

Add or Change Home Page...

Remove

Set up your home page

Can't decide on just one home page? Thanks to tabbed browsing, you can have multiple home pages. In Step 3 above, choose ADD THIS WEBPAGE TO YOUR HOME PAGE TABS. Then click on YES.

Another way to change your home page is to go to TOOLS, then INTERNET OPTIONS. In the GENERAL tab, just type in the Web address of your desired home page. Or, if you're already on that Web page, click on USE CURRENT. You can add more home page tabs here, too, by typing each address on a separate line.

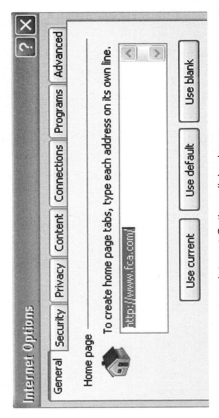

Internet Options dialog box

Get a fix on favorite sites

You may not be able to recapture favorite moments from your youth — but you can easily go back to your favorite Web sites. Just designate them as Favorites. Also called Bookmarks in other browsers, Favorites are a collection of select Web pages — perhaps those you visit most often. And with Favorites, you don't have to memorize long Web addresses to get back to a site you like. It's easy to set them up in Internet Explorer 7.

First, find the star icon with a plus symbol to the left of your tabs. Then, when you're visiting a Web site you want to save as a Favorite, just click on this icon. Select the first option from the drop-down menu, ADD TO FAVORITES. Now you'll see the ADD A FAVORITE dialog box. The title of the current Web page automatically appears in the NAME field, but you can change the name to something shorter or easier to remember if you want. Then click on ADD.

Favorites Center and Add a Favorite icons

Add as many Favorites as you want. To access them, click on the large star icon — with no plus sign. This opens the FAVORITES CENTER. Scroll down and find the name of the site you want to visit. Click on it and — presto! — you've found your way back to a favorite Web site.

211

Fantastic ways to organize your favorites

Now that you have accumulated a bunch of favorite sites, your FAVORITES CENTER has become quite cluttered. Follow these suggestions for tidying things up.

Try the ABC approach. One easy way to bring order to chaos is to arrange your list of Favorites in alphabetical order. Click on the FAVORITES CENTER icon to bring up your list of Favorites. Hover your pointer over any item in the list and right-click. Find SORT BY NAME in the drop-down menu and click on it.

Have fun with folders. Maybe you visit several Web sites dealing with gardening. Rather than have your gardening sites scattered among your list of Favorites, you can store them all in a folder labeled Gardening. Here's how to create folders within your Favorites.

1. Click on the ADD TO FAVORITES icon — the star with a plus sign — then choose ORGANIZE FAVORITES. An ORGANIZE FAVORITES dialog box appears.

2. Create a folder by clicking on NEW FOLDER. Type in a name, then press ENTER on your key board. Create as many folders as you want.

3. Drag any Favorite into an appropriate folder. You can even move folders, like your Gardening folder, into another folder, perhaps one called Hobbies.

4. Single-click on a folder to see what Favorites are stored inside.

5. While you're here in the ORGANIZE FAVORITES dialog box, you can also rename or delete Favorites or folders.

6. Close the ORGANIZE FAVORITES dialog box.

Another way to move a Favorite or folder is by selecting it in the ORGANIZE FAVORITES dialog box with a single-click. Then click on the MOVE button. From within the BROWSE FOR FOLDER dialog box, choose which folder to put it in.

Once you have your Favorites organized into folders, it's easy to keep them nice and tidy. Next time you add a Web site to your Favorites, you can send it straight to the appropriate folder. When you click on ADD TO FAVORITES, before clicking on ADD, specify which folder it should go to. Just click on the arrow in the CREATE IN field and scroll down to the folder you want. You can even create a new folder to house your latest link.

Speed launch favorites from the Taskbar

For even quicker access to your preferred Web sites, add your Favorites folder to your Windows Taskbar.

1. Right-click on your Taskbar.

2. Point to TOOLBARS and click on NEW TOOLBAR.

3. In the dialog box, navigate to Favorites. You can usually get there by going to MY COMPUTER → LOCAL DISK (C:) → DOCUMENTS AND SETTINGS → YOUR USER NAME → FAVORITES.

4. Click on your FAVORITES folder. Then click on OK.

Now your Favorites folder appears on your Taskbar. Single-click on the double arrows, then navigate to the site you want and single-click. You won't even need to launch Internet Explorer first. Use the same steps to add any folder you want to your Taskbar.

Web favorites to go: take them with you

You love your old Favorites, and you never want to lose them. Luckily, you can import and export them — which comes in handy in several situations, including:

◆ switching from one browser to another, such as from Internet Explorer to Firefox.

◆ switching from an old computer to a new computer.

✦ creating a backup for emergencies.

✦ switching from your home computer to an office computer or laptop.

In Internet Explorer, click on the ADD TO FAVORITES button, then click IMPORT AND EXPORT. This brings up the Import/Export Wizard, a built-in program that walks you through this task. Just follow the prompts. The Wizard creates a standard HTML file named *bookmark.htm* and saves it in your MY DOCUMENTS folder. When you import your Favorites to a new browser, the Wizard looks for that file.

If you're going from one computer to another, copy the *bookmark.htm* file to a disk or flash drive. Then import your Favorites from the disk or flash drive to the new computer. You can also copy this file onto a disk, just so you have a backup.

Cookies aren't always a treat

Just like the Cookie Monster, some Web sites love cookies. They can make surfing easier for you — but they can also cause problems.

So what is a computer cookie? Simply put, it's a small file that contains information, such as your log-in name, password, or preferences. A Web site sends a cookie to your browser, and it's stored on your hard drive. When you return to a Web site that sent a cookie, it will retrieve the cookie and recognize you. This makes certain things easier. For instance, you don't have to log in every time you go to a subscription site. Other sites might greet you by name or recommend items based on what you've bought previously from the site.

Contrary to popular belief, most cookies don't follow your every move online — but they can track some things. Those from banner ads do track you from site to site and rotate the ads you see. Malicious cookies, usually caught by anti-virus programs, keep a trace on your surfing habits in an attempt to build a profile of your interests. Mostly though, cookies are a way for Web sites to keep track of unique visitors.

Say no to cookies. If you're concerned about your privacy, you can take steps to restrict cookies. You can block them all, but that makes surfing the Web almost impossible. You can set your browser so you'll be prompted to accept or decline each cookie, but this can be a hassle. Your best bet is to selectively block cookies.

1. Go to the TOOLS menu → INTERNET OPTIONS and click on the PRIVACY tab.

2. Adjust the slider setting as you wish. It ranges from ACCEPT ALL COOKIES to BLOCK ALL COOKIES.

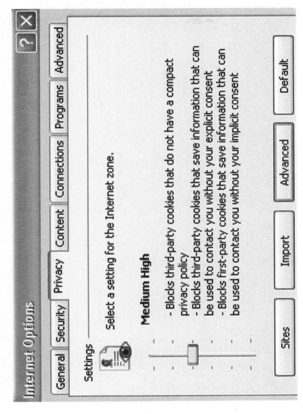

Adjust your cookie settings

3. Or click on the ADVANCED button to override the automatic setting and choose your own options. First-party cookies are those that come come from the Web site you are visiting. Third-party cookies come from content — mostly advertising — on the site you're viewing. You can check ALWAYS ALLOW SESSION COOKIES. These track only a single visit to a Web site.

215

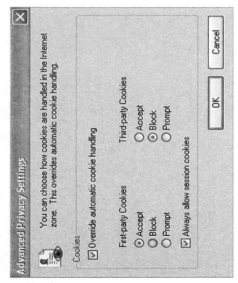

Advanced Privacy Settings dialog box

You can also allow or block cookies from specific Web sites. While on the PRIVACY tab of the INTERNET OPTIONS dialog box, click on SITES. This opens the PER SITE PRIVACY ACTIONS dialog box. Type in the address of the Web site and click on either BLOCK or ALLOW.

Burn those cookies. You have a few ways of getting rid of the cookies already on your computer.

◆ To delete all cookies, go to TOOLS → INTERNET OPTIONS → GENERAL tab. Under BROWSING HISTORY, click on DELETE. Click on DELETE COOKIES, then click on YES. Remember, this may cause some Web pages not to work properly.

◆ You could pick and choose which cookies you delete. While you're on the GENERAL tab, click on SETTINGS under BROWSING HISTORY. Then click on the VIEW FILES button. Scroll down until you see files that begin with "cookie." Right-click on the ones you want to get rid of, then click on DELETE.

Put a stop to pop-ups

You're watching your favorite TV show when all of a sudden, a commercial interrupts the action. Not a regular commercial, but one that appears right on top of the actors' faces while the show is going on.

That's kind of what happens when you try to surf the Web and get bombarded with pop-up ads — small windows, usually advertisements, that open on top of your current browser window.

But not all pop-up windows are bad. Because they let Web sites display information without disrupting the page you're currently viewing, they can be useful. For instance, a pop-up may help you fill out a form on a Web page by explaining something without forcing you to leave — and then navigate back to — the page.

> Pop-under ads are similar to pop-up ads except you don't notice them until you close your browser window.

Block pop-ups. If you have Internet Explorer 7, it contains a built-in pop-up blocker. By default it should be turned on. To make sure, go to TOOLS → POP-UP BLOCKER. If it's on, you'll see TURN OFF POP-UP BLOCKER. You'll also see POP-UP BLOCKER SETTINGS. Click on this option to adjust how your browser handles pop-ups.

You can change the filter level to low, medium, or high — which blocks all pop-ups. Choose how you want to be alerted to a blocked pop-up. A sound may play or an information bar may appear to let you know when a pop-up is blocked. You can even enter Web sites that you will accept pop-ups from.

Firefox comes with similar pop-up protection. Just go to TOOLS → OPTIONS → CONTENT and check the BLOCK POP-UP WINDOWS option. To set exceptions for safe Web sites, click on the EXCEPTIONS button and enter Web addresses in the ALLOWED SITES → POP-UPS dialog box.

You may want to consider Adblock Plus, a free add-on for Firefox that blocks ads even more thoroughly.

Get a power boost. If your browser's pop-up blocking isn't working well enough for you, you can download software for greater power — programs like Ad Muncher, PopUp Ad SmasheR, or Ad Annihilator. Free add-ons, like the Google Toolbar, IE AdBlock, and IE7Pro also fight pop-ups.

Avoid pop-up perils

If a pop-up ad manages to get through your pop-up blocker, don't click on it. Closing that pop-up window could cause automatic charges to your credit card. It could also deliver malware to your computer.

One common marketing trick, known as a negative option scam, happens after you buy something online. You make your purchase, and then a pop-up appears. You most likely close it without thinking. But what you've actually done is enroll in some sort of buyers club. Because the store is partnered with the marketer, they have your credit card number. You will be billed every month until you cancel or opt out of the service.

To close a pop-up safely, do not click on the X — or anywhere else within the pop-up. Bring up the WINDOWS TASK MANAGER dialog box by pressing CTRL + SHIFT + ESC or CTRL + ALT + DELETE. Select the pop-up and click on END TASK.

Digital history: see where you've been

Can't remember where you found that great recipe on the Internet? Here's how to find any visited Web site easily — even days later.

Become a history buff. Your computer keeps track of Web sites you've visited in its "history." This is a handy way to see where you've been online. To view your history in Internet Explorer, just click on the big star button, or FAVORITES CENTER. Then click on HISTORY. Scroll down the list to find the site you're looking for, and click on it. If you click on the small arrow next to HISTORY, you'll get a drop-down list with options. You can view your Web browsing history by date, by site, by most visited, or by the order visited today. You can even choose SEARCH HISTORY, then enter a word or phrase. So, if you're looking for a chicken recipe, type **chicken** and you'll get a list of Web pages you've visited that mention chicken.

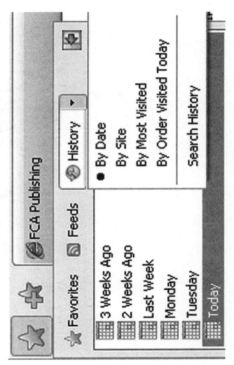

Change the way you view your History

Cover your tracks. You don't always want your browsing history to be so readily available. Perhaps you share the computer with someone else and want to protect your privacy. To completely wipe out your history, go to the TOOLS menu, then click on INTERNET OPTIONS. In the GENERAL tab, under BROWSING HISTORY, click on DELETE. Then click on DELETE HISTORY.

You can also delete individual sites. When viewing your history, just right-click on any site, then click DELETE.

Limit the clutter. Maybe you don't want such a long record of where you've been on the Internet. You can change your history settings. Again, go to TOOLS → INTERNET OPTIONS → GENERAL tab. Under BROWSING HISTORY, click on SETTINGS. You can specify how many days Internet Explorer will save the list of Web sites you've visited. You can even set the number of days to "0" so you will leave no history.

chapter 21

Secrets to safe surfing

"In 1998 the U.S. Congress made identity theft a federal offense."

Associated Content

Control content with Web filters

Thanks to its wide-open nature, the Internet features plenty of questionable Web sites. Pornography, violence, hate groups, and other disturbing content litters the Web. Luckily, you can take steps to keep offensive material off your computer screen.

Flip on the filter. Accidentally pull up a naughty site? Protect yourself and any children who use your computer with Internet Explorer 7's built-in filter — it's free and easy to use.

1. Under the TOOLS menu, click on INTERNET OPTIONS, then go to the CONTENT tab.

2. Under CONTENT ADVISER, click on ENABLE.

3. Click on a category and adjust the slider to control content.

4. Use the other tabs to specify approved or disapproved sites or to create a password to unlock the filter.

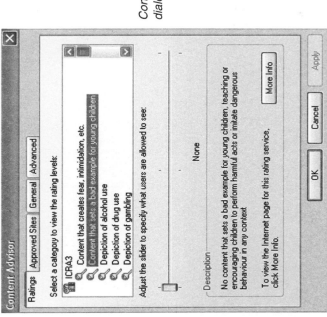

Content Advisor dialog box

Pick some plug-ins. Other browsers may not come with built-in filters, but you can download plug-ins, or add-ons, that let you filter Internet sites based on settings. For example, Firefox features these two filters.

✦ FoxFilter, which works with Windows and Macs, has password-protected features and lets you designate safe sites.

✦ ProCon Latte blocks all sorts of material, including pornography and gambling. It also comes with a profanity filter.

To download these plug-ins, go to **www.mozilla.com** and click on ADD-ONS.

Sanitize your searches. If you're tired of bringing up objection-able material during your Web searches, use a searching filter that restricts Internet searches by content. Here's how to make your Google search more family-friendly, with its SafeSearch option.

1. Go to **www.google.com.**

2. Click on PREFERENCES. This option sits next to the search box in the middle of the page.

3. Scroll down to SAFESEARCH FILTERING. You'll get three filtering options: strict, moderate, and none. Choose the one that best fits your needs, then click on SAVE PREFERENCES at the bottom of your screen.

Shop for software. You can also purchase filters for more control. Prices range from about $30 to about $60, and common features include e-mail filtering, pop-up blocking, and chat room monitoring. When shopping for software filters, consider ease of use and effectiveness. You want to find the perfect balance between not filtering out enough offensive material and filtering too much. One important feature to look for is foreign language filtering. This counteracts a common trick of teens — entering the foreign language equivalent of certain blocked keywords to circumvent filters. Here's a quick look at some popular filters and where to download them.

Net Nanny	*www.netnanny.com*
CYBERsitter	*www.cybersitter.com*
Safe Eyes	*www.safeeyes.com*
CyberPatrol	*www.cyberpatrol.com*
MaxProtect	*www.max.com*

Remember, no filter is 100 percent effective. What's offensive to some people may not be offensive to others. But filters reduce your risk of viewing Web content you're not comfortable with.

For information about safe downloading from the Internet, see page 165 in the *Straight talk about software* chapter.

ActiveX: cut through the confusion

ActiveX controls are small computer programs used to create interactive Web content. They let you play games with other Internet users, display stock tickers, and view animation sequences. Some Web sites or Internet tasks require them. For the most part, they make Web browsing more enjoyable and effective. In fact, Windows Update even uses an ActiveX control to compare installed patches and updates on your system with those available on Microsoft's servers.

> If an ActiveX control contains the signature of a known virus or worm, your anti-virus software will intercept it and refuse to allow the installation to proceed.

But there is a dark side to ActiveX. They can be used to collect or damage information on your computer, install software without your consent, or even allow someone else to control your computer remotely.

You can raise the security levels on your computer to keep out ActiveX controls.

1. Go to TOOLS → INTERNET OPTIONS → SECURITY tab.

2. Adjust the security level to HIGH. Realize that this may limit your Web browsing.

3. Click on the green check mark above TRUSTED SITES, then click on the SITES button. Here you can add Web sites that are safe. This will loosen up some of the restrictions on sites you frequently visit.

Security tab options in the Internet Options dialog box

For more control over your settings, you can click on CUSTOM LEVEL. Then scroll down to the ACTIVEX CONTROLS AND PLUGS-INS section to make changes. These settings can be complicated, and changes here can cause error messages.

For instance, if a Web site needs to install an ActiveX control and either your browser or your security settings prevent it, you will see an Information Bar pop up at the top of the Web page. You'll have to click on the message for more information or to take action. From this point, you're in control of your computer's security. Only install ActiveX programs if you completely trust the publisher.

Stay up-to-date on Internet safety

Protecting your computer from hackers and scammers is a constant battle. Visit the following Web sites to keep up with the latest tips for staying safe online.

U.S. Chamber of Commerce Security Toolkit	www.uschamber.com/sb/security
staysafe.org	www.staysafe.org
Stay Safe Online	www.staysafeonline.org
OnGuard Online	www.onguardonline.gov
NetSmartz	www.netsmartz.org
GetNetWise	www.getnetwise.org
i-SAFE	www.isafe.org
AARP	www.aarp.org/netsafe

Spot new Internet scams

The Internet gives you access to a whole world of information and excitement. Unfortunately, it can also be very dangerous territory, full of scams and fraud. In fact, the FBI says that consumers lost close to $240 million from online swindles in 2007. Don't be a target. Catch fraud alerts.

Online scams have many of the same telltale signs as those conducted by phone or mail. Offers that sound too good to be true, vague promises of easy money, and pressure to act now should all raise red flags. Learn how to protect yourself from high-tech scams, like phishing, identity theft, and credit card fraud. These two Web sites can help keep you informed of the latest Internet scams.

◆ The National Consumer League's Fraud Center at **www.fraud.org** provides general information and helpful tips about fraud, including Internet fraud and scams that target the elderly. It's also a good place to report fraud, using an online complaint form.

◆ ScamBusters at **www.scambusters.org** is also a recommended source for trusted information on Internet scams, identity theft, and urban legends. You can even subscribe to a free weekly e-mail newsletter that keeps you in the loop about the latest scams making their way through cyberspace.

File sharing: 5 tips help sidestep dangers

You probably taught your children the value of sharing. But when it comes to sharing the files on your computer, the risks may outweigh the rewards.

File sharing, as its name implies, lets you swap files with other computer users, by way of a peer-to-peer (P2P) network. With software like LimeWire, BearShare, and Morpheus, once you are connected to the network, you can search for and download copies of files that other users have shared from their hard drives — music, videos, games, software, documents, and PDFs. It's convenient, useful, and fun.

It's also potentially dangerous. In order to share files on your computer and sometimes in order for you to access files on other computers within a P2P network, you must open a specific port through your firewall. Once you open the port, you are no longer protected. Remember, everyone on the network is anonymous — they could be anyone from anywhere in the world.

An alternative to peer-to-peer networking is to put files you want to share online. For example, Microsoft Office Live Workspace lets you store documents online for free. No software is required. You can even set up passwords so only those you trust can access your files. Go to **workspace.officelive.com** for more details.

If you decide to use P2P file sharing, take the following precautions recommended by the Federal Trade Commission.

Set up file sharing carefully. Any changes you make to the P2P software's default settings during installation could cause problems.

Unless you want your personal and financial information to become public knowledge, use public computers with caution. Never use the computers in the library or Internet cafe to make online purchases or do online banking. You may not even want to check your e-mail. These computers are often contaminated with spyware. Scammers can steal your passwords and gain access to all your important information.

For instance, generally, there is a default folder for sharing designated during the software installation. Never change it to the root "C:" drive. This allows everyone on the P2P network to see and access virtually every file and folder on your entire hard drive, including sensitive files like your tax returns. The risk for identity theft is very real.

Know what you're sharing. Make sure your shared folder contains only files that you want others on the P2P network to be able to view and download.

Control your connection. Close it when you're not using it. Exit the file-sharing program rather than just close the window. Also make sure it does not start automatically when you turn on your computer.

Screen for viruses. Use an effective anti-virus program and update it regularly. Without it, your computer could become infected with malware or adware.

Talk with your family. Make sure everyone understands the risks and precautions. It's possible you could unintentionally download pornography or copyrighted material — and find yourself in legal trouble.

For information on how to share files with other computers on your home network, see page 45 in the *Home network options* chapter. And for information on using your operating system to make folders private, see page 104 in the *Organize files & folders* chapter.

chapter 22

Successful Web searching

> ❝Google is a version of the word Googol, which is the number 1 followed by 100 zeroes, representing the large number of Web pages Google searches.❞
>
> Associated Content

In search of the perfect search engine

Before you can even begin looking for something on the Internet, you must pick a search engine. These wonderful tools give you a quick, convenient way to make sense of the vast amount of information on the World Wide Web.

Search engines work by constantly scouring the Internet for new and updated Web pages, using automated programs called "spiders" or "robots." These programs copy everything they find and send it back to the search engine database, which stores and indexes each item.

All you have to do is go to a search engine's Web site and type in a keyword — you'll have results in seconds.

Because you're really searching the search engine's copy of the Internet, each engine will yield different results in a different order. So you may want to try more than one.

Pick and choose. Google, found at **www.google.com**, is probably the most popular search engine. The word "google" is even used as a verb these days. Google is also considered the best of the bunch — but it's not your only option.

Ask	www.ask.com
Windows Live Search	www.live.com
Yahoo!	www.yahoo.com
AOL Search	search.aol.com
Lycos	www.lycos.com
AltaVista	www.altavista.com

Metasearch engines combine results from several other search engines. Here are a few of the most common metasearch engines.

Dogpile	www.dogpile.com
Search.com	www.search.com
Mamma Metasearch	www.mamma.com

Some searches may require multiple searches using multiple engines to find what you're looking for. Other times, you may get lucky on your first try.

Search from your browser. You don't really need to go to a search engine's home page to perform an Internet search. Most browsers, including Internet Explorer 7, come with a built-in search bar in the top right corner of the browser window. Just enter your search term and press ENTER. You can move your cursor to the search bar quickly by pressing CTRL + E.

The default search engine for Internet Explorer 7 is Windows Live Search, but you can use other engines — or even change the default.

1. Click on the arrow to the right of the blue magnifying glass in the top right corner of IE7's window.

2. Click on FIND MORE PROVIDERS.

3. Click on the search provider you want to add, and the ADD SEARCH PROVIDER dialog box appears.

4. You can check the box next to MAKE THIS MY DEFAULT SEARCH PROVIDER.

5. Then click on ADD PROVIDER.

Internet Explorer 7's built-in search bar

When you perform a search, you can use your default engine or select a different one. Your options appear in a drop-down menu when you click on the arrow.

Super search strategies make surfing simple

Sometimes it seems searching the Internet is like looking for a needle in a haystack. But these search engine tips help you find anything on the Web, without being overwhelmed.

Be specific. Successful searchers say to use four or five keywords, rather than just one or two.

Tweak the top 10. Just as David Letterman has his Top 10 list, search engines usually display their results 10 at a time. Rather than scroll through multiple pages, stick to these top results. They should be the ones the search engine considers the strongest. If they're not, tweak your search until you get a useful top 10.

Refine your search. Most of the time, you need to narrow, or limit, the search to make it more specific. But sometimes, you may need to broaden it. Here are some helpful techniques.

◆ Put quote marks around your keywords. This is great for proper names, phrases, quotes, book or movie titles, and song lyrics. The search engine will look for Web pages where the words within the quote marks appear side by side on the page.

◆ Subtract keywords. Use a minus sign (-) to exclude a keyword or phrase. This is a good way to limit your search. Say you want to find information about Paul McCartney, but not the Beatles. Type **"Paul McCartney" -Beatles**. Note, the minus sign must be touching the keyword you want to exclude.

◆ Expand your search with OR. Instead of finding pages that include both terms, you'll find pages with either one.

Tap into terrific tricks. Really narrow your searches with these simple, yet little-known pointers.

◆ Need a definition? Type **define:** plus the term you need defined into the search engine.

◆ Want to limit your search to a particular Web site? Type **site:** followed by the site's Web address and your keyword or phrase.

◆ Looking for a specific type of file? Type **filetype:** then the type of file you want — for instance, **PDF** — before your keyword or phrase.

◆ Seeking the name of a specific Web page? If you type **allintitle:** before your keywords, it will limit your search to Web page names.

For even more focused searches, explore the Advanced Search options on your search engine. You can do things like limit your search to sites that end in ".gov" or ".edu" or even search in other languages.

Find old friends and long-lost relatives

What ever happened to your high school buddy? Thanks to the Internet, it's easy to find out. You have a variety of options for tracking down friends, relatives, and former classmates. You'll wonder why you didn't do this sooner.

Give Google a go. The Internet search engine Google also includes a phonebook directory, which makes it easy to find phone numbers and street addresses. Just type the first and last name of the person you're looking for, followed by a comma, then the city, another comma, and the state or zip code. For instance, type **Joe Smith, Philadelphia, Pa.**

Search online white pages. You can also turn to hundreds of online white pages. One of the best sources is Switchboard.com at **www.switchboard.com**. If you don't find who you're looking for there, try some of these other useful directories.

Superpages	*www.superpages.com*
AnyWho	*www.anywho.com*
PeopleFinder	*www.peoplefinder.com*
Yahoo! People Search	*people.yahoo.com*
411.com	*www.411.com*

To find more white pages directories, simply type **white pages** into your favorite search engine. Not all directories will include the same information, and some listings may be out of date. That's why it's important to try several sites before giving up.

Register for more resources. Looking for an old classmate? A fraternity brother? A military buddy? Some sites specialize in these groups. They require you to register in order to search their listings — which means that someone may also find you.

◆ Find fellow alumni at **www.classmates.com** or **www.reunion.com**.

◆ Locate fraternity brothers or sorority sisters at **www.findagreek.com**.

♦ Reconnect with military buddies at **www.militarylocator.com** or **www.militaryconnections.com.**

Pay for information. If you're coming up empty in your search, you can also use pay sites. In addition to finding phone numbers or addresses, these sites can conduct background checks or look up court records. It's best to use these sites as a last resort and for legitimate reasons. Otherwise, it may cross the line into stalking.

Online Yellow Pages mean business

Instead of rifling through a large phone book, let your fingers do the walking across your keyboard. With the Internet, it's easy to find a business phone number or address, even if you're not sure how to spell the name.

Just type in the name of the business along with the city or zip code into your search engine. Even if you spell the name wrong, Google can help. Most likely, you'll get a message that reads "Did you mean" followed by the correct spelling.

Most of the directories you use to find people also let you search for businesses. Switchboard.com, for instance, even includes a directory of businesses by town. Just type in the zip code and get category-by-category listings. As with white pages, you can also search for more online directories by typing **yellow pages** into your search engine.

Here are some other handy online yellow pages.

Yellowpages.com	www.yellowpages.com
Yellow.com	www.yellow.com
Yahoo! Yellow Pages	yp.yahoo.com
Yellowbook	www.yellowbook.com

Online directories search out the specific

Ever wonder which company makes a certain product? Or where exactly a famous landmark is? To answer very precise questions like these, you may want to use a directory rather than a search engine.

A directory is simply a collection of Web sites organized by subject. You can click on a topic and browse the resources related to it. Unlike search engines, which use automated computer programs to constantly look for new and updated Web pages, directories are maintained by people. So they are limited to those pages known by the people who run the directory.

You can find professional and academic directories, as well as commercial ones. The most famous of these is Yahoo! Directory, which now also includes a search engine. For a shortcut, go to **dir.yahoo.com.** Other examples of directories include GoGuides.org and About.com.

If you're just looking for one or two pages from a specific source about a popular topic, use a directory. You'll get fewer results than if you used a search engine, but they will be relevant.

High-speed scan finds it fast

You think you've found the Web page you want — but it's packed with too much information. It might take forever to read through it all. Here's an easy way to find exactly what you're looking for on a Web page.

1. Press CTRL + F to bring up the Find box. You can also go to the EDIT menu and choose FIND ON THIS PAGE.

2. Type the word or phrase you're looking for on the page and press ENTER. Watch the screen. Your found word(s) will be highlighted.

3. Click on NEXT or PREVIOUS in the Find box to move from one instance of the word or phrase to another within the Web page.

23

chapter

Internet deals & steals

❝The Internet is becoming the town square for the global village of tomorrow. **❞**

Bill Gates

9 must-know tips for safe online shopping

The Internet is a shopper's paradise. It's like a giant mall that's open 24 hours and features an unlimited selection of products. But, along with the convenience and choices comes risk.

Stick to big names. Sometimes, bigger is better. Large, established companies you know and trust, like Amazon, Target, or Wal-Mart, come with more safeguards and less risk than smaller, lesser known ones.

Spot security signs. Look for these two security indicators before giving your credit card number online. They mean the information you type will be encrypted, or coded, so no one will be able to view it except the receiving site.

✦ The prefix for the Web site in your address bar should switch from "http" to "https."

✦ You should see a padlock symbol, either in your address bar or at the bottom right of your browser window.

Be careful, though. Sometimes scammers try to fake these well-known safeguards. For example, scam Web sites can include "https" in their Web address. You might see "http://https.www." Remember, a truly safe site begins with "https."

Pay with a credit card. Debit cards can help keep you from spending money you don't have. But there are times when you absolutely shouldn't use one. Shopping online is one of them. When you use a credit card, you generally have zero liability for fraudulent purchases. And, because the money does not come right from your checking account — as it does with a debit card — it's easier to dispute charges. Banks are quicker to settle disputes when it's their money — not just yours — on the line.

Other safe options include third-party escrow services like PayPal or virtual credit cards, also known as single-use credit card numbers. These card numbers are usually limited to one transaction and often one merchant. See if your bank or credit card company issues these.

> Don't get ambushed by state sales tax when making an online purchase. Check the bottom of the Web page or footnotes to prices to see which states will be charged. If you get surprised by tax, simply cancel the transaction.

Track down the seller. While it's safer to buy from big stores that you already know, that doesn't mean you can't give a smaller store a chance. Just make sure you can find a street address and a working telephone number posted on the Web site. Beware of sites with no contact information.

Do some research. If you're unsure about an online retailer, check with the Better Business Bureau. Go to **www.bbb.org** to look for negative reports.

Keep a paper trail. Print a record of every transaction, including your receipt and any e-mails between you and the seller, in case of a dispute.

E-mail with care. Never send personal financial information by e-mail.

Understand the terms of the transaction. Know the refund policy and the company's privacy policy. Make sure you can return your item if you're not satisfied and that the company will not be sharing your information with other parties.

Beware of suspicious questions. If a company asks for your date of birth or Social Security number during checkout, stay away. The company is probably up to no good — and could be planning identity theft.

Why savvy shoppers use the Internet

Here are just a few of the reasons why it's smart to shop online.

◆ Save money. Lower overhead means lower prices.

◆ Save gas. No need to drive from store to store when you can shop from home.

◆ Save time. No more standing in line at stores.

◆ Compare prices easily.

◆ Save on shipping — it's often free.

◆ Take advantage of online coupons.

◆ Research your options.

◆ Shop anytime — 24 hours a day, seven days a week.

◆ Shop a nearly limitless selection.

Comparison shop for instant savings

Wonder if you're getting the best deal on that computer or printer? They can cost thousands of dollars. Find the one you want at the price you want with a price comparison Web site. You can see prices from several retailers at once.

AOL Shopping	shopping.aol.com
Google Product Search	www.google.com/products
MSN Shopping	shopping.msn.com
PriceGrabber.com	www.pricegrabber.com
Shopping.com	www.shopping.com
Yahoo! Shopping	shopping.yahoo.com

Use these sites for anything — from gas to groceries to appliances. Just use them wisely. Remember, some retailers pay more to be listed higher on the page. Take the time to scroll down in case of better deals. Read the user comments or reviews — and beware of sellers with very few of them. And pay attention to shipping calculators so you don't get ambushed at checkout.

Popular comparison Web sites include Shopzilla at **www.shopzilla.com** and BizRate at **www.bizrate.com**. You can shop for products in a variety of categories, including computers, electronics, furniture, clothing and accessories, home and garden, and toys and games.

Other sites have a more focused approach. For example, you can shop for computers, televisions, and other electronics through Shopper.com at **shopper.cnet.com**.

For prescription drugs, contact lenses, or beauty products, try HealthPricer at **www.healthpricer.com**.

One good way to make sure you get the lowest price is through a Web site called Price Protectr at **www.priceprotectr.com**. It keeps tabs on prices in case they drop — so you don't have to.

Why stop at groceries? You can find online coupons, rebates, and deals for almost anything — like appliances. Double up on savings. When you buy your next appliance, save money month after month with an energy-efficient model. Find out more by going to Energy Star at **www.energystar.gov**. This Web site will find local sales and rebates for you. You might even get a tax break.

Online coupons save big bucks

More than $350 billion of packaged goods coupons are offered every year, according to the Promotion Marketing Association (PMA) Coupon Council. Are you getting your fair share of this money-saving pie? Experts say it's worth the effort. Spend a little time each week clipping coupons from your local paper or printing them out online, and you could cut your grocery bill by 33 percent. Get a little more creative with shopping strategies and you could cut it in half. For instance if you combine coupons with a grocery store's loyalty card, you could cut $20 off your bill every week — that's a savings of $1,000 a year.

There are several ways you can use your computer to take advantage of coupons for groceries and more.

◆ Print free coupons off a couponing Web site, specific store's home page, or manufacturer's Web site.

◆ Join a subscription service — often for a fee — and order the coupons you want.

◆ Download electronic coupons directly to your store loyalty card.

◆ Sign up to have coupons and deals e-mailed to you.

◆ Enter the product's name plus the word "coupon" into your favorite search engine.

◆ Enter a special coupon code while making a purchase online.

If you do print coupons, be aware of some drawbacks. Often, you'll have to download special software from the site, and it may include spyware. If you have to provide your e-mail, you could become swamped with spam, or junk e-mail. Consider using a special e-mail address just for this purpose. Here are just a few great sources for online coupons.

CoolSavings	www.coolsavings.com
Coupon Mom	www.couponmom.com
Coupons.com	www.coupons.com
MyGroceryDeals.com	www.mygrocerydeals.com
The Coupon Clippers	www.thecouponclippers.com

When an order goes wrong

Not every transaction on the Internet goes smoothly. Maybe you receive a damaged or incorrect item. Or perhaps your purchase never arrives. Just in case, follow these tips.

Keep a paper trail. Always keep records of your transaction, including receipts and any e-mails you exchanged with the retailer. When you have documentation, it makes resolving disputes much easier.

Go direct. Deal head-on with the online seller first. Look for an address, phone number, or e-mail address. You should be able to clear up most disputes this way.

File a complaint. If you can't work things out with the seller, you can always file a complaint with the following organizations.

✦ Better Business Bureau at **www.bbb.org**

✦ Federal Trade Commission at **www.ftc.gov** or 1-877-FTC-HELP

✦ Your state attorney general's office

✦ Your county or state consumer protection agency. Check the blue pages of your phone book.

Internet Crime Complaint Center at **www.ic3.gov.** This is only for serious, criminal situations.

Remember, some problems may just be a case of poor customer service rather than a violation of the law. You can always take your business elsewhere next time.

Bidding to win at online auctions

One man's trash is another man's treasure. That's the theory behind online auction sites. You can find almost anything you want — if you're willing to pay for it.

Online auctions work much like regular auctions — people place bids on products and the highest bid wins. By far, the most popular site is eBay, which was started in 1995. Now, tens of millions of people buy and sell there every day. That's because you can find almost anything. Go to **www.ebay.com** to browse through countless categories and subcategories, or search for an exact item. Just be on the lookout for questionable products or deals that are clearly too good to be true.

Whichever online auction site you use, make sure you play it safe. Never pay with a wire transfer. Always use a credit card or escrow service, like PayPal. Be suspicious if the seller insists on a shady escrow service that you haven't heard of. Understand the terms of the transaction, including shipping and the return policy, before-hand. Ask the seller for details if you're unclear. If the seller won't agree to a shipping price ahead of time, walk away.

Here are some more tips for successful bidding.

◆ Learn the value of the item you're bidding on. Establish your top price and stick to it.

◆ Don't bid on an item you don't intend to buy. You might get stuck with it.

◆ Understand exactly what the item is. Always read the descrip-tion carefully.

♦ Try to learn about the seller. Pay attention to the feedback from other buyers.

♦ Take time to learn the rules of any auction site. Don't assume they're all the same.

One trick you can use to win an online bid is called "sniping." It simply means swooping in and making a winning bid at the last minute. To do that, you have to be alert and online as the auction winds down, which isn't always possible. However, there are ways to do this automatically. For instance, you can try a service called eSnipe at **www.esnipe.com**.

Although it's the most popular, eBay is not your only option for online auctions. You can also bid for items on the following sites.

Bidtopia	www.bidtopia.com
Bidz Online Auctions	www.bidz.com
Overstock.com	auctions.overstock.com
uBid	www.ubid.com
WeBidz	www.webidz.com

For information on selling things on eBay and other online auction sites, see page 250 in the *Ins & outs of online selling* chapter.

Save hundreds on your next car

Never ask a car salesman about car prices. Instead, use the Internet for research. When you know a car's real value, you're armed with information — your best weapon — when you go to the dealership. You won't only save money, you'll also save precious time. In fact, people who use the Internet for research spend an average of 80 minutes less at the dealership and 25 minutes less negotiating and going on test drives. Here are just a few things you can do on the Internet.

- Compare prices and features of various makes and models.
- Learn the true value for new and used cars.
- Find deals in your area.
- Read reviews of cars you're considering.
- Discover the true value of your trade-in.
- Gather helpful tips and advice on buying cars.

Where should you start? Check out these valuable online resources for automobile information.

Autobytel.com	www.autobytel.com
AutoTrader.com	www.autotrader.com
Cars.com	www.cars.com
Edmunds.com	www.edmunds.com
Kelley Blue Book	www.kbb.com
National Automobile Dealers Association	www.nada.com

You can also visit the Web sites of dealers in your area. That's a good way to browse their inventory before making a trip to the lot. Another good resource is CARFAX at **www.carfax.com**, a service that lets you see a vehicle's history by checking its Vehicle Identification Number, or VIN. That way, you don't get stuck with a used car with costly hidden problems.

Pocket pennies at the pump

With gas prices out of control, every cent you can save makes a difference. Use the Internet to find the lowest gas prices in your area.

Check out sites like GasPriceWatch at **www.gaspricewatch.com** or GasBuddy at **www.gasbuddy.com**. Just enter your zip code or city and state to discover which local gas stations boast the best deals.

You can also go to **www.fueleconomy.gov**, a government site with links to gas price data for U.S. cities in every state.

Ever wonder if it's actually worth driving to a gas station farther away to save money? Find out with GasEdge at **www.gasedge.com**. Enter the distance and gas prices for your local gas station. Then do the same for the alternate station. Finally, enter your car's gas tank capacity and usual city miles per gallon. It will calculate your savings — if any.

Pay less for computer extras

Computers are wonderful — but, like even the most wonderful outfit, they need some accessories. Things like ink cartridges and memory can add to your computer budget. Luckily, you can save on these items through the Web.

Good one-stop shopping sites for computers, accessories, and electronics include TigerDirect at **www.tigerdirect.com** and Newegg at **www.newegg.com**. You can find great savings here or try other sites that specialize in specific accessories.

Sink the high cost of ink. You don't have to pay full price for printer ink cartridges. It's possible to save up to 80 percent on ink by shopping online. Just visit these money-saving sites.

123Inkjets	www.123inkjets.com
ABC co	www.abcco.net
InkSell.com	www.inksell.com
Pacific Ink	www.pacificink.com
PrintPal	www.printpal.com

Remember how to save on memory. Don't pay three times more than you need to when you upgrade your computer's memory. Here's where to find the best prices.

4 All Memory	*www.4allmemory.com*
Memory Store	*www.memorystore.com*

Curb costs with a refurbished computer

Instead of paying big bucks for a brand new, state-of-the-art computer system, look for a refurbished model. You could save an average of 10 to 25 percent off the retail price.

These are not-quite-new or used computers that have been restored to like-new working condition. Your best bet is to get them directly from manufacturers. In many cases, these are computers returned by customers, previously leased systems, or those used as store models. Here's where to find refurbished computers online. Search on the word "refurbished" or "used" and, in some cases, you will be rerouted to the manufacturer's outlet store.

Dell	*www.dell.com*
HP	*www.hp.com*
IBM	*www.ibm.com*

You can also find good deals on refurbished computers from independent resellers, like TigerDirect at **www.tigerdirect.com** — called recertified — and Newegg at **www.newegg.com** — open box items. Of course, you can also find them at eBay and other online auction sites. But be careful.

When shopping for a refurbished computer, make sure it has enough memory and processing speed to fit your needs. Is there warranty coverage or an option to return it? If you buy from an individual seller, make sure the seller deleted all files, spyware, browser history, cookies, and other programs. You should also insist on receiving the original software and license keys.

Save big on software

Freeware and shareware are two alternatives to commercial software that can save you money. Freeware is software you can download, pass around, and distribute without payment. In other words, it's free. Shareware is often free for a trial period, but you must register the software and eventually pay a small fee.

Besides the obvious benefit — the cheap price — these low-cost options are usually problem-free, well-designed programs. They're easy to install and update, and simple to find on the Internet. And because they boast so many users, any bugs get spotted and fixed quickly. Even if you're not satisfied with the program, all you have to do is uninstall it. No need to haggle for a refund for something you didn't have to pay for in the first place.

Of course, you should use some caution whenever you download anything from the Internet. Only download from sites you trust, and make sure you have a good anti-virus program installed, updated, and running.

For information on how to install software from downloads, see page 165 in the *Straight talk about software* chapter.

So, before you buy that expensive software, look at these Web sites. You just might be able to get the same thing for free. At these sites, you can learn more about applications and developers, read reviews, and download what you want. Whatever your interests — health, games, money, education, video, music, and more — you can find free software for it.

Download.com	www.download.com
Shareware.com	www.shareware.com
Tucows	www.tucows.com

Find low-cost insurance

Insurance should help you feel safer — but high premiums make you feel poorer. Thanks to the Internet, you can easily shop for cheaper auto, health, home, or life insurance. Get the most insurance you need for the lowest price available — guaranteed.

Research is key, but it takes some effort. Visit at least 10 Web sites to compare policies. Take into consideration agencies, premiums, and coverage. Some sites offer rate comparisons, so it's easy to see multiple options. Just make sure to do the math, pay close attention to details, and find out what's not included.

You'll also want to double-check the company and agent. Make sure they're licensed in your state, and look at their record of handling policy complaints. One good resource is the National Association of Insurance Commissioners at **www.naic.org**. Among other things, this site has links to each state's insurance department Web site. Here are just some of the helpful insurance Web sites available on the Internet.

Insure.com	*www.insure.com*
InsWeb	*www.insweb.com*
NetQuote	*www.netquote.com*
Quotei.com	*www.quotei.com*

You may prefer to take the quotes and information you found from the Internet to a local insurance agent, who can help you make sense of them — and maybe match or beat what you found online.

Take a vacation from pricey vacations

Enjoy cut-rate, first class vacations — without paying a travel agent. Learn where to look online for discounts, surplus tickets, last-minute specials, no hassle packages, and more.

In 2007, almost half of all travel-related reservations were booked online. That's because the Internet makes it easy to plan your own vacations. There are a wealth of travel Web sites, and you should visit several of them while planning your next vacation. Many provide booking options, including flights, rental cars, hotels, cruises, and packages. Some even offer resources like weather reports, maps, and travel guides.

So, be your own travel agent. Take a trip around the Web to explore these sites — then head off on your next adventure.

Feeling spontaneous? Book a domestic trip as late as three hours before departure on Lastminute.com at **www.lastminute.com**.

CheapTickets	*www.cheaptickets.com*
Expedia	*www.expedia.com*
FareCompare	*www.farecompare.com*
Hotwire	*www.hotwire.com*
Orbitz	*www.orbitz.com*
Priceline	*www.priceline.com*
Travelocity	*www.travelocity.com*
Yahoo! FareChase	*farechase.yahoo.com*

You can also go directly to the Web sites of major airlines, like Delta, United, Continental, or AirTran, to book your flights, hotels, and rental cars.

Prescription for online drug discounts

Feeling sick over the high cost of medicine? You can find good deals on prescription drugs on the Internet. And while it's hard to beat the convenience of shopping for medicine online, you must use caution. If you buy from a shady Web site, you run the risk of receiving counterfeit or mis-labeled drugs. You could end up with diluted, contaminated, stolen, mishandled, or expired drugs or those not approved by the FDA. Furthermore, you may be putting your privacy and financial information at risk. Never buy from any pharmacy that contacts you through spam. And stay away from sites that:

> Don't pay another cent for things you can get for free. And don't throw something away just because you don't want it anymore. Thanks to the Freecycle Network, you can donate and receive items in your area. To find a Freecycle group near you, go to **www.freecycle.org.**

♦ are not licensed by the state board of pharmacy where the Web site is operating.

♦ do not require a prescription or give you one based on an online questionnaire.

♦ have no phone number or street address.

♦ require you to sign a waiver.

♦ feature a limited choice of medicine.

♦ boast prices that are too good to be true.

♦ do not have a pharmacist you can talk to.

Play it safe and stick with sites that meet the National Association of Boards of Pharmacy (NABP) standards. Look for the Verified Internet Pharmacy Practice Sites (VIPPS) logo.

You can find a list of approved sites at **www.nabp.net.** Popular pharmacies like Walgreens, CVS, and drugstore.com are among those that meet NABP standards.

Verified Internet Pharmacy Practice Sites (VIPPS) logo

chapter 24

Ins & outs of online selling

" eBay was started in 1995; more than $1 billion worth of merchandise are sold each month by its users. **"**

Associated Content

Earn money with your computer

Got something to sell? Instead of holding a garage sale, post your stuff on eBay or other online auction sites. It's a great way to make some extra cash. Some people even make a living buying and selling on eBay. Discover the secrets to successful selling online.

Connect with buyers. The Internet gives you access to more potential buyers. Your best bet is probably eBay, since it's the most popular online auction site. But it's not your only option. For instance, you can sell handmade crafts at Etsy at **www.etsy.com.**

Learn how to cash in. While you can sell virtually anything online, some items sell better than others. Pick something that's not too common or easy to find. It should also be in good condition and easy to ship. If you're not sure what to sell, try these standbys and "hot" items.

> Of course, auctions aren't the only way to sell things online. You can even sell items on Amazon. Just go to **www.amazon.com** and click on SELL YOUR STUFF. Or place an online classified ad on Craigslist at **www.craigslist.org**.

◆ Clothing and accessories. Did you know that some costume jewelry from the 50s is now selling for hundreds of dollars?

◆ Household furnishings or antiques, like clocks or china.

◆ Electronics, like cell phones, scanners, or DVRs.

◆ Camcorders and cameras.

◆ Hobbies and collectibles, like model railroads, vintage sewing machines, and comic books.

◆ Musical instruments, like banjos, accordions, guitars, or ukuleles.

◆ Sports equipment, like golf clubs.

◆ Your own hobby or craft items.

◆ Locally made goods, or products unique to your region.

You can even check eBay for the current most popular items at **pulse.ebay.com**.

Make a perfect pitch. Now that you know what you want to sell, here are some tips for successfully selling those items.

◆ Research. Find out what your item is worth and what similar items have sold for. Then price it right.

◆ Browse eBay — or whatever site you choose — to get a feel for the site.

◆ Hook potential buyers with an attention-grabbing title.

◆ Write a good description of your item. Include lots of detail. Specify if the item is new or used.

- Use photos.

- Be up front about the terms of the sale, including your return policy, shipping options, and accepted methods of payment.

- Build trust. You may want to buy and sell a few small things to build up positive feedback from other users before trying to sell something truly valuable.

- Respond quickly to any questions from potential buyers.

- Take advantage of convenient shipping options. You can get free shipping supplies from the U.S. Postal Service through eBay. You can even print your postage from home, saving you a trip to the post office.

For information on buying items at online auctions, see page 241 in the *Internet deals & steals* chapter.

Sidestep scams when selling online

As a savvy consumer, you know to be careful when making purchases online. But sellers face risks, too. Know your responsibilities, and make sure you don't get cheated.

Foil fake checks. Swindlers may send you a counterfeit check or money order as payment. While it may look legitimate enough to fool the bank teller at first, the bank will eventually spot the fraud. The problem is, in the meantime you already shipped your goods.

A similar trick, known as an overpayment scam, works like this. The buyer sends you a check for an amount higher than the selling price. He contacts you, claiming he made a mistake and asks you to send

> Go to the government's OnGuard Online Web site to play Auction Action, a "Jeopardy"-like game that teaches you about online auctions. You can find it at **www.onguardonline.gov/ games/auction-action.aspx.**

the difference back. You do so, but then the bank tells you that the original check was fraudulent.

Protect yourself from these scams by accepting only a cashier's check from a local bank for the exact amount you are due. Or refuse to accept checks at all.

Steer clear of shady services. As a buyer or seller, be suspicious of escrow services you're not familiar with. Stick with only trusted, legitimate services. PayPal, an online payment service, is a good option. In fact, eBay encourages using this form of payment.

Resolve problems. If you sell on eBay, you can use its Resolution Center to handle disputes, such as not receiving payment. Following this step-by-step guide should clear up the matter. You can also report fraud to eBay.

Dodge unwanted phone calls. Maybe you've sold your item long ago, but you keep getting phone calls about it. Maintain your privacy with a disposable phone number. Several companies provide this service, sometimes even for free.

My AdBox	www.myadbox
Vumber	www.vumber.com
inumbr	www.inumbr.com
Tossable Digits	www.tossabledigits.com

Play by the rules. As a seller, you must know your legal obligations. Always advertise your product and terms of sale honestly and accurately. You're also required to ship your product in a timely manner. Web sites, like eBay, post lists of restricted or prohibited items. Familiarize yourself with them. Never use "shill" bids to boost the price of your item or write fake testimonials to improve your feedback.

253

chapter 25

Use the Internet for fun & learning

"A computer once beat me at chess, but it was no match for me at kick boxing."

Emo Philips, comedian

Find fast answers to any question

Have a question, but don't know where to find the answer? Look online for the solution. You can find several how-to Web sites that can help with almost any question. Whether you need to know how to change a tire, tie a tie, or cook a meal, answers are just a few clicks away.

Step-by-step solutions. These sites provide handy guides that walk you through a process from start to finish. You'll find out what materials you'll need and how to go about completing any project.

eHow	www.ehow.com
HowToDoThings	www.howtodothings.com
Instructables	www.instructables.com
wikiHow	www.wikihow.com

Watch and learn. If you learn best by observing, you're in luck. Several Web sites feature how-to videos that let you see exactly how to do something.

Howcast	www.howcast.com
VideoJug	www.videojug.com
ViewDo	www.viewdo.com
WonderHowTo	www.wonderhowto.com

Ask and receive. You can find sites dedicated to answering questions. Search these sites to see if your question has been answered already. If not, just submit a new question. You can even help others by providing answers to their questions.

Answers.com	www.answers.com
Live Search QnA	qna.live.com
Yahoo! Answers	answers.yahoo.com

Build basic knowledge. Other Web sites work like encyclopedias to provide information. Browsing these sites is a good way to find answers to common questions or solutions to common problems.

About.com	www.about.com
HowStuffWorks	www.howstuffworks.com
Wikipedia	www.wikipedia.org

255

Keep in mind that sites like *Wikipedia*, called *wikis*, can be edited by users. That means entries can be modified with incorrect information. The same applies to several how-to sites, so you may want to find more than one source for a tip just to be safe.

Search for knowledge. Of course, you can also use a trusty search engine to find answers to your questions. Some search engines even specialize in how-to Web sites. They work like regular search engines, where you enter a keyword and they search the Internet. But they focus their search on instructional sites to match you with the information you need. Here are two worth trying.

| FindHow | *www.findhow.com* |
| HowDoYa | *www.howdoya.com* |

Don't give up if you don't find an answer right away. Keep trying other Web sites. No matter how unusual your question, you should eventually find an answer online.

Become computer savvy for free

If you can get online, you can learn how to do anything on your computer. Several Web sites provide tutorials or tips, and you can even find free computer classes for seniors near you. For online computer lessons, check out these helpful Web sites.

AARP	*www.aarp.org/learntech/computers*
About Internet for Beginners	*netforbeginners.about.com*
GCFLearnFree.org	*www.gcflearnfree.org/computer*
Learnthat	*www.learnthat.com/computers*
Living Internet	*www.livinginternet.com*
Stimulus: Internet 101	*www.stimulus.com/education*

A new UCLA study finds that searching the Internet may be even better for your brain than reading or working crossword puzzles. Searching the Web helps stimulate and improve brain function in seniors, according to the study. Both reading books and searching the Internet spark activity in the regions of the brain that control language, reading, memory, and visual ability. But Web searching also affects the areas of the brain that control decision-making and complex reasoning. The interactive aspect of the Web, such as making decisions about where to click, probably helps. So does practice. Experienced Internet users showed even more benefit in the study. So keep searching the Web — and keep your brain in shape.

You can learn at your own pace, pick up handy tips, and find out everything you always wanted to know about computers and the Internet.

While these sites can help you improve your computer skills, maybe you'd prefer an actual classroom with an actual instructor. Use the Web to find free computer classes.

◆ Use your regular search engine. Just enter the terms **free computer classes for seniors** plus your city and state.

◆ Check the Web sites of local colleges, community colleges, or libraries to see if they offer classes.

◆ Try the official Web site of your city as well. You might be able to find something like the program offered in Berkeley, California. You can view the Division on Aging: Computer Classes for Seniors Web page at **www.ci.berkeley.ca.us/seniors/ computers/computers.htm.**

Explore health breakthroughs online

Stay out of the waiting room and find up-to-the-minute health information from your living room. Join the growing numbers of seniors who are exploring health breakthroughs online. No doctor's fees, no newsletter subscriptions, no waiting — just the facts, all for free.

The key is to choose where you get your health information carefully. It doesn't do you any good to read about bogus treatments or shady products from quack doctors. Keep these factors in mind when evaluating a health-related Web site.

◆ Consider the source. Government sites, university or medical school sites, medical centers, and non-profit groups are usually the best sources of health information.

◆ Avoid sites that are obviously trying to sell you something, like a product or service.

◆ Check for a date stamp to make sure you're reading the latest information. Things change quickly in the health field.

◆ Make sure it's fact and not opinion. The Web site should cite legitimate sources for its information.

◆ Understand the target audience. Look for sites or portions of sites targeted to consumers. If the site is strictly for professionals, like doctors, it may be too confusing or not appropriate for your needs.

Now that you know what to look for in general, take a look at these wonderful health resources on the Web.

American Cancer Society	*www.cancer.org*
American Diabetes Association	*www.diabetes.org*
American Heart Association	*www.americanheart.org*
Mayo Clinic	*www.hotwire.com*
MedlinePlus	*www.medicineplus.gov*
National Institutes of Health	*www.nih.gov*
PDRHealth	*www.pdrhealth.com*
WebMD	*www.webmd.com*

For information about online support groups for health-related issues like diseases or caregiving, see page 322 in the *Social networks enrich your life* chapter.

Find top doctors and hospitals

When you're sick, you deserve the best care possible. Get the best doctor in town. Simply use the information from these Web sites to examine your doctor before he examines you.

Go to the American Medical Association's Web site at **www.ama-assn.org** and click on DOCTORFINDER. This gives you access to information on more than 800,000 doctors. Search by doctor name and location or specialty and location. You can review a doctor's educational history and credentials and contact one that suits your needs.

Make sure your doctor is certified in his chosen specialty at the American Board of Medical Specialties Web site. Go to **www.abms.org** and click on IS YOUR DOCTOR CERTIFIED? to find out. You can search by doctor's name or area of certification and your state's name.

Just as you can examine your doctor, you can also give your hospital a check-up. A few Web sites rate hospitals, based on quality of care and safety. They also focus on how well each hospital treats certain conditions or performs high-risk surgical procedures.

Discover the top 50 hospitals for treating whatever ails you. As with doctors, you can search by hospital name or location. Make sure your hospital is up to snuff using these handy Web sites.

Having trouble accessing a Web site? Find out whether the site is down or if the problem is with your computer or Internet connection. Go to **www.downfor everyoneorjustme.com.** Type in the name of the site in question and click on JUST FOR ME? You'll get your answer right away.

Quality Check	www.qualitycheck.org
The Leapfrog Group	www.leapfroggroup.org
U.S. Department of Health and Human Services	www.hospitalcompare.hhs.gov

Check out supplement safety

You can easily find herbal supplements online. It's not quite as easy to find information about them. Before you use an herbal supplement, make sure it's safe by checking these helpful Web sites. Information is your best protection against harmful reactions.

United States Pharmacopeia. This public health organization verifies the identity, strength, purity, and quality of dietary supplements and their ingredients. Those that meet their standards may display a "USP Verified" mark on their product labels. Go to **www.usp.org**, then click on USP VERIFIED to learn more about the verification process, find out which manufacturers participate, and discover where to buy these verified supplements.

Office of Dietary Supplements. This government office of the National Institutes of Health evaluates information, supports research, and educates the public about dietary supplements. Visit its Web site at **dietary-supplements.info.nih.gov**. Then click on HEALTH INFORMATION. You'll get links to background information, tips for older supplement users, databases of research, and helpful fact sheets about specific supplements.

Memorial Sloan-Kettering Cancer Center. The world's oldest and largest private cancer center focuses on patient care and research into new treatments. These include herbs, botanicals, and supplements. To search the About Herbs database, go to **www.mskcc.org**. Then click on CANCER INFORMATION. Click on INTEGRATIVE MEDICINE. Then click on ABOUT HERBS, BOTANICALS & OTHER PRODUCTS, or go directly to **www.mskcc.org/mskcc/html/11570.cfm**.

In an emergency, your medical records should be easy to access. Unfortunately, disasters — like hurricanes — can strike hospitals, too. Keep your medical records safe by storing them online. Several Web-based storage services let you securely house your medical history, prescriptions, and other health information. Only you and those you authorize have access to your records. MyMedicalRecords.com at **www.mymedicalrecords.com** comes with a free trial, then charges less than $10 per month. Others, like WebMD's Health Manager, iHealthRecord, and Google Health, are free. To learn more about these services, go to **www.webmd.com**, **www.ihealthrecord.com**, or **www.google.com/health**.

8 best sites for seniors

The Internet may seem like the domain of young people — but there are plenty of sites just for seniors. Here are some of the best ones.

Senior Citizens' Resources at USA.gov. Your taxes paid for it. Get free info and assistance with retirement, Social Security, taxes, prescriptions, veterans' benefits, and more at this site just for seniors. Just go to **www.usa.gov** and click on SENIORS.

ThirdAge. This site caters to people ranging in age from their early 40s to their late 60s and features a variety of topics, including health and wellness, money, work, beauty, and leisure. Read articles, chat, post your opinions on discussion boards, play games, and participate in free online classes at **www.thirdage.com**.

AARP. Like the organization, the AARP Web site is dedicated to people over 50. You can join online and take advantage of hundreds of member benefits and discounts. Even if you're not a member, you can enjoy the wealth of information about health, money, leisure, family, and more at **www.aarp.org.**

SeniorLaw. This site provides legal information in plain language that anyone can understand. Features include basic explanations of

Medicaid and Medicare, links to resources on elder abuse, and information about wills. You can also find attorneys in your area who specialize in elder law. Just go to **www.seniorlaw.com.**

ElderWeb. At this site focusing on senior issues, you can find lots of information about assisted living and long term care. It also has links to resources, including legal matters, insurance, education, and finance. Explore for yourself at **www.elderweb.com.**

Elderhostel. If you like to learn "on the go," you should check out the world's largest educational travel organization. Elderhostel offers nearly 8,000 programs in more than 90 countries. Study art in Paris, jazz in New Orleans, or wine in Italy. You can browse by location at **www.elderhostel.org.**

SeniorSite. Geared toward seniors, this site features information about retirement, finances, and health. You can also chat with other seniors, meet that special someone, and even ask questions of experts. Find out what else this site has to offer at **www.seniorsite.com.**

The National Council on Aging. The mission of this non-profit service and advocacy organization is to improve the lives of older Americans. They do this by working with thousands of organizations across the country to help seniors live independently, find jobs and benefits, improve their health, and remain active in their communities. Visit them at **www.ncoa.org.**

Get smart on government programs

There are approximately 50 to 70 government programs in your state alone — all designed to benefit older adults. Simple ways to sort through them all and get what you deserve can be found at the following Web sites.

www.benefitsCheckUp. This service of the National Council on Aging lets you find and enroll in federal, state, local, and even private programs that help pay for prescription drugs, utility bills, meals, health care, and other needs.

www.eldercare.gov. The U.S. Administration on Aging provides this helpful site to link you to state and local agencies on aging and community-based organizations that serve older adults. Find help with legal issues, health insurance, long-term care, prescription drugs and more.

www.ssa.gov. The official Web site of the U.S. Social Security Administration allows you to apply for benefits online, check the accuracy of your personal records, and estimate future benefits. You'll also find many other helpful features, including easy-to-understand explanations of confusing Social Security rules and regulations.

www.medicare.gov. Unravel the secrets of Medicare at an official government site. Learn about the various plan options, including those in your area. Compare plans and nursing homes, find a doctor, and find out what Medicare covers. Read about billing, preventive services, long-term care, and more. You can even get a replacement card.

www.pbgc.gov. You may be due pension benefits you never knew existed. A quick research tool at The Pension Benefit Guaranty Corporation helps reunite people with missing pensions. Click on PENSION SEARCH DIRECTORY to see if you're among the people PBGC has been unable to contact about your pension.

Hear the verdict on legal advice

Worrying about drafting your will or other important legal documents? It should be a crime not to take advantage of the vast amount of free legal advice on the Web.

www.uslwr.com. Perhaps you're asking yourself, "What is a living will? Do I need one? How do I get it?" The U.S. Living Will Registry can help. This one source answers all your questions about this very important document. You can also store it and make it available to health care providers across the country. The site even provides resources for preparing a living will and links to download the appropriate forms in your state.

www.abanet.org. Click on PUBLIC RESOURCES and this American Bar Association Web site will help you find a lawyer, get definitions of legal terms, find free legal help, learn about the court system, and read about topics like family law, real estate transactions, wills, and more. There's even a search tool where you can type in a topic — like living wills — and read various free articles.

www.nolo.com. This one-stop provider of legal information sells several things, like legal forms, software, and books. But it's also a great resource for good, free legal information. Read articles about wills and estate planning, patents and copyright, property and money, family law and immigration, and rights and disputes. There's even a lawyer directory to help you find legal help.

www.legalzoom.com. Create legal documents right at home with this online service.

Remember, the Web is a great way to get legal information and advice. But you may want to consult an actual lawyer before taking any action.

Give wisely: check out charities

Everyone likes to help someone in need — but no one wants to be ripped off. So you don't get taken when you give, you can make sure a charity is legitimate by checking IRS Publication 78, available at **www.irs.gov**. This is a list of organizations eligible to receive tax-deductible contributions. You can also ask the charity for written literature, a copy of their exemption letter, and an annual report of the organization's income and expenses. Check up on charities at these watchdog sites.

American Institute of Philanthropy	*www.charitywatch.org*
Charity Navigator	*www.charitynavigator.org*
GuideStar	*www.guidestar.org*

If you're looking for a worthy charity, check out Cell Phones for Soldiers. This non-profit organization, started by teenagers Robbie and Brittany Bergquist of Norwell, Mass., turns your old cell phone into prepaid calling cards for U.S. troops stationed overseas. Visit **www.cellphonesforsoldiers.com** to find out how your old cell phone can help servicemen stay in touch with their families.

Trace your family tree

With the Internet, learning about your ancestors was never so simple — especially now that other folks have done so much of the legwork. See how many branches of your family tree have already been drawn through these genealogy Web sites.

www.ancestry.com. This subscription site gives you access to census and military records; birth, marriage, and death certificates; immigration and emigration data; newspapers; periodicals; and more. Luckily, it comes with a free trial so you can test it before committing.

www.rootsweb.ancestry.com. This free sister site to Ancestry.com lets you connect with other genealogists. It's a good way to match family trees with other branches of your family.

www.myheritage.com. Share your family tree with others, search for ancestors, and connect with other genealogists on message boards.

www.geni.com. Build and store your family tree at Geni. It's a free, safe place to keep your family history and share it with others in your family.

www.ellisisland.org. Because many families got their start in America through Ellis Island, the free Port of New York passenger records search can be very useful.

www.legacy.com. Look up death notices and obituaries.

Other good, all-around genealogy resources include the following Web sites.

FamilySearch	www.familysearch.org
Genealogy.com	www.genealogy.com
Genealogy.org	www.genealogy.org

Harvest free gardening advice

Love gardening? If this is your favorite hobby, your computer can dig up all sorts of tips for you. The Internet is fertile ground for all things gardening.

One great resource and starting point is the National Gardening Association's Web site at **www.garden.org**. Landscape your yard for the cost of materials with their how-to projects. Get free landscaping and gardening advice from experts, regional reports, and helpful tips. You can look through reference materials and connect with others on message boards.

Explore these other helpful Web sites, which serve as good all-around gardening resources.

| GardenWeb | www.gardenweb.com |
| Garden Guides | www.gardenguides.com |

Pick a perfect plant. Want to learn more about plants? Which ones fare best in your climate zone or soil type? Get all the answers at these searchable online plant databases and encyclopedias.

USDA Plant Database	www.plants.usda.gov
LandscapeUSA.com	www.landscapeusa.com/plantfinder.asp
Botany.com	www.botany.org

Call on the experts. You can always go to names you know and trust, like corporations and national or local nurseries, for a wealth of gardening information. Here are just a few examples.

Pike Nurseries	*www.pikenursery.com*
Better Homes and Gardens	*www.bhg.com*
The Old Farmer's Almanac	*www.almanac.com*
Home & Garden Television	*www.hgtv.com*

Seek out more advice. As usual, a search engine can come in handy for gardening tips. Just enter a keyword, like **perennials**, to get more information on any garden-related topic. Search engines are also a good way to look for cooperative extension programs and Master Gardener classes in your area.

Turn old pennies into big bucks

With the Internet, you can find out what your coins — and other collectibles — are worth.

Cash in on small change. Valuable information for coin collectors can be found at these Web sites.

✦ Professional Coin Grading Service. Go to **www.pcgs.com** to learn more about this service, find links to other coin-collecting resources, and discover the prices of rare coins. Just click on PRICE GUIDE to see which coins have gone up or down in value or how much they sold for at auction. You'll get a good idea of the value of your collection.

✦ United States Mint. At **www.usmint.gov,** you can buy coins online. Click on COLLECTOR'S CLUB to learn more about coin collecting and find links to more resources, including a coin dealer database that lets you find dealers near you. The HISTORIAN'S CORNER provides lots of interesting tidbits, including images of old coins.

Collect more info on collectibles. Get expert tips and specific details on just about any type of collection.

✦ Use a search engine to find more price guides. Enter key-words such as **coins collect price guide** and see what you come up with. Of course, the same strategy works for any other hobby, like stamps or comic books.

✦ For good general information about collectibles, check out About.com's Collectibles page at **collectibles.about.com**. You'll find advice for buying and selling as well as links to price guides.

✦ If you're looking to buy collectibles, including coins, comics, sports memorabilia, toys, dolls, and figures, check out Collectibles.com at **www.collectibles.com**.

✦ For a searchable collectors' price guide and other helpful resources for antiques and collectibles, go to the Kovels Web site at **www.kovels.com**.

Laugh at online punchlines

The Internet has serious powers — but that doesn't mean you need to take it so seriously. Sometimes, you'd rather giggle than Google. Just for laughs, tickle your funny bone with these free online joke sites.

CleanJoke.com	*www.cleanjoke.com*
Find Jokes.net	*www.findjokes.net*
Free Jokes Online	*www.free-jokes-online.com*
FunPike.com	*www.funpike.com*
GCFL.net: The Good, Clean, Funnies List	*www.gcfl.net*
JokeJam.com	*www.jokejam.com*
Jokes Gallery	*www.jokesgallery.com*
Jokes Warehouse	*www.jokeswarehouse.com*

Most joke sites organize their funnies by category. Others include a search feature that lets you look for the kind of jokes you like.

You may even be able to sign up to receive a joke of the day via e-mail. It's a good way to brighten your day.

Online games: not just for kids

All work and no play makes for a pretty dull computer session. Whether you play against the computer or match wits with other Internet users around the world, you can find a host of fun, free games online.

Windows comes with a few built-in Internet games. To access them, go to START → ALL PROGRAMS → GAMES. You'll see the following options:

◆ Internet Backgammon

◆ Internet Checkers

◆ Internet Hearts

◆ Internet Reversi

◆ Internet Spades

While these are certainly fun and challenging, you're not limited to them. Several Web sites let you download or play online games. Here are just a few of them.

games.yahoo.com. Yahoo! Games offers board games, arcade games, puzzle games, card games, word games, and more.

www.puzzleFactory.com. You'll find more than 7,000 free online games here.

thinks.com. Want to keep your mind agile? Try these games when you're tired of the crossword — they're especially designed to boost your memory and cognition. Try Sudoku, the Japanese logic-based number placement puzzle, or other brainteasers, puzzle games, and word games. You can even do crossword and jigsaw puzzles or play chess, checkers, and Chinese checkers.

www.gammoned.com. Learn all about the rules and strategies for backgammon. You can even play against others, when you get up to speed.

Maybe you're looking for a bigger challenge than a simple one-on-one game. In that case, you can join in any number of multiplayer games. Like Dungeons and Dragons, these games often involve fantasy or science-fiction worlds and role-playing. Others involve building cities or waging wars.

The beauty of Internet games is that you can always find an opponent. Thanks to the magic of the Internet, you can play with anyone in the world, day or night.

Get real-time real estate info

Whether you're looking for a new home or trying to sell your current one, the Internet can help. In fact, a 2006 National Association of Realtors survey found that 80 percent of recent home buyers used the Internet to search for a home. These Web sites can help you determine the value of your house and others like it, find a real estate agent, and get tips for buying and selling a home.

www.cyberhomes.com. Find out what your house is worth — or your neighbor's. All you need is an address and this Web site. You can also find homes for sale, schools, and neighborhoods. It lets you refine your search by features including number of bathrooms or bedrooms, home and lot size, and price range.

www.zillow.com. This site estimates your home's worth with a special home-value calculator. It also includes a neat aerial map feature; helpful guides; directories to help you find a real estate agent, appraiser, inspector, lender, or contractor; and discussion groups about a variety of real estate topics.

www.realtor.com. The official site of the National Association of Realtors lets you browse listings from all over the country. It also features several helpful tools, articles, and links to more resources.

www.trulia.com. Chat with locals in your prospective neighborhood at this handy site. There's no need to register to get full access to listings, maps, and other data.

If you're interested in bypassing an agent and selling your home by yourself, check out FSBO.com and Fizber.com for all the advice, tips, and resources you need. Just go to **www.fsbo.com** or **www.fizber.com**.

Watch TV on your PC

You don't need to go to the movie theater — or even use your remote control — to watch movies and TV. You can enjoy your favorite films and TV shows right on your computer. Check out these two main sources of online video entertainment.

Streaming TV shows. Whether you've missed the latest episode of your favorite police drama or you're nostalgic for old family sitcoms, you can probably find it free online. You have several options here.

✦ Try the Web site of the network that carries your favorite show. You may find full recent episodes, although you'll have to watch commercials.

✦ Aggregate sites collect links to popular shows, which you can watch free with commercials.

Hulu	*www.hulu.com*
Fancast	*www.fancast.com*
AOL Television	*television.aol.com/video*
Joost	*www.joost.com*

✦ For a small fee, say around $2 dollars per episode, you can watch TV shows without commercials. Buy them at these popular sites.

iTunes Store	*www.itunes.com*
Amazon Unbox	*www.unbox.com*

Pay-per-download movies. Skip driving to the video store or waiting for DVDs to arrive in the mail when you download movies to watch on your PC. Film rentals cost about $4 each at these sites, or you can buy them for around $20 each.

Blockbuster	www.blockbuster.com
iTunes Store	www.itunes.com
CinemaNow	www.cinemanow.com
Amazon Video On Demand	www.amazon.com

Fantastic sites for film buffs

Read movie reviews, find local show times, and buy movie tickets online. You can also learn more about your favorite movies or actors.

Read reviews. Not sure which movie to see in the theater or rent on DVD? Several Web sites provide online movie reviews. One of the best resources is the Internet Movie Database. You'll find it at **www.imdb.com.** Much more than reviews, this site lets you look up all kinds of information for any movie, actor, director, or TV show. From interesting trivia to continuity goofs to memorable quotes, this site has it all.

Another good resource for parents is Screen It. In addition to reviewing movies, this subscription service, at **www.screenit.com,** screens movies for language and other objectionable material.

Filmcritic.com, at **www.filmcritic.com,** provides over 7,500 movie reviews. You can also check out the Web site of famous film critic Roger Ebert. Just go to **rogerebert.suntimes.com** to read reviews of current and classic films. You'll give his site two thumbs up.

Buy tickets. You don't have to line up to buy movie tickets at the theater. Thanks to the Internet, you can buy them online. Find out which moves are playing at your local theaters, what times they're playing, and snag tickets before they sell out. That gives you more time to buy popcorn and other snacks once you get to the theater. Go to these Web sites for show times and tickets near you.

AMC Theatres	*www.amctheatres.com*
Carmike Cinemas	*www.carmike.com*
Cinemark	*www.cinemark.com*
Fandango	*www.fandango.com*
Moviefone	*movies.aol.com*
MovieTickets.com	*www.movietickets.com*
Regal Entertainment Group	*www.regmovies.com*

Find fan sites. Can't get enough of your favorite movie or movie star? Use a search engine to find fan sites of actors, actresses, and movies. Just enter the name of the actor or movie, then add the word **fan** or **fansite**. You can also try adding the word **official** to your search.

Listen closely. Here's a great way to secretly slack off at work. Go to **www.listentoamovie.com**. You can access the complete audio soundtracks to some of your favorite films. While there's no picture, you get the entire musical score and every line of dialogue — plus every footstep, sound effect, and ominous moment of silence. It even comes with a "stealth mode" feature that replaces the movie player with a spread-sheet so it looks like you're working.

Capture clip art online

Need something to jazz up your family newsletter, party invita-tions, or greeting cards? Try clip art. It's easy to download samples at Microsoft Office Online. However, you must have a program called Microsoft Clip Organizer that comes with Microsoft Office installed on your computer to download this way.

1. Go to **office.microsoft.com** and click on the CLIP ART tab.

2. Enter a keyword in the SEARCH box. For example, type **snowman** if you're looking for a winter theme.

3. Select CLIP ART from the drop-down list next to the SEARCH button. Notice you can also search for PHOTOS, ANIMATION, and SOUNDS.

4. Choose the snowman pictures you want by checking the box beneath each one. Your selections go to the SELECTION BASKET on the left.

5. When you're through choosing, click on DOWNLOAD ITEMS.

Your clips will be imported to Microsoft Clip Organizer, where they will be stored for easy access. You can access your Microsoft Clip Organizer folder by going to the START menu, and navigating to your MY PICTURES folder.

You don't have to limit your search for clip art to Microsoft Office Online. Simply search for **clip art** in your favorite search engine, and you'll end up with countless sites to choose from. Just make sure you use a reliable site, since you'll be downloading from it.

Take a high-tech path to higher education

Get your college degree without spending time on a college campus. Several schools offer online degrees — a convenient way to continue your education that lets you learn at your own pace, at your own hours, from the comfort of your own home.

Spot shady schools. Before you pay for any classes, make sure you're dealing with a legitimate school. The Better Business Bureau advises you to watch out for these red flags:

✦ claims that degrees can be earned in less time than traditional colleges

✦ list of accrediting agencies sounds a little too impressive

✦ heavy emphasis placed on credits for real-world experience

- tuition paid on a per-degree basis, with discounts for multiple degrees

- name that's similar to a well-known university

- address is just a P.O. box or suite number

To check out a school, make sure it appears on one of these accreditation lists.

| U.S. Department of Education | www.ope.ed.gov/accreditation/Search.aspx |
| Council for Higher Education Accreditation | www.chea.org/search/default.asp |

Look for learning. One good place to find Web sites for colleges and community colleges that interest you is DegreeTutor at **www.degreetutor.com.** You can search by zip code, subject, or degree.

Maybe you're not interested in getting a degree or competing for grades — you just want to learn and be exposed to new things. No problem. You can find plenty of non-degree programs as well. Several schools, including MIT and Yale, provide free lectures online. Watch a video, and feel like you're in the classroom. Auditing classes, for a nominal fee per class, is a great idea for seniors looking to fill time or expand their horizons. Check the Web sites of local schools to see if this option is available.

Seniors for hire: find jobs online

Just because you're retired doesn't mean you're ready to stop working and ride off into the sunset. Or maybe the current tough economy has postponed your retirement plans.

Seeking seniors. Several employment Web sites are dedicated to seniors. No matter how bad the economy is, experts will always be in demand — and who has more experience than older workers?

275

Go here to get the scoop on job openings for seniors. You'll also find a host of resources to help you land a new position.

Employment Network for Retired Government Experts	www.enrge.us
SeniorJobBank	www.seniorjobbank.com
Seniors4Hire	www.seniors4hire.org
Workforce50.com	www.workforce50.com
YourEncore	www.yourencore.com

Help wanted. Of course, you don't have to limit your job search to senior-specific sites. Give the many general employment Web sites a shot. Search for job openings by location or field, post your resume, and get helpful tips for your job search at these popular sites.

CareerBuilder.com	www.careerbuilder.com
Jobs Online	www.jobsonline.com
Jobs.com	www.jobs.com
Monster	www.monster.com
Salary.com	www.salary.com
SimplyHired	www.simplyhired.com
Yahoo! HotJobs	hotjobs.yahoo.com

Another good option is Craigslist, at **www.craigslist.org**, where you can find help wanted classified ads online.

Cutting-edge way to read the classics

If you love to read, you'll love the Internet. Think of it as the world's largest library — all in the comfort of your own home.

Some Web sites let you download print or audio books, while others just let you access them online. Most free books are classic titles that are no longer in copyright, but some contemporary works are also available. Have fun browsing the shelves of these online resources.

Classic literature. The big boys in this arena are Project Gutenberg, at **www.gutenberg.org** and Bartleby, at **www.bartleby.com**. Browse their vast catalogs of classic works or use their search engines to find exactly what you're looking for.

Another good source is Classic Bookshelf, at **www.classicbookshelf.com**. This site lets you change fonts, text size, background, and text color to make it easier to read on your monitor.

ManyBooks.net, at **manybooks.net**, lets you download free classics and some newer works in a variety of formats, including PDF and large-print editions. If you prefer audio books, LibriVox offers audio versions of books in the public domain. Just go to **librivox.org**. Here are some more destinations for great books.

Access the Great Books	www.anova.org
Bibliomania	www.bibliomania.com
Classic Authors.net	www.classicauthors.net
Classic Reader	www.classicreader.com
FullBooks.com	www.fullbooks.com
Great Books Collection	www.greatbookscollection.org
Page By Page Books	www.pagebypagebooks.com
The Literature Network	www.online-literature.com

Short stories. While the previous sites may include poems, short stories, and plays in addition to novels, a few sites specialize in short stories. For classic and contemporary examples of this genre, go here.

| East of the Web | www.short-stories.co.uk |
| The Short Story Classics | members.lycos.co.uk/shortstories |

Library services. Enjoy the benefits of a public library without being hushed by a librarian. The Internet Public Library, at **www.ipl.org**, is a great resource, with lots of links to online books, magazines, reference materials, and more. If you have a reference question, click on ASK AN IPL LIBRARIAN to get an answer.

WorldCat.org, the world's largest network of library content and services, lets you search several libraries for the titles you want. It also provides links to those libraries, which may let you download or check out these books. Go to **www.worldcat.org** to find out more.

University Web sites. Another good way to find online books is to Google the title of a classic book. Often, you'll be able to download it for free on a university Web site. For example, check out The Online Books Page at **onlinebooks.library.upenn.edu.**

You can also try EServer, an e-publishing co-op based at Iowa State University which provides novels, short stories, biographies, and more online. Check it out at **www.eserver.org.**

Virtual bookshelf. Want to know which books your friends are reading? Want to share recommendations with others? Build a virtual bookshelf at Shelfari. This site lets you discover new books, share reviews of books you've read, and see what others are reading. You can't actually access the books here, but you can view and post images of the covers at this social network site. Go to **www.shelfari.com** to get ideas for your reading list.

New way to get your news

Stop the presses! Now you can say goodbye to costly newspaper subscriptions, newsprint-stained hands, missed deliveries, and soggy morning papers. Just go online to read the latest news — for free — from newspapers all over the world.

Most newspapers have online versions now — go right to their Web sites. Usually, a newspaper's Web address is easy to figure out. For instance, the New York Times Web address is simply **www.nytimes.com.**

You can always type a newspaper's name into a search engine to find its Web site, too. Or, if you don't know the name of the news-paper in a particular city, just search for the city's name plus the word **newspaper.** You may have to register at the site by providing your name and e-mail address, but access is usually free.

You can also find links to thousands of online newspapers all in one place at the following Web sites.

Newspapers.com	*www.newspapers.com*
Online Newspapers	*www.findnewspapers.com*
AllYouCanRead	*www.allyoucanread.com/newspapers*
News and Newspapers Online	*library.uncg.edu/news*

The Internet makes it easy to read many newspapers each day instead of just one. You can stay up-to-date and get multiple points of view. If you plan to relocate or go on vacation, check out the local papers before you go. You'll feel like a local before you even arrive.

Get cooking with your computer

Whether you're an expert chef or a novice in the kitchen, the Internet can help you put meals on the table. Learn basic cooking terms and techniques, find free recipes, and organize your grocery list online.

Begin with the basics. A great all-around source for any cooking question you have is Epicurious at **www.epicurious.com.** Unsure about a cooking term? Consult the site's food dictionary. You can also get details about ingredients, read articles and guides, and even find recipes at this one-stop culinary site.

Consider your cupboard. Having a hard time deciding what to make for dinner? Get some hints based on what you already have in your pantry. Just go to RecipeMatcher at **www.recipematcher.com**, where you'll find recipes based on the ingredients and groceries you have on hand. Just enter the items you have, and you'll get options. It will even let you know of any additional ingredients you may need for a particular recipe.

Find free recipes. Maybe you saw a celebrity chef whip up something delicious on TV. Go to the Food Network Web site at **www.foodnetwork.com** to search for featured recipes.

Perhaps you want to recreate a meal you had at a restaurant. Top Secret Recipes tells you how to make "kitchen clones of America's favorite brand-name foods" at **www.topsecretrecipes.com**.

Several other Web sites provide a smorgasbord of tasty recipes online. Whet your appetite here.

All Recipes	*www.allrecipes.com*
Bon Appetit	*www.bonappetit.com*
Cooking.com	*www.cooking.com*
FabulousFoods.com	*www.fabulousfoods.com*
iChef	*www.ichef.com*
Meals For You	*www.mealsforyou.com*
Recipezaar	*www.recipezaar.com*

Make healthy choices. While you can certainly find healthy recipes — as well as other helpful cooking tidbits — at the above sites, other sites specialize in healthy eating. For example, the Centers for Disease Control (CDC) has recipes for fruits and vegetables at **apps.nccd.cdc.gov/dnparecipe/recipesearch.aspx**. You can also find healthy recipes at the following Web sites.

American Heart Association	www.americanheart.org/deliciousdecisions
FATFREE	www.fatfree.com
FoodFit	www.foodfit.com

Shop smarter. Recipes aren't the only things you can print online. You can also find printable grocery lists at the Organized Times Web site. Just go to **www.organizedtimes.com/grocery.htm.** This handy shopping list is divided into categories, like baked goods, deli, dairy, frozen foods, and so on. This will help you get in and out of the supermarket quickly.

Collect recipe cards. If you like to save or share recipes on attractive recipe cards, you can find those online, too. Here are just a few examples of cute, printable recipe cards.

Original Country Clipart by Lisa	www.countryclipart.com/recipecards.htm
Alenka's Printables	alenkasprintables.com/free_recipe_cards.shtml
Gramma Hugs Recipe Cards	grammahugs.com/cookies/rcards1.html

Go gourmet. Some Web sites help you feel like a gourmet chef. Go online to get all the essential tools, from chef's hats to kitchen gadgets to fancy ingredients.

Williams-Sonoma	www.williams-sonoma.com
Chefs' Warehouse	www.chefswarehouse.com
Chef Depot	www.chefdepot.com
The Chef Hat	www.thechefhat.com

Redecorate with help from cyberspace

Why hire an interior decorator when you can find all sorts of help online — for free? Check out these Web sites for home decorating tools and tips.

Move furniture with your mouse. Go to Better Homes and Gardens at **www.bhg.com.** Click on DECORATING, then SEE ALL TOOLS. Choose ARRANGE-A-ROOM. You must provide your name and e-mail address to use this free program, which gives you a bird's-eye view of your room. Start with a blank grid, then add walls, windows, and furniture. It's easy to move furniture around with your mouse — much easier than lugging your sofa and coffee table around your living room. Print the layouts you like or save your designs to check later.

Get advice from experts. Several Web sites provide decorating tips and tricks. For a whole host of projects, including painting and putting up wallpaper and other wall coverings, go to DoItYourself.com at **www.doityourself.com** and click on DECORATING. If you're decorating on a budget, check out The Thrifty Decorating Blog at **www.thriftydecorating.com.**

Big names like HGTV, at **www.hgtv.com,** and Martha Stewart, at **www.marthastewart.com,** also feature several decorating ideas and resources.

Pick the perfect paint. Agonizing over paint choices? Online tools and software can help you choose the right colors for any room in your house. Often, you can upload photos of your own rooms and "paint" them online. That way, you get a preview of what each room will look like — without having to paint your walls first.

◆ Behr, at **www.behr.com,** offers ColorSmart, which helps you coordinate colors. There's also the subscription Paint Your Place option, which lets you preview colors on photos of your own home.

◆ Benjamin Moore has a Personal Color Viewer. Go to **www.benjaminmoore.com** and choose FOR YOUR HOME from the drop-down menu. Then click PAINT NOW under the Personal Color Viewer. You can "paint" sample photos or upload your own.

♦ Colorcharts.org, an online database of manufacturers' standard colors, offers a free trial for its CBN Selector, which lets you color your own digital photos. Just go to **www.colorcharts.org.**

♦ Bob Vila's Web site, **www.bobvila.com,** also lets you envision your paint projects from start to finish. Under the HOME IMPROVEMENT LIBRARY tab, click on PAINT DESIGNER.

Keep in mind that paint colors may appear slightly different on your computer monitor than they do on your wall. So, after you narrow down your choices to a few finalists, you may still want to buy a quart or a sample to test.

Safety first: what to know before you go

There's more to planning a trip than finding the lowest airfare and hotel rates or getting good directions. You also want to make sure you get there safely.

♦ Get traffic or road closure information from the Federal Highway Administration at **www.fhwa.dot.gov/trafficinfo.**

♦ Discover safety tips from the National Highway Traffic Safety Administration at **www.nhtsa.dot.gov.**

♦ Learn which items you can't take on a plane and uncover packing tips to help you sail through airport security screenings with fewer delays at **safetravel.dot.gov** or **www.tsa.gov.**

♦ For helpful links about travel by air, land, or sea, check out the U.S. Department of Transportation site. Visit **www.dot.gov** and click on the SAFETY link. Learn everything from how to drive safely around eighteen-wheelers to ways to help keep your passengers safe.

chapter 26

RSS & podcasts: fun & free

❝When I was a teenager in the late 30's and early 40's, electronics wasn't a word. You were interested in radio if you were interested in electronics. ❞

Kenneth Olsen
American engineer speaking to the World Future Society in 1977

News you can use comes to you

Let's say you like to read news headlines at the BBC's Web site, but you want to read stock reports at the New York Times Web site and you need weather forecasts from your local newspaper's site. It takes time and effort to visit all these Web sites every day, wading through the abundance of information to get to the nuggets you're looking for. There's a better way.

Skip all the Internet navigating and have what you want sent directly to your computer. Sign up for free RSS feeds, and your favorite news comes to you.RSS stands for Really Simple Syndication, and it really is quite simple.

Get yourself a reader. A feed reader, also called a news aggregator, is software that will locate and organize your news links so you can read them all in one place. Some programs show news items by headlines with summaries, while others add in graphics or arrange them into folders based on topic. You can choose whether you prefer a stand-alone program or a plug-in to a Web browser like Internet Explorer. You can also opt for a Web-based reader, which lets you check your RSS feeds from any computer, even while you're away from home. Some good feed readers are available free, while others are for purchase.

AmphetaDesk	www.disobey.com/amphetadesk	software download
Bloglines	www.bloglines.com	Web-based program
Google Reader	www.google.com/reader	Web-based program
NewsGator	www.newsgator.com	software download
RSSReader	www.rssreader.com	software download

Add your favorite news links. The next step is locating links to the sites you're interested in. You'll be able to link to most of the major news outlets, like *The New York Times*, *The Wall Street Journal*, BBC News, CNN, MSNBC, and so on. You can also find RSS feeds from specialty Web sites if you're interested in, say, Washington Redskins football, happenings at your grandson's college, or taking care of your flower garden. Look for the orange button that indicates an RSS feed at that Web site, and click on it to subscribe.

Examples of buttons that indicate links to RSS feeds

Sit back and enjoy the show. After your feeds are set up, you'll be able to open your RSS reader every day and see what's new. Headlines will be updated automatically, so you don't have to lift a finger. You'll have some control over how the page looks, how often the headlines are updated, and whether you receive an alert about updates. Check the preferences in your RSS reader.

Podcasts: free broadcasting on demand

Some people like to read for information and fun, but others prefer to use their ears. If you like listening to the radio more than reading a newspaper or magazine, then podcasts are for you.

A podcast — taken from the words "iPod" and "broadcast" — is a short bit of audio that you can download from the Internet, then listen to on your computer or MP3 player. It's similar to a tape of a radio broadcast, but you can listen to a podcast whenever you want rather than at a certain time. That makes listening to podcasts akin to watching television shows that you've recorded on your DVR or TiVo machine. And now there are podcasts that aren't just audio — they incorporate photographs and even video.

If you subscribe to a podcast series, then all the episodes on that series will be downloaded to your computer. Or you can pick and choose, listening to a single episode of a podcast whenever you find one that's interesting. You'll find podcasts of all kinds of material:

◆ news and current events

◆ readings of poetry or fiction

◆ talk shows on subjects as diverse as parenting, coin collecting, and pro basketball

◆ episodes of old radio shows like *The Jack Benny Show* and *The Lone Ranger*

Fire up your software. Just like with RSS feeds, you first need to get software that will allow you to download and listen to podcasts. Many good programs are available for free.

iTunes	www.apple.com/itunes/download
Juice	www.juicereceiver.sourceforge.net
iPodderX	www.download.com
Zune	www.zune.net

But don't forget how podcasts got their name — the option to play them on an iPod or similar MP3 player. You can download podcasts from the Internet to your player, then listen to them while you're on the go.

Find the podcasts. You can locate podcasts on just about any topic by searching through podcast directories. Try these.

Digital Podcast	www.digitalpodcast.com
Find Podcasts	www.findpodcasts.com
Podcast	www.podcast.com
Podcast Pickle	www.podcastpickle.com
Podomatic	www.podomatic.com

You can also get podcasts through some of the same software you use to listen to them, including the free iTunes program. In iTunes, click on the ITUNES STORE link, then scroll down to the TOP PODCASTS section. You can subscribe to thousands of popular podcasts without opening an iTunes account.

For information on how to create your own podcasts, see page 341 in the *Audio magic* chapter.

chapter 27

High-tech banking

66 Once a new technology rolls over you, if you're not part of the steamroller, you're part of the road. 99

Stewart Brand, author and creator

of the *Whole Earth Catalog* and *CoEvolution Quarterly*

Bank on online benefits

Do all your banking on your PC and you'll save time — no more driving to your bank and standing in line for a teller. You'll gain peace of mind — with just a few security rules, online banking is safer than using your mailbox. And you'll cut banking costs.

Save money 3 ways. Most banks let you pay your bills online. If you set up automatic withdrawals, you'll avoid paying late fees. Plus you won't need to spend money on stamps and envelopes to mail payments. You may even get a lower interest rate if you sign up for automated loan payments.

Get control of spending. When your bank account is available online, you can monitor just exactly how you're spending money. This makes forming and sticking to a budget much easier. You'll also know quickly when a check clears or a payment is made — no need to wait for your monthly statement.

Stay secure. Convenience counts, but be sure to protect your bank account when paying bills with automatic withdrawals. Follow these rules to keep your personal information from being broadcast all over the Internet.

✦ Use anti-virus and anti-spyware software on your computer.

✦ Don't connect to your bank using a public computer.

✦ Become familiar with your bank's Web site so you'll notice suspicious changes.

✦ Select a strong password, and change it every three to six months — even if your bank doesn't require it.

For information on picking a powerful password, see page 161 in the *Security matters* chapter.

Sidestep scams. Don't click on a link in a suspicious e-mail message, even if it looks like it's from your bank. It could be a phishing message, and the link will lead to a fake Web site that looks just like the real one. Scammers set up these sites to try to access your personal information. Your bank's Web site should include "https" at the start of the URL, and you should see a closed lock symbol at the bottom of the page.

For information on avoiding phishing scams, see page 304 in the *E-mail essentials* chapter.

If something seems odd while you're banking online, stop and report the problem. Look up your bank's phone number and call in a report, or contact the United States Computer Emergency Readiness Team (US-CERT) at **www.us-cert.gov.**

Keeping track of your credit score can help you save money with a lower interest rate. But beware of following an online promotion to get a free copy of your credit report. If you see ads on the Web site, you're being scammed. You may be charged for another service if you order a report from this site. Instead, get a free credit report every year from the three major credit-reporting agencies at **www.annualcreditreport.com.**

Make sense of credit card perks

You use your credit card because it's convenient. But why not use a card that gives you free money? Credit cards with rewards programs and cash-back incentives pay you just for using them. This cash-back option gives you the most flexibility, but if you shop around, you can probably find a card that offers:

✦ airline points toward free plane tickets

✦ contributions to your retirement account

✦ a discount on your next car purchase or lease

✦ tickets to amusement parks

✦ gift cards at various stores, including Macy's, Home Depot, or L.L. Bean

Since there are lots of rewards cards out there, you might want help comparing the offers. Start with these informational Web sites.

CreditCards.com	www.creditcards.com
Bankrate	www.bankrate.com
MSN	www.moneycentral.msn.com

Beware of an offer that seems too good to be true — it probably is. Before you sign, read the fine print on a credit card agreement to be sure you're getting the deal you think you're getting. And pay off your balance every month. If you don't, the rewards cards are not for you, since your "free money" will be eaten up by interest and fees.

Kick the bricks with an Internet bank

An Internet-only bank is one you access strictly through a Web site, mail, or telephone. There's no brick-and-mortar building to go to. That means you save, since the bank doesn't have to pay for upkeep of physical buildings or keep tellers on call. Your benefit — better interest rates and lower fees. But using an Internet-only bank could cause you some headaches if you don't select one carefully.

✦ Watch out for ATM transaction fees.

✦ Look for the FDIC logo on the bank's Web site, meaning it's backed by the Federal Deposit Insurance Corporation. Or check the FDIC's Web site for confirmation at **www.fdic.gov.** Click on the BANK FIND/INSTITUTION DIRECTORY link.

✦ Look for "deposit at home" technology, letting you scan in and deposit checks from your home PC.

You can do a side-by-side comparison of Internet banks, checking their interest rates, services, and fees at **www.bankrate.com.**

Click on the CHECKING & SAVINGS button at the top of the screen, then use the tools to compare banks. And check with an affinity group you belong to for special banking services, like USAA banking for retired and active duty military personnel or NEA accounts for educators.

Find a local bank without leaving home. Use the Web site **www.mybank.com** to locate FDIC-insured financial institutions with branches in your town. You can search by the bank's name or by entering your city's name or local ZIP code, then specify how many miles you're willing to drive.

chapter 28

E-mail essentials

❝I'm a great believer that any tool that enhances communication has profound effects in terms of how people can learn from each other, and how they can achieve the kind of freedoms that they're interested in. ❞

Bill Gates

Send your next letter for free

Stay in touch with family and friends — without licking one stamp. Thanks to e-mail, you can spend less money on stamps and envelopes but write more often than ever before. It's like getting free mail with a click of a button.

Before you begin. You need three things to send and receive e-mail — an e-mail program, an e-mail address, and how-to information from your Internet Service Provider (ISP). You already have one e-mail program that won't cost you a penny.

It's called Outlook Express, and it comes with every copy of Windows XP. You can get your e-mail address from your ISP. In fact, it may already be waiting for you in papers your ISP gave you. Just look for a series of words and numbers with the @ sign in the middle — such as john.smith@mindspring.com. Your ISP may also have provided important information on how to set up your e-mail.

If you don't find your e-mail address or information about setting up your e-mail, call your ISP. Be sure to read through the information once you have it.

Set it up. Before you can use Outlook Express, you must set it up to work with your e-mail address. To start Outlook Express, click on START, then ALL PROGRAMS, and OUTLOOK EXPRESS.

After the program opens, the Internet Connection Wizard should automatically appear. This *Wizard* walks you through the process of setting up your e-mail. Don't forget to follow your ISP's instructions for setting up your e-mail, too.

If you'd like Outlook Express to pop up anytime you click on the E-MAIL CUSTOMER SERVICE link or any other MAIL TO link on a Web page, make it your "default" mail program. Here's how.

1. In the Outlook Express menu bar, click on TOOLS, then OPTIONS.

2. Click on the GENERAL tab.

3. Near the bottom, find THIS APPLICATION IS THE DEFAULT MAIL HANDLER. Check MAKE DEFAULT button beside it. If Outlook Express is already your default, the button may be dimmed.

4. Click on OK.

Find help. If you need help with anything in Outlook Express, press F1 on the keyboard or, in the menu, click on HELP, then CONTENTS AND INDEX. This opens your online help which can assist you with all sorts of things in Outlook Express.

Hot new e-mail features in Vista

Try to find Outlook Express in Windows Vista and you'll come up empty. That's because the new and improved version of Outlook Express is called Windows Mail. And while you'll recognize most things, this new mail program has also added some cutting-edge features.

Smart Screen. *Windows'* Smart Screen technology monitors your incoming e-mail, grabs suspected spam, and tosses it into the Junk e-mail folder. You can also right-click on any message, click on JUNK E-MAIL, then click on ADD SENDER TO BLOCKED SENDERS LIST. All future e-mails from the sender will be tossed into the Junk e-mail folder.

Anti-phishing. *Windows* Mail has added anti-phishing technology to help protect against those sneaky scammer e-mails that try to trick you into supplying passwords, account numbers, and other sensitive information. It also includes anti-phishing settings to protect against phishing e-mails in your Inbox.

Instant Search. If you have a large number of e-mails in your folders, finding the one you need just got easier. Windows Mail offers a Search bar to help you search for one or more e-mails.

Unfortunately, one change in Windows Mail may come as an unpleasant surprise. Outlook Express allows you to check your old Hotmail account online, but Windows Mail does not.

Avoid a hacker favorite

Outlook Express is widely used, which makes it a favorite target of hackers and virus writers. That's why some experts suggest you use a different e-mail program. Fortunately, you have two kinds of free alternatives to choose from. You can use software-based e-mail programs that work like Outlook Express or try Web mail services that handle your mail on the Web.

Software-based programs. Software-based programs usually transfer e-mail from the e-mail server to your hard drive — and then delete the mail from the server. This means you can compose e-mails, delete e-mails, or do other e-mail tasks without being logged into the Internet. But it also means the only copy of your e-mail is the one you have on your computer — unless you make backups. Thunderbird (**www.mozilla.org**) is a popular software-based program.

Web-based servers. Web-based servers or Web mail keep your e-mail on a server so you must log in on the Web to check, compose, or read your e-mail. You must also remember to log in regularly or you won't know whether you have new e-mail. Even if you lose all the files on your hard drive, your e-mails are still on the Web.

Be aware that Web mail services may require you to establish a different e-mail account and address with them than the one your ISP provided to you. Yet, some Web mail services allow you to use their service to check multiple e-mail addresses — including your ISP address. Or they may let you check your Web mail address with a software e-mail program. In fact, some people keep one ISP address and one Web e-mail address — one address for anything that may lead to spam and the other for personal e-mails.

If you're considering Web mail, ask these questions.

◆ How much storage are you allowed for your e-mails?

◆ Is the Web mail service you want compatible with your favorite browser? Will the service's spelling checker work with your browser?

◆ Can you check other e-mail addresses from your Web mail? Can you check your Web mail from your software e-mail program?

◆ How will you know when you have new mail?

Popular Web mail sites include these:

Gmail	*gmail.com*
Yahoo! Mail	*mail.yahoo.com*
Windows Live Hotmail	*mail.live.com*

Whether you're picking a Web mail service or e-mail program, consider these features.

◆ Organization. Some e-mail programs — or services — let you file messages in folders while others let you label messages instead. Find out which products offer the method you prefer.

◆ Troubleshooting. Find out what kind of learning and troubleshooting help each product has. Options may include tutorials, online help, user forums, Frequently Asked Question lists, and a "knowledge base" of known problems and their solutions.

◆ Security. Determine which programs give you a spam filter, virus filter, and phishing protection. If the e-mail product includes ads, find out whether they'll be text ads, animated ads, or ads targeted to the topics of your e-mails.

◆ Search options. Find out what search options you'll have if you need to find one message in a sea of messages. Also, check whether you can search attachments and messages or just messages.

Add e-mail addresses to your address book

Your hardback address book can't address your mail for you, but your online address book can. Here's what you need to know to get started.

Your online address book needs your e-mail addresses, but you may have already added addresses without even trying. Reply to any e-mail and the sender's name is automatically added to your address book. You don't have to do a thing.

If you don't need to reply to the person, just find one of their e-mails in your Inbox message list. Right-click on the message and click on ADD SENDER TO ADDRESS BOOK, and you're done.

You can also create e-mail groups or distribution lists, so you can send e-mails to several people at once.

Addresses

Addresses button

1. Click on the ADDRESSES button on the toolbar.

2. In the ADDRESS BOOK dialog box, click on FILE, then NEW GROUP.

3. In the PROPERTIES dialog box, click in the GROUP NAME box and type a name for your e-mail group.

4. To add e-mail addresses from your address book, click on SELECT MEMBERS.

5. For each person you'd like to add, find that person's name in the list, click on it and then click on the SELECT button.

6. Each name you add should appear in the MEMBERS box.

7. If you'd like to add an e-mail address that is not in your address book, click on NEW CONTACT. Otherwise, skip to step 13.

8. When the PROPERTIES dialog box appears, type in the person's name.

9. Click in the E-MAIL ADDRESSES box and type in the person's e-mail address.

10. Click on the ADD button.

11. Click on OK.

12. In the SELECT GROUP MEMBERS dialog box, find your newly added contact in the list, click on the name, and click on the SELECT button.

13. If you're done adding members, click on OK.

14. Click on OK in your group's PROPERTIES dialog box.

Now you can send e-mails to everyone in this group just by typing the group name in the TO box of any e-mail.

Manage multiple e-mail addresses easily

You might be surprised to discover that your household can have more than one e-mail account. In fact, each family member can have several e-mail addresses. Some people never need more than one e-mail account, but others do. For example, you might have:

✦ a work e-mail address with your employer's e-mail server

✦ a personal e-mail address with your ISP

✦ a free account from Hotmail or another free e-mail vendor so you can use it when ordering online, participating in chat rooms, or doing anything else that might invite spam

✦ a free Google Gmail address for e-mails related to your club, church group, or home business

Unfortunately, extra addresses can also lead to confusion and Inbox overload unless you know the right tricks. Here are two of the best ones.

Check multiple accounts quickly. Keeping multiple e-mail accounts can be a great way to stay organized and help manage spam. Yet, the problem is you must remember to check them separately. That's a lot of time and hassle, and it's easy to forget. Standard programs like Outlook Express and Thunderbird offer options to add extra e-mail addresses to the list of addresses the program checks.

Google's Gmail provides a way to funnel all your e-mail into Gmail. This also lets you check all your e-mail in one place. Either use Gmail's Mail Fetcher feature to retrieve e-mail from your other e-mail addresses. Or, if that doesn't work, forward e-mail from your other e-mail addresses to Gmail. You can even set up

You can address your mail in as few as three key-strokes. As long as the person's e-mail address is in your address book, all you have to do is type the first few letters of their name in the TO box of an e-mail. Outlook Express will pop in the rest of the name, and e-mail address, for you.

rules or filters to label which e-mail address each e-mail has been sent to. What's more, you can write messages in Gmail that will appear to come from your other e-mail addresses. Visit **gmail.com** to learn more.

Keep messages organized. If everyone's e-mail comes to the same Inbox, how do you know which ones are yours? To prevent confusion, you can create a folder for each e-mail address. Then you can create rules to funnel all the e-mails for a particular address into the folder reserved for it.

However, this may not be necessary if you use the Outlook Express Add New Identity option to assign each person their own "identity." Each person's e-mails, folders, rules, and contacts are kept separate from everyone else's. The identity can even be password protected so no one else can access it. You must also add a new e-mail account for each identity before a person can use it.

E-mail huge pictures without error messages

E-mail attachments are a wonderful way to send photos, PowerPoint presentations, PDFs, videos, and even plain old word processor documents. In fact, you can normally send and receive the latest pictures of your loved ones in minutes — just by downloading pictures from your digital camera and e-mailing them.

But sometimes your e-mailer digs in its heels and won't send an e-mail with an attachment. This happens because the file is too big. Fortunately, Windows offers an easy way to shrink a file by 50 to 90 percent without changing the file's contents. It's called compressing or zipping and best of all, it's free.

1. Click on START and then click on MY COMPUTER.

2. Navigate to the file you want to compress.

3. Right-click on the file's icon and choose SEND TO COMPRESSED (ZIPPED) FOLDER.

4. The compressed version of the file appears in the same folder as the original, but the compressed file has a .zip at the end of its file name and a file icon that looks like this.

9771a.zip

Compressed file icon

Now you can e-mail the file to anyone with Windows XP. They'll be able to uncompress the file back to its normal size just by double-clicking on the compressed file's icon.

For more information on how to compress a folder or even your entire hard disk, see page 118 in the *Keep your PC problem-free* chapter.

Get help from a free application

Some videos, pictures, and files are so big that even compressing them can't shrink them enough to fit your e-mail program's size limits. When that happens, experts from *The Wall Street Journal* recommend Pando software.

Download this free software and you can successfully send files — or groups of files — up to 1 gigabyte in size without triggering an error message from your e-mail provider. When you send files to someone, they must download Pando before they can receive your files, but Pando works for both Windows and Macintosh computers. Visit **www.pando.com** to learn more.

For more information on photo-sharing, see page 360 in the *Make the most of your digital images* chapter.

Protect yourself from viruses and scammers

Protect your credit, keep your personal information private, and squelch viruses with these e-mail tips. Practice defensive e-mailing the same way you practice defensive driving and you may even prevent identity theft.

Share information cautiously. Never send your Social Security number, any password, any kind of account number, or any other sensitive information in an e-mail — even if the request for this information comes directly from your bank, credit card company, law enforcement organization, or government agency. Instead, look up the company's number and call to confirm that the e-mail came from them.

Even sending sensitive information to a family member could be dangerous — if you do it by e-mail. That's because e-mails don't pass directly from your computer to another computer. Instead, e-mail may pass through several places where it might be opened and read before the intended receiver downloads it.

Beef up security. Your spyware checker, firewall, and anti-virus software should all be set up and turned on to protect you. In particular, your anti-virus software should be set up to scan your e-mails and their attachments. But you can also beef up your Outlook Express security settings. Here are a few tips to help you take your first steps

1. Open Outlook Express, click on TOOLS → OPTIONS and then the SECURITY tab.

2. For SELECT THE INTERNET EXPLORER SECURITY ZONE TO USE, Microsoft recommends you click on RESTRICTED SITES ZONE (MORE SECURE).

3. Microsoft also recommends you click on WARN ME WHEN OTHER APPLICATIONS TRY TO SEND MAIL AS ME. This prevents viruses or other infiltrators on the Internet from using your computer to send e-mail.

Also, consider clicking on BLOCK IMAGES AND OTHER EXTERNAL CONTENT IN HTML E-MAIL. Some graphics in unsolicited e-mails can actually notify a marketer that your e-mail address is valid, which invites more unsolicited e-mails. Blocking these graphics may prevent you from getting unsolicited e-mails.

Be wary of attachments. Never open an unexpected e-mail attachment. It may contain viruses or worse. Viruses and hackers can generate e-mails that look as if they came from someone you know well. That means e-mail attachments from friends and family can be unsafe.

Outlook Express comes with Do Not Allow Attachments To Be Saved Or Opened That Could Potentially Be A Virus already turned on. If your favorite cousin calls and says she's sending you an e-mail with an attachment, but you never get the attachment — this may be why.

To fix the problem, make sure your anti-virus protection is running and it's set up to protect e-mail and attachments. Then click in the DO NOT ALLOW ATTACHMENTS TO BE SAVED OR OPENED THAT COULD POTENTIALLY BE A VIRUS check box to clear it — for now.

Click on OK and ask your cousin to resend the e-mail with the attachment right away. As soon as it arrives, turn DO NOT ALLOW ATTACHMENTS TO BE SAVED OR OPENED THAT COULD POTENTIALLY BE A VIRUS back on.

For more information on anti-virus software, see page 151 in the *Security matters* chapter.

10 terrific tips to cut down on junk e-mail

You don't have to drown in a sea of junk e-mail called spam. Get the inside scoop and keep it to a mere trickle. Learn how spammers "harvest" your email address, how to stop them, and discover 10 terrific tips to get rid of annoying junk email.

Go undercover. Avoid displaying your e-mail address in newsgroup postings, chat rooms, online services' membership directories, Web sites, or any other online public places. Spammers use automated software to trawl these places and scoop up addresses for their mailing lists.

Try two e-mail addresses. Use one for regular e-mail correspondence and the other for Web sites, chat rooms, newsgroups, discussion boards, and e-mailing lists that require an e-mail address. You might think e-mail lists are safe if they don't display your address, but know this before jumping on e-mailing lists. Spammers have several ways to trick e-mail servers into giving up mailing list addresses.

Stop harvesting by 'masking.' If you must submit your e-mail to a Web site, chat room, or newsgroup, mask it. For example, instead of JoeCool@example.com, write JoeCool at example dot com. A Federal Trade Commission (FTC) study found this can help prevent spammers from harvesting an e-mail address.

Protect your privacy. Never submit your e-mail address to a site that won't let you "opt out" of having your e-mail address sold or put on a mailing list. Read the Web site's privacy policy to discover whether you can opt out and how to do it.

Choose a spam-resistant address. Spammers use "dictionary attacks" to guess e-mail addresses, especially if they have a common domain name, like yahoo.com. Spammers are less likely to guess an e-mail address with numbers in the middle, such as Joe234Cool@example.com. They are also less likely to guess e-mail addresses from domain names that aren't well known.

Change to low tech. Either turn off your e-mail program's option to display graphics in e-mails or turn on the setting that lets you read e-mails as plain text. Spammers often include tiny, nearly invisible graphics in their e-mails. These graphics can notify a spammer when an e-mail address is valid.

Don't reply to spam. Many spam e-mails may also be scams, especially chain letters that promise money or e-mails promising weight loss, work-at-home options, or credit repair. Even if the e-mail isn't a scam, replying just tells a spammer he has found a valid e-mail to use again. Also, be aware that some experts suspect unsubscribing may have the same effect as a reply.

Filter it out. Choose an e-mail program with a good spam filter or buy a third-party spam filter. To find the best one, read reviews in computer magazines and reliable sites, such as **www.cnet.com.** Be wary of Web sites that offer free spam blockers you've never heard of. These may be spammer tools that will make your spam problem worse.

Thwart viruses. Keep your anti-virus protection up to date and make sure it scans your e-mail and attachments. Scammers use viruses to collect e-mail addresses from your computer, including those visible in e-mails you've received and sent. Addresses in the TO and CC boxes of e-mails are visible. When you forward jokes and other e-mails to groups of people, put their addresses in the BCC (blind carbon copy) address box to hide them. Ask your friends to do the same.

Blow the whistle. Forward copies of spam to your ISP's e-mail address abuse desk and to spam@uce.gov at the Federal Trade Commission. Be sure to include the full e-mail header. The FTC will pass it on to law enforcement and consumer protection agencies so they can fight spam, while ISPs may use it to help stop spam directly.

More than 100 billion spam e-mails are sent every day. According to McAfee's Avert Labs, more than half of those are about health or medicine.

Dodge dangerous phishing scams

The e-mail you just received from your bank, credit card company, eBay, PayPal, or even the IRS asking for personal information could be a fake. Scammers pose as everything from government regulators to retailers.

That's why you should never give out your user name and password for anything. If someone claiming to be from your bank, credit card company, or Internet provider asks for it, you're being scammed. In fact, some scammers are very good at creating e-mails that look like they came from organizations like these. These e-mails may even include the institution logo and graphics. The e-mail will say there's a problem and offer a link where you can enter information to fix the problem so your account won't be closed. You might be asked to visit the site and enter your user name, password, and bank account number, supposedly for verification.

The site will look genuine, but it will actually be a scammer site for collecting personal information for identity theft. This scam is called phishing.

As people wise up to phishing, scammers try new ways to trick you. For example, the e-mail may:

◆ appear to come from your favorite airline, your employer, or even a friend.

◆ take you to the real Web site and then a pop-up window from the scammer site appears asking for personal information.

◆ contain personal information about you taken from a social networking site.

◆ ask you to provide information so you can get a tax refund or claim sweepstakes winnings.

◆ ask you to call a phone number rather than visit a Web site.

Outwit scammers with these great tips:

◆ Don't click on an e-mail link that asks for personal information. Clicking on the link may take you to a fake site or invisibly download software that records your keystrokes and sends them to a scammer. Instead, find it in your bookmarks or look up the site on your own and manually type in the address. Whenever you type an address, double-check to make sure you typed it correctly so you aren't directed to a look-alike site.

◆ Call the organization and verify that they really need this information. Don't use the number from the e-mail or any Web site it sends you to. Find the number in the phone book or on account statements you've received.

◆ Use a browser that will block phishing sites or warn you about them.

◆ Use anti-virus software and a spyware blocker.

For more information on Internet banking and phishing, see page 288 in the *High-tech banking* chapter.

Stay safe against new 'vishing' swindle

An urgent e-mail from your bank suggests calling a local number instead of visiting a Web site, but that doesn't mean it isn't a scam. Internet scammers can fake call-in numbers. The good news is you don't have to be a victim.

Once upon a time, scammers only used official-looking e-mails from your "bank" to trick you into giving out account numbers and other personal information on the Web. But now they've found a way to use phones, too. Here's how it works.

You get an e-mail claiming to be from your bank, credit card company, someone you do business with, or even a company you've never heard of. Just as with phishing, the e-mail looks very official, and you're told there's an urgent problem or threat you must resolve — or a reward if you act right away.

You're given a number to call. Before the problem can be resolved, you must say or key in information first, such as your account number or password, just what the scammer needs for identity theft.

This is called vishing because Voice Over Internet Protocol, or making phone calls over the Internet, makes this scam possible. As if that's not bad enough, scammers also try these ingenious ways to fool you.

◆ The phone number in the e-mail shows your area code. Internet callers can choose any area code no matter where in the world they're located, which makes it difficult to track them down.

◆ A prerecorded message may ask for your information, tell you to call a different number, or send you to a fake Web site.

306

◆ A real person may ask for your personal information. The scammer may have some of your personal information already in order to appear legitimate.

◆ You may be invited to join a research project by putting special software on your computer. The software is spyware.

Beware any phone call or e-mail that asks for your personal information. Instead of supplying the information, look up the company's contact number in your account paperwork and call to ask if the request is legitimate. If you discover the call was not legitimate, file a complaint with the Internet Crime Complaint Center at **www.ic3.gov.**

What you must do when forwarding messages

Forward an e-mail to a group and everyone in the group can see the e-mail address of every other person in the group. Some people find this very disturbing, so be mindful of protecting other's e-mail addresses. Fortunately, Outlook Express makes this surprisingly easy to do.

Most e-mail programs feature a header called Bcc (blind carbon copy). Type the e-mail addresses of your recipients here, and everyone will get the e-mail, but none of their addresses will appear at the top of the e-mail. Now you're protecting the privacy of friends in group e-mails. That's friendly forwarding.

The Bcc feature is hidden in Outlook Express so after you click on FORWARD, do this.

1. At the top of the e-mail window, click on VIEW, then ALL HEADERS.

2. A slot labeled BCC will appear.

3. Add your e-mail addresses here.

Rescue your computer from hackers

You've started getting e-mails accusing you of sending spam, and your computer is running very slowly. You've even found messages in your Outbox or Sent Items folder you know you never sent. Your computer might be part of a botnet.

A botnet is a network of computers created by a hacker or spammer. The botnet master creates this network by infecting computers with robot software. The robot software is usually hidden in an e-mail attachment or planted on malicious Web sites.

Once the software gets on a PC, it turns the computer into a "zombie" — a computer that takes orders from the botnet master. But the owners of zombie computers may have no idea their computers have become zombies.

Meanwhile, the botnet master can use these zombies to send spam, commit identity theft, steal your personal information, and spread spyware. If your computer has shown signs of being a "zombie," take these steps.

◆ Report the problem to your ISP and ask if they have any advice on removing the botnet software.

◆ Report the problem to the FBI at **www.ic3.gov.**

◆ Update your anti-virus and anti-spyware software. Disconnect from the Internet and scan for viruses and spyware.

You can protect your computer from becoming a zombie with these tips.

◆ Use anti-virus and anti-spyware software and keep it up to date.

◆ Make sure Windows is set up to automatically download security patches as soon as they become available.

◆ Never open an e-mail attachment — even from friends, family, and co-workers — unless you're expecting it and know what it contains.

◆ Use firewall software and make sure it is turned on.

◆ Disconnect from the Internet when you're away from your computer.

◆ Only download free software from reputable sites you know and trust.

◆ Check your e-mail Outbox or Sent Items folder for messages you did not send.

Deliver your e-mails from future doom

To keep Outlook Express from getting top-heavy and sluggish, clean out your e-mails regularly. Otherwise, your e-mails can eventually get corrupted, and you could lose them all.

Visit each of your folders, including the Sent Items folder, and clean out e-mails you no longer need. To do this, simply go to your list of messages, right-click on the e-mail, and click on DELETE. But don't stop there.

E-mails deleted from other folders go to the Deleted Items folder. To permanently get rid of these e-mails, move your mouse to the Outlook Express menu bar and click on EDIT, then EMPTY 'DELETED ITEMS' FOLDER. A dialog box will ask ARE YOU SURE YOU WANT TO PERMANENTLY DELETE THE CONTENTS OF THE 'DELETED ITEMS' FOLDER. Be aware that you can't look at these e-mails again once you click on YES.

Attach a Web page to your e-mail

Why send the URL of a Web page in an e-mail when you can send the page as an e-mail attachment? Here's how to do this in Outlook Express. First, turn on the Outlook Express setting that allows you to send Web pages.

1. In the menu, click on TOOLS, then OPTIONS.

2. Click on the SEND tab.

3. In the section labeled MAIL SENDING FORMAT, click on the HTML radio button.

4. Click on OK.

Now you're ready to send your Web page. Before you begin, make sure you have the URL of the page. Your best bet is to visit the page, click in the URL box in your browser, double-click to select the URL, and press the CONTROL and C keys at the same time. This copies the URL so you won't have to type it. Return to Outlook Express so you can send the page.

1. Find the menu above the buttons and click on MESSAGE, then NEW MESSAGE USING, and WEB PAGE.

2. Click your cursor in the box under ENTER THE URL OF THE WEB PAGE YOU WANT TO SEND.

3. If you copied the URL from your browser, paste in the URL by pressing the CONTROL and V keys at the same time. Otherwise type in the URL.

4. Click on OK.

5. When the e-mail appears, type your recipient's e-mail address in the TO box.

6. Click in the SUBJECT box and type a subject line.

7. Click on SEND.

Personalize your mail with a 'signature'

The e-mail signature is text that can be automatically added at the end of any e-mail. Unlike a handwritten one, this signature is printed lines of text, but it tells your recipient who you are.

To add your signature in Outlook Express, from the menu, click on TOOLS, OPTIONS, SIGNATURES tab, and then NEW button.

Type in your signature. For example, you might type your name on one line and your address on the following lines. Click on OK to save the signature for future e-mails. To add it to a finished e-mail, click on INSERT and then SIGNATURE.

Dazzle them with e-mail stationery

Whether you want to dress up your e-mail for a special occasion or express your personal style every day, e-mail stationery can help.

Outlook Express comes with several standard stationery options. These include attractive backgrounds, picture letterheads or borders, and fun fonts and font colors. Here's how to add one to your next e-mail.

1. Find the Outlook Express menu above the row of buttons. Click on MESSAGE and then NEW MESSAGE USING.

2. Click on one of the first seven options in the list.

3. Your new e-mail appears with the stationery showing in the section where you'll compose your message.

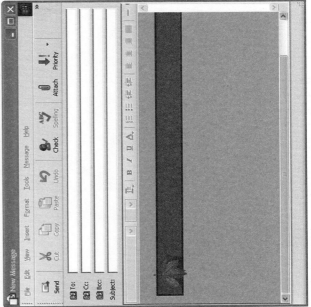

Example of Outlook Express stationery

4. Address and compose the e-mail as you normally would.

If none of the standard stationery choices suit your needs, try this.

1. In the Outlook Express menu, click on MESSAGE → NEW MESSAGE USING → SELECT STATIONERY.

2. A list of stationery files appears. Click on a choice. If the SHOW PREVIEW box is checked, you'll see a preview picture in the PREVIEW box.

3. When you find one you like, click on it and click on OK.

4. As before, your new e-mail appears with the stationery showing in the section where you'll write your message.

Some people like stationery, while others don't. In fact, one expert recommends against using it for business correspondence. To remove stationery from an e-mail, find FORMAT in the menu at the top of your e-mail. Click on APPLY STATIONERY, then NO STATIONERY.

Tame inbox overload

Your Inbox is so full of new e-mails every day you're beginning to miss out on the ones you really need to read. No problem. Just instruct your e-mail program to look through your e-mails and set aside the important ones where you'll be sure to find them.

Perhaps you'd like to make sure you read all e-mails from your family or a particular daily newsletter. Just make a new folder for each e-mail category you want to read and create a rule that sends the correct e-mails to their new home.

Here's how you could use Outlook Express to funnel e-mails from your family into a particular e-mail folder. First, create a new folder.

1. In the FOLDERS pane, click on LOCAL FOLDERS.

2. In the menu, click on FILE → NEW → FOLDER.

3. In the CREATE FOLDER box, type the name of the new folder you'd like to create.

4. Click on OK. The new folder will appear in the FOLDERS pane.

Now create the rule.

1. Find an e-mail message from one of your family members.

2. In the menu, click on MESSAGE then CREATE RULE FROM MESSAGE.

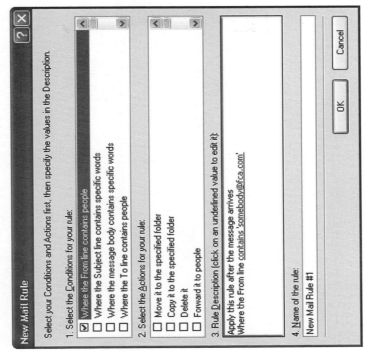

New Mail Rule dialog box

3. Under SELECT THE CONDITIONS FOR YOUR RULE, notice what has been selected with a check mark. Scroll down to make sure you see them all.

4. Make sure the choice or choices selected are the ones you want. Make changes, if needed.

5. Under SELECT THE ACTIONS FOR YOUR RULE, click the check box for MOVE IT TO THE SPECIFIED FOLDER to fill the check box.

6. Under RULE DESCRIPTION, read the underlined sections.

7. One line should say WHERE THE FROM LINE CONTAINS followed by an e-mail address. Click on CONTAINS to add the rest of your family's e-mail addresses.

8. Type in each address and click on ADD to add it to the list.

9. When you have added all the addresses, click on OK.

10. Return to the remaining underlined sections in RULE DESCRIPTION.

11. Find MOVE IT TO THE SPECIFIED FOLDER. Click on SPECIFIED to indicate which folder the rule should use.

12. When the MOVE box appears, click on the folder name and click on OK.

13. Click on OK in the NEW MAIL RULE dialog box.

14. A message appears saying THE RULE WAS SUCCESSFULLY ADDED.

Now the e-mails from your family members will go to their own mailbox every day.

Stop e-mail notification sounds

You don't have to listen to annoying sound effects every time an e-mail arrives. It's easy to stop the noise.

1. In the menu, click on TOOLS, then OPTIONS.

2. Click on the check mark in the PLAY SOUND WHEN NEW MESSAGES ARRIVE check box until it disappears.

3. Click on OK.

Instant messaging: when e-mail's too slow

❝ I think, therefore IM. **❞**

New York Times 2003 article

Boot up without starting Windows Messenger

Every time you log into *Windows*, *Windows* Messenger starts up, and people start bombarding you with instant messages before you can get anything done. You're caught between a rock and a hard place. You don't want to ignore your friends, but you need time to do other work on your computer first.

Windows Messenger wasn't meant to become the bane of your existence. Instead, it's meant as a convenience — an instant messaging program to exchange online messages with others in the blink of an eye. To keep it convenient, the program's makers included a setting to stop Windows Messenger from starting up each time Windows starts. This means people won't automatically know when you're online, and you won't get buried in instant messages the minute you boot up. It's easy to put this setting to work.

*Windows
Messenger icon*

◆ Click on START → ALL PROGRAMS → WINDOWS MESSENGER if Windows Messenger isn't already open.

◆ Click on TOOLS → OPTIONS → PREFERENCES tab.

◆ Find RUN WINDOWS MESSENGER WHEN WINDOWS STARTS and click in the check box to clear it.

You'll know it works the next time you boot up because the Windows Messenger icon will no longer appear in your Taskbar.

When you get ready to use Windows Messenger again, just click on START → ALL PROGRAMS → WINDOWS MESSENGER.

Be invisible online

You can still make yourself invisible to chatterboxes with time on their hands — even if you're signed into Windows Messenger. Just ask yourself how you prefer to disappear and how long you want your "invisibility" to last. If you need to be invisible to everyone, change your status to APPEAR OFFLINE.

1. Click on your name in the WINDOWS MESSENGER window.

2. Select APPEAR OFFLINE from the menu that appears.

Your status will change to Not Online, and you're the only one who will know you're still logged on. But what if you only need to be invisible to a particular person? To block someone in your sender list, right-click on the name and click on BLOCK.

From now on, you will always appear offline to that person. If you later decide to unblock the person, right-click on the name again and click on UNBLOCK.

If you begin receiving unsolicited advertisements from a stranger, you can block that person, too.

1. Click on the BLOCK button in the box where the message appears.

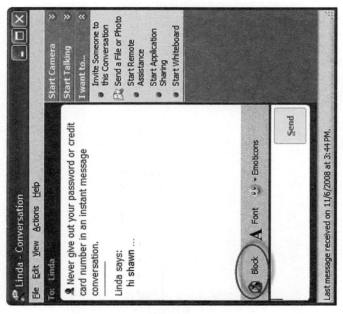

Block an individual with the Block button

2. You may see a dialog box saying IF YOU BLOCK THIS PERSON, HE OR SHE WILL NOT BE ABLE TO HAVE ONLINE CONVERSA-TIONS WITH YOU, SEE YOUR PHONE NUMBERS, OR SEE YOUR ONLINE STATUS.

3. To block the person, click on OK.

4. Click on the Close button to close the conversation window. From now on, that person will always see your status as Not Online.

Never put any information in an instant message that could be used for identity theft. And don't share any information you'd like to keep secret. Reports suggest hackers may be able to capture logs of instant message conversations. Also, be as cautious with files received from instant messaging as you would with e-mail attachments. Viruses can hide in any file. Scan your newly arrived file with your anti-virus program before you open it.

Get the message with other IM programs

You've just found out that none of your friends or family uses Windows Messenger — which means your instant messaging (IM) program won't talk to theirs. Switching to a new program probably won't cost you a penny, and some new programs offer more exciting bells and whistles than Windows Messenger.

The most important feature in any instant messaging program is this — the person you want to message with already uses it. But IM programs can be loaded with all sorts of interesting features that may also affect your choice.

You may find options for video or audio chat, IM and file sharing from both your computer and cell phone, "emoticon" pictures to show when you're smiling or frowning, and all sorts of ways to personalize your instant messaging experience.

To learn more about what features each program offers, read reviews from reliable sources, such as computer magazines or **www.cnet.com**. Meanwhile, here's a quick primer to help you discover some of the most popular and promising programs.

AOL Instant Messenger (AIM). You don't have to be an AOL subscriber to use this free, popular IM program. Not only will it talk to other AIM users but to people using Macintosh iChat, as well. Download this for free from **www.aim.com**.

Google Talk. You must get a free Gmail address from Google before you can use this instant messenger — and the program will only communicate with other people who also have Google Talk. Visit **www.google.com** to get your Gmail address and download the free IM software.

Yahoo! Messenger. Download this free instant messenger from **messenger.yahoo.com**. When installing this software, be sure to look for opportunities to opt out of changes to your browser home page and other settings.

Trillian. Imagine instant messaging people on Google Talk, Windows Messenger, Yahoo! Messenger, AIM, and others all from the same program. That's what Trillian can do — and you can keep all your IM buddies in the same window. You can even keep logs of your conversations. Download a free or for-pay version from **www.ceruleanstudios.com**.

Meebo.com. IM anyone without downloading any software. Meebo is a Web site where you can do all your instant messaging. IM friends on AIM, Yahoo! Messenger, Google Talk, and several other message services.

Social networks enrich your life

❝MySpace reports over 110 million registered users. Were it a country, it would be the tenth largest, just behind Mexico. ❞

PC.com

Play it safe on Facebook

Your grandson wants you to look at his "Facebook page," but you've heard social networking sites, like Facebook, are dangerous. The truth is — social networking sites may enrich your life in ways you never imagined, if you learn to protect yourself.

Get to know social networks. Social networking sites can help you connect with friends, family, coworkers, or even strangers who share common interests with you. Usually, you must register with the site to use it, but registration grants you a sort of Web page or profile page. Profile pages often include your picture and personal information, such as your age and location. You can also add other information including photos, videos, and personal commentary or descriptions related to your interests.

But the sites also help you find and make friends with other site members. This may include posting their profile site links on your page, chatting with them, interacting on forums, and more.

When it can be dangerous. Scammers can harvest information from your profile page to make themselves sound like friends, bank workers, and others you might trust. They may use this information to trick you and steal your identity offline. What's more, some "new friends" you meet on a social networking site may be scammers looking for a victim. And, of course, spammers also try to harvest e-mail addresses from social networking sites.

Precautions to take. Before you try social networking, read up on ways to protect yourself. You can start with these tips.

◆ Join as a guest or only fill out the information that is absolutely required to register.

◆ Before signing up with a social networking site, get a free e-mail address from Google, Windows Live Mail, or Yahoo! Use that address exclusively for social networking.

◆ When you register, use a password you never use for anything else.

◆ Don't provide any information you're not comfortable sharing when registering and creating your profile. And don't fill in any field or add any information that isn't required.

◆ The moment you register, find out about your privacy options and settings. Set up your account to be as private as possible.

◆ Never display your full name in online profiles. Use a nickname instead.

◆ Never reveal your phone number, Social Security number, address, or financial institutions you use on social networking sites and keep your e-mail address secret.

◆ Avoid posting any information on your profile that you wouldn't want broadcasted worldwide or in your local newspaper.

◆ Never give out your birthday, birthplace, mother's maiden name, or any other information financial institutions use to verify your identity.

Super social sites for seniors

Facebook, MySpace, and LinkedIn may be the most famous social networking sites, but other sites may be more interesting, more beneficial, and good for your health.

Chat with health professionals. A recent study found that 74 percent of those participating in an online diabetes discussion group felt better able to cope with their disease. If you'd like to try something similar, look for discussion groups moderated by a health professional. When you find one, don't use it as a substitute for medical care. Instead, get your doctor's approval before trying any new ideas you find there. Visit **www.webmd.com** to see examples of moderated forums.

Share your wisdom. Become an advisor at **www.elderwisdomcircle.org.** You'll join a group of 600 "advisors" over age 60 who offer answers to questions about everything from sex to family life to careers.

Try AARP message boards. To talk about health or hobbies with people close to your age, visit the message boards at **www.aarp.org.** You can sign up as a guest or fill out your profile and post a picture.

Help for caregivers. Visit the Alzheimer's caregivers support group at **www.webmd.com.** Or visit **thePatientPartnerProject.org** or **carepages.com** to make a Web page where family members can get updates about the person you're caring for.

Discover the blogs you've been missing

Al regularly posts pictures and stories from his scenic hikes in the mountains. Millie tells entertaining tales about life after 80. Some people write about diabetes, gardening, current events, and many other fascinating topics. They're the bloggers, and you're going to love what they have to offer.

Express your thoughts. Once upon a time, you had to be a reporter or professional writer to publish your opinions, commentaries, or stories. Blogs allow anyone to publish on the Internet, and they're less complicated than a Web site. In fact, "blog" is short for Web log — a Web page where the writer or blogger can publish text, pictures, and even video about any topic she wants to write about.

Some bloggers use blogs as an online diary or scrapbook. Others write about current events or politics. Many use blogs as a place to post information about a particular subject, such as saving money, weight loss, or scrapbooking. And some blogs cover all of the above. Blogs often feature links to other blogs on similar or related topics. That's why finding one good blog may lead you to many others. You may even find blogs by celebrities or experts.

Good blogs are updated regularly with the newest entry, called a post, appearing at the top. The posts get older as you read down the page. The best part about blogs is that you choose your level of participation. You may read blogs and do nothing more, read a blog and post your comments, or take up writing blogs yourself.

Find great blogs. Finding blogs is almost as easy as doing a regular Google search. Just visit Google's blog search at **blogsearch.google.com** and search by typing in words or phrases as you normally would.

Become a blogger. You can sign up for your own free blog at **www.blogger.com**. Just remember to protect your privacy, write responsibly, and don't write anything that could come back to haunt you.

Create your own Web page

It's easier than you think to create your own Web page — and it's free. You'll need these four things.

◆ Content. Decide what you'd like to write on your Web site and what to include, like pictures or links to other pages.

◆ A way to create and lay out your pages. This can be software or a tool provided online.

◆ Web space. Even if you create your site on your PC, you must send it to a computer called a Web server for others to see it.

◆ A way to get Web pages to your Web server.

Some sites offer free space on their server for your Web page but may or may not offer tools or templates to help create the page. This may mean you need to buy software to help create the page and then choose a place to host the site. If you pick this option, visit your local bookstore or **www.amazon.com** to find books about creating Web pages. Read software reviews in computer magazines or at sites like **www.cnet.com** to learn which Web editor may suit you best. The web hosting service Angelfire also recommends **www.lissaexplains.com** as a good place to learn about HTML, the language of Web pages.

Free, all-in-one sites may be the simplest way to create a Web page. These sites not only give you Web space, they may also supply tools to help you create and lay out the page. The best sites may offer tutorials, Web page templates, and Web page editors to help create your site. For example, SynthaSite says you need no technical knowledge to use their tutorials and Web page editor to create a Web page. Creating a Web page may be more like using a word processor than you expected. Sites that can help you build a Web site for free include:

SynthaSite	*www.synthasite.com*
Angelfire	*www.angelfire.com*
Yahoo! GeoCities	*geocities.yahoo.com*

Options vary by site but you may find free images or the ability to simply drag and drop images into the page. You may also have ways to add videos, maps, and other multimedia content. What's more, these sites may solve the problem of getting content from your computer to the Web server.

Before you choose a site, check what they offer. At the very least, find out the answers to these questions.

◆ Do they supply space on their server for your site?

◆ How much space do they offer in megabytes or gigabytes? This can range from 15 megabytes to 999 megabytes.

◆ Will they put ads on your page?

◆ Is there help to create your page, like tools and tutorials?

◆ How much technical knowledge must you have to create a page?

◆ Are there templates for Web pages?

◆ How big a file can you transfer to the site?

Get free product reviews before you buy

Online reviews by people like you could help you make smarter decisions about everything from choosing a doctor to picking a washing machine. Be aware that some reviews may be written by the businesses or people being reviewed, while others may be penned by people with their own agendas. But if a product has more than 100 reviews, biased reviews are less likely to be a problem.

Explore sites, like **www.yelp.com**, that provide reviews of local retailers and services, as well as sites like **www.epinions.com** and **www.amazon.com** that offer product and service reviews.

chapter 31

Chat for less — use the Net

❝ Approximately 365 million people in the world have computers while half of the world's 6.5 billion population has never seen or used a telephone. ❞

PC.com

Make talk cheap with free Internet calling

Don't pay another cent for phone service when you can get it for free. What makes this possible is VoIP or Voice over Internet Protocol. This allows you to make calls over an Internet connection instead of a phone line.

One way to do this is to download the free Skype software from **www.skype.com.** If you already have a high-speed — not dial-up — Internet connection, a microphone, and a headset or speakers, calling is free.

Just download and install the software, open a free Skype account, and get your friends and family to do the same. Then use the Skype software to call someone with Skype for free. It's like free phone calls with the click of a button.

But even if all your friends aren't Skype users, you can still get discounts. Skype lets you call people with regular phones for just a few cents per minute. People can also call your Skype number if you pay a small monthly fee. But Skype isn't your only discount option.

You can also get discounts with services like Vonage and Magicjack. With these services, you connect a special hardware adapter to your computer and plug your phone into the adapter. The adapter converts your phone signal so it can pass through the Internet instead of regular phone lines.

Regardless of whether you use Skype, Vonage, or another service, ask these questions before you try them.

◆ Can you use your current phone number with VoIP service? How many weeks will it take that number to be transferred?

◆ What happens to phone service during a power outage or when a high-speed Internet connection goes down? A power outage may take down your phone service unless your VoIP provider offers call forwarding to a working phone during outages. A few cable VoIP providers now include batteries in their modems so your phone service won't go out during a power outage.

◆ Can you call 911 with this service? Will the 911 operator be able to pinpoint your location if you can't provide it?

◆ Does your computer have to be on for you to make and receive calls?

◆ How much technical knowledge will you need to install, maintain, and troubleshoot your phone connection?

◆ Are call forwarding, voicemail, call waiting, and caller ID free?

◆ Do you have to buy software, hardware, or other supplies? Are there extra charges for shipping or setup?

◆ What is the cancellation policy? What will you be charged if you cancel?

Be aware that *Consumer Reports* recommends against using VoIP to completely replace your regular land line phone because you may need it for emergencies. However, VoIP may still help reduce or eliminate charges in land line local and long-distance bills.

Make video phone calls from your computer

It's not science fiction anymore. You'll be able to hear and see the person on the other end when you make video phone calls. You'll need both hardware and software to video chat. Best of all, many computers come equipped with everything you need. Check for these items.

◆ a Web cam — a digital camera connected to your computer that can send digital pictures or movies over the Internet

◆ a sound card

◆ either a microphone and speakers or a headset including headphones and microphone for both you and the person you want to video chat with

Windows Messenger comes with *Windows XP* and is equipped to allow video chat on a dial-up connection. Make sure the person you want to chat with also has Windows Messenger. Before using video chat, click on TOOLS, then AUDIO TUNING WIZARD in Windows Messenger. To learn how to video chat with Instant Messenger, visit its online help.

If you aren't satisfied with the quality of *Windows Messenger's* video chat, consider a free alternative, like SightSpeed. You must have a high-speed or broadband Internet connection to use SightSpeed and other Windows Messenger alternatives.

But an expert reviewer says getting started with SightSpeed is easy. Visit **www.sightspeed.com** and be sure to pick the free version of the software to download. When you install the software, it helps you adjust your audio and video settings to get a better video chat experience. To learn how to install and use the software, visit **www.sightspeed.com**, click on SUPPORT and then USING SIGHTSPEED PERSONAL.

Other good — and free — choices for video chat include Windows Live Messenger (**messenger.live.com**) and Yahoo! Messenger with Voice (**messenger.yahoo.com**). Video chats may only be free if you call computer to computer. Avoid calling anyone's phone number or you may be charged.

> If you can't find the Fax Console as described in step 1, here's how to install the Fax Services yourself. Click on START → CONTROL PANEL → ADD OR REMOVE PROGRAMS → ADD/REMOVE WINDOWS COMPONENTS. Insert your Windows XP CD and click on the check box for FAX SERVICES. When you're done, go to START → ALL PROGRAMS → ACCESSORIES → COMMUNICATIONS again. FAX CONSOLE should now appear in the menu.

Set up Windows XP to fax documents

You don't need to buy a fax machine. You can fax documents to and from your computer if you have a fax-capable modem. You just need to type in a little information first.

1. Click on START → ALL PROGRAMS → ACCESSORIES → COMMUNICATIONS → FAX → FAX CONSOLE. If you don't see the Fax Console, install Fax Services from your Windows CD.

2. In the FAX CONSOLE menu bar, click on TOOLS → CONFIGURE FAX.

3. When you see the WELCOME TO THE FAX CONFIGURATION WIZARD screen, click on NEXT.

4. Type in your name and fax number when the SENDER INFORMATION dialog box appears. Additional information —

such as your voice phone number, e-mail address, and company — is optional, but be aware any information you type in will appear on every fax cover letter you send. Click on NEXT.

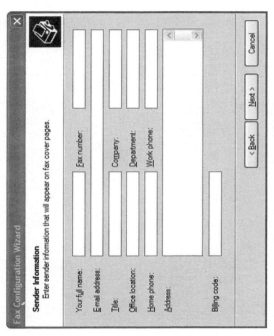

Sender Information in the Fax Configuartion Wizard dialog box

5. Click on the drop-down arrow under PLEASE SELECT THE FAX DEVICE and choose your modem.

6. To send faxes from your computer, click on the ENABLE SEND check box.

7. To receive faxes on your computer, click on the ENABLE RECEIVE check box. New options appear. If you click on the radio button for AUTOMATICALLY ANSWER AFTER and then click on the drop-down box for number of rings, the fax automatically picks up after the phone rings that number of times. If you click on the radio button for MANUAL ANSWER, your computer notifies you when the phone line rings, and you can pick up the phone and click an option to tell the computer to accept a fax.

8. Click on NEXT.

9. Click in the TSID (Transmitting Subscriber Identification) box. What you type here appears at the top of any page you fax to others. Type in your fax number and click on NEXT.

10. If you chose to ENABLE RECEIVE, you'll see the CSID (Called Subscriber Identification) box. Otherwise, skip to the last step. The text you type in the CSID box can help people sending faxes to you know whether they've reached the correct number. Type in your fax number and click on NEXT.

11. If you chose to ENABLE RECEIVE and you'd like to print all incoming faxes, click on the PRINT IT ON check box and select a printer from the drop-down list. If you'd like to store copies of your faxes on your computer, click on the STORE A COPY IN A FOLDER check box, click on BROWSE to select the folder, and click on OK when you're done. Click on NEXT.

12. Click on FINISH.

In the FAX CONSOLE menu, click on HELP and HELP TOPICS to learn how to send and receive faxes.

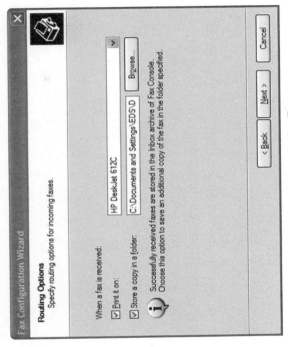

Routing Options in the Fax
Configuration Wizard dialog box

chapter 32

Audio magic

" The iPod remains the top MP3 player, with more than 70% of the market, and Apple is now the top retailer of music in the nation, ahead of Wal-Mart stores. **"**

Nick Wingfield, The Wall Street Journal, 2008

Play music your way with Media Player

Your computer does more than just work. It's also for fun, like listening to music and watching videos. Customize your music-playing software, Windows Media Player, so it's easy to use.

You have the program if your computer's operating system is Windows XP or Windows Vista. The Media Player is a program that lets you play music CDs, download songs from the Internet, and put music onto a CD.

Before you start using Windows Media Player, be sure you have the latest version. You can download it free at **www.microsoft.com**.

Under the list of POPULAR DOWNLOADS, click on WINDOWS MEDIA PLAYER 11 or a more recent version, then follow instructions for downloading. When it's done, you can open it by clicking on START → ALL PROGRAMS → WINDOWS MEDIA PLAYER.

You don't have to use the player as it comes. You can customize it to fit your needs and your mood. One great option is changing from the full-screen mode to something called "skins mode."

This turns the player into a tiny graphic controller, which you can drag around your screen or hide behind another open window. Like a snake shedding its skin to reveal something new and fresh underneath, a different skin makes the player look different, but it still behaves the same way. You'll still be able to start or stop a song or change the volume.

To switch to skin mode, click on the menu option VIEW at the top of the page, then click on SKIN MODE. You can change to a different skin from the same menu by selecting SKIN CHOOSER. Preview the available skins, then click on APPLY SKIN.

When you're tired of the standard skins, just download a new one from the Internet. You can choose a rubber ducky skin for when your grandkids come to visit, switch into a holiday mood with a gingerbread man skin, or add a tough Batman skin if you're a superhero fan. Check out the free options at **www.wmplugins.com**.

Label your tunes for an easy-access library

You could put a music CD in your computer's CD drive and listen to the songs, then remove it when it's done and find another. But that's tedious. An easier way to listen to music on your computer is by copying, or ripping, songs from your entire CD collection onto the PC, then organizing them into a music library. You can listen to your favorite songs any time.

Even better, Windows Media Player can keep track of your songs by title, album, artist, and genre — if you do one little thing. Be sure your computer is connected to the Internet before you start the ripping process. That way, *Windows Media Player* will be able to retrieve information about the song titles, album titles, and artist names. The player gets these details from a database maintained by Microsoft. Why is this information so important?

◆ Song title. Without the names of each song and album, Windows Media Player will assign a generic name, like Unknown Artist and Track 1. That's not too helpful if you're trying to find a certain song.

◆ Album art. This is what the cover of the CD looks like. It will appear on your screen so you can easily find your favorites at a glance.

◆ Genre. If you later decide to move music onto an MP3 player, you'll be able to play all your songs in the folk music genre, or all the songs by The Beatles.

If you can't access the Internet before you rip a CD, go ahead and do the copying. Next time you connect to the Internet, the Windows Media Player will automatically check the database to update missing information.

Check this setting so your computer will automatically start copying songs into Windows Media Player when you insert a music CD. Under the TOOLS menu, select OPTIONS. Click on the RIP MUSIC tab, and be sure there's a check mark in the box next to RIP CD WHEN INSERTED. Also, be sure ALWAYS is marked.

Pick a file format to fit your player

MP3, WAV, AAC — digital music files come in numerous formats. How do you know which one works with your computer or music player?

When you put a music CD in your computer to copy the songs into Windows Media Player, the default setting copies them in Windows Media Audio (WMA) format. That'll play just fine in your computer. But you could copy the songs you download in MP3 format instead — if you make the change before you copy the songs. That way, you'll be able to play them on both your computer and your MP3 player, which may not play WMA files.

Here's how to set up Windows Media Player (version 10 or higher) to rip songs as MP3 files. It's a simple matter of changing a couple of settings. First, change the format the files will be copied in. Click on TOOLS, and then OPTIONS. Select the RIP MUSIC tab. In the FORMAT drop-down menu, select MP3. Then click on OK.

Change the bit rate, or the speed at which the songs are copied. Under the RIP tab at the top of the screen, pull down to BIT RATE. There's probably a check mark next to the slowest speed, 128 KBPS (kilobits per second), if you haven't changed it yet. Place a check mark next to 192 KBPS or higher instead. Now you're ready to rip.

So why are those other file formats out there? Uncompressed formats, like WAV, are huge files that contain all the digital details of a song. These files are useful to people who want the highest-quality music and music professionals who do audio editing.

Compressed formats, like MP3 and AAC (Advanced Audio Coding), are smaller and quicker to copy, but they've lost some of the digital details. You probably won't notice any difference when you listen to your favorite tunes.

Burn a music CD

It sounds dangerous, but it's not. "Burning" is what they call it when you copy files to a blank CD, including music files. You can pick all your favorite songs from your Windows Media Player library and load them onto one CD, then take it with you to play in your car.

All you need is a CD burner on your computer and a blank CD. The kind called CD-R is your best bet, since it'll play in a regular music CD player. The basic steps involve creating what's called a burn list in Windows Media Player, then putting all the songs onto the blank CD at once.

Pick your songs carefully, because you won't be able to add more songs to the CD after it's been burned. Here's what you do.

1. Open Windows Media Player and click on the BURN tab at the top of the screen. A BURN LIST pane will open to the right.

2. Insert your blank CD into the computer. The player will recognize it and tell you how many minutes of music you can fit. Check the top of the right-hand pane for minutes remaining.

3. Add songs or entire albums to the burn list by dragging them from your music library, in the left-hand pane, into the BURN LIST pane. As you do this, you'll notice the minutes remaining to fill the CD going down. Keep an eye on this counter so you don't select more songs than will fit on your CD.

4. If you drag more songs than will fit, you'll see a new list titled NEXT DISC at the bottom of the BURN LIST pane. Unless you want to put those songs on a second CD, delete some titles from the list until they fit. Give yourself some leeway here. Even if your songs seem to fit in the minutes available, they may not fit when the burning occurs. That's because Windows Media Player adds two seconds of silence after each track. You can't change that feature.

5. When you're ready, click on START BURN at the bottom of the screen.

Be patient. The process takes several minutes, because Windows Media Player has to first convert files into a new format, then copy them onto the blank CD. Don't work on your computer while this is going on — just let it run.

Label the CDs you burn with a felt-tip pen — not a sticker. You may be surprised to learn you can write on your newly created CDs, but it's true. You can safely write the date and name of the collection you've created in the clear inner ring. But if you use a stick-on label, you risk putting the label on crooked, so the CD is out of balance when it plays. That could damage it. And if it came off in your CD player, it could trash the drive.

Shop online stores to save money on music

A music CD can easily set you back $15 or more, and you may not like all the songs on the album. Instead, buy just the song you like online for less than a dollar. What do you get when you "buy a song"? You won't have a physical record, tape, or CD with your music. Instead, you'll have the digital music file that you can play on your computer, copy to a CD to play in your car's stereo, or move to your MP3 player.

Some online music stores give you the option of buying a subscription, so you can download a certain number of songs every month. The rules about how — and for how long — you can listen to a song vary by store, so read the fine print before you purchase. Shop around and consider these features before you settle on your favorite music store.

✦ prices of individual songs, which are usually around 89 to 99 cents

✦ subscription rules and costs

✦ restrictions on how you use the songs — do you get full ownership or are you allowed to copy the song only a certain number of times?

✦ selection of music at that site — some offer mostly pop music, while others are heavy on jazz or classical

✦ file formats offered — do you want WMA files to play on your computer, or would you prefer MP3 files for your portable player?

✦ ease of navigation and use of the Web site

These popular Web sites offer large lists of songs.

iTunes	www.apple.com/itunes
Napster	www.napster.com
eMusic	www.emusic.com
Rhapsody	www.rhapsody.com
Classical.com	www.classical.com

But if an offer looks too good to be true, it probably is. You may find free music downloads from Web sites you've never heard of, or offers to share music.

Stay away from music-sharing sites, which may be illegal. Numerous court cases have determined it's not legal to share copyrighted music files with others who have not purchased them.

Enjoy musical mobility with an MP3 player

Who says you have to be in the same room with your computer to enjoy the songs in your music library? With an MP3 player, you can carry those songs all over the house — or anywhere you go. Other nifty accessories let you go one step further, turning your player into an entire stereo.

Those little gadgets with headphones that store music and some-times videos aren't just for your grandkids. They're handy — and increasingly affordable. This basic setup will let you take your music anywhere, and you can probably find the whole list for less than $150.

◆ an MP3 player with ear bud headphones

◆ a transmitter so you can play songs from your MP3 player through your car stereo; this lets you avoid wearing headphones while you drive, which can be dangerous and is illegal in many states

◆ a docking station for your kitchen, sewing room, or wherever you'd like to hear your music without wearing headphones; it works like a tiny stereo and recharges your MP3 player while it's docked

You'll find numerous sizes, features, and prices of the many MP3 players on the market. Consider how you'll use it before you buy.

Will you watch videos or just listen to music? If video is important, find a player with a color screen that's at least 2 inches measured diagonally.

How important is size? You can buy an MP3 player that's as small as a matchbook, but you lose some features and capacity to hold songs. Do you really need it small enough to clip on your sleeve while you jog, or is a player the size of a deck of playing cards small enough?

How long will you play music at one time? That'll help you decide what battery capacity you need.

Is brand important? The popular Apple brand of player, iPod, offers benefits like easy compatibility with iTunes software and the iTunes Store and lots of accessories. But other brands of MP3 players may be cheaper, and they have other great features. Some include an FM radio tuner, while many can hold music in a greater variety of file formats, like both MP3 and WMA.

Can you work the darn thing? Stop by an electronics store and test drive some floor models to see if you can easily use the controls and read the screen. And be sure it's compatible with your computer's operating system.

If you decide you don't really want an MP3 player, you can still listen to your songs on some cell phones, personal digital assistants (PDAs), and portable CD players.

Don't put off buying a new computer simply because all your good music is on your old one. You can easily move your music library to another computer. First, copy — or burn — your song files to a blank CD. Don't bother trying to compress these files. MP3 and WMA files are already compressed. Just copy them to as many CDs as it takes to fit them all. Then you can transfer the files to your new computer. Save the CD you used to move the songs as a backup copy.

Get your groove on for free with Internet radio

Free stuff is good, and Internet radio is free. You can listen to Internet radio stations while you're working on your computer. Internet radio may be even better than what you hear over the airwaves.

It works by streaming audio, which means you can start listening to the music before all the data has reached your computer. It's useful for large sound and video files that would otherwise take a long time to download. Listening to radio over the Internet works best if you have a DSL or cable connection. It'll also work if you connect with a dial-up modem, but the sound quality may not be as good.

You may decide Internet radio is better than your local radio stations. That's because you can find a huge selection of music styles on the Internet, with many stations playing only the type of music you really like. Most stations don't interrupt your music with commercials.

Seek out your favorite Internet station at **www.radio-locator.com**. Click on the pull-down menu beneath FIND INTERNET STREAMING RADIO, and select the type of music you like. Then click on GO. Whether it's jazz or classical, news or nostalgia, you'll get a list of stations you can listen to for free.

If you still haven't found the perfect station, you can make your own. Some stations let you design a custom music selection that fits your tastes, offering suggestions based on songs you like. Try one of these on for size.

Pandora	*www.pandora.org*
Slacker	*www.slacker.com*
Yahoo! Music	*new.music.yahoo.com*

Be your own broadcaster with podcasting

What do you get when you cross "iPod" with "broadcast"? A podcast or short bit of audio you can download from the Internet to listen to on your computer or MP3 player. Not surprisingly, today's podcasts aren't just audio. They often contain photographs and videos.

You can easily create your own podcasts. With a podcast, you can share your knowledge about knitting or bass fishing, or express your opinions about local politics or the newest James Bond movie. You can use a podcast to share the details of your last trip to Mexico with family and friends, or send out holiday greetings as an audio file.

You could even start a regular podcast in which you read a bedtime story to your grandchildren. Be aware that once your podcast is postet on the Internet, the whole world can download and listen to it. You don't need much equipment to get into podcasting.

A computer. Even an old one will work, because editing audio doesn't require lots of processor speed.

A microphone connected to your computer. Almost any microphone will work, but if you want really good sound you may want to splurge for a professional-quality model for about $50 to $100.

A program to record and edit audio files. You can find software that's free or for purchase. You'll have to decide if you want it to merely do the audio recording and editing, or post and publish your podcast online, too. Here are some good choices.

Audacity	www.audacity.sourceforge.net
Easy Recorder	www.easyrecorder.com
Record for All	www.recordforall.com
WildVoice	www.wildvoice.com

After you record and edit your podcast, you'll need to post it on a host server on the Internet, then set up something called an RSS feed so your listeners can find it. Some free Web sites, like OurMedia at **www.ourmedia.org**, will help you do these tasks.

For information on finding and listening to podcasts, see page 286 in the *RSS & podcasts: fun & free* chapter.

Steps to end the sound of silence

You set up your Windows Media Player, load up your favorite songs, then sit back to relax and enjoy the music. But no sound comes out. What's up?

Lots of little things could keep you from hearing sounds from your computer. Start by checking the simplest problems first, then move on to the more complicated ones.

Check your wire connections. Unplug and plug in your speakers to both the back of your computer and the electrical outlet, then restart your computer.

Look at your speakers. See if the volume control knob is turned down, muting the sound.

Check the audio and speaker settings. Click on START, open CONTROL PANEL, then click on SOUNDS, SPEECH, AND AUDIO DEVICES. Click on ADJUST THE SYSTEM VOLUME, then be sure the volume is turned up and the MUTE button is not checked.

For information on how to change volume settings in Windows XP, see page 56 in the *Get to know your XP desktop* chapter.

Make sure your computer has a sound card. Click on START
→ CONTROL PANEL → SOUNDS, SPEECH, AND AUDIO DEVICES.

Click on ADJUST THE SYSTEM VOLUME. Open the AUDIO tab and look at the SOUND PLAYBACK pane. Your computer's sound card should be listed here.

Be sure the correct sound card device drivers are installed.
Every piece of hardware needs a little piece of software, called a driver, to make it work right. To check on the sound card's driver, click on START → CONTROL PANEL → SOUNDS, SPEECH, AND AUDIO DEVICES → ADJUST THE SYSTEM VOLUME.

Under the HARDWARE tab, you'll see a list of devices on your computer. Select your sound card from the list and click on PROPERTIES. The DEVICE STATUS window should tell you if it's working correctly. If not, you may need to reinstall the sound card's driver.

For information on updating your device drivers, see page 126 in the *Fast fixes you can do yourself* chapter.

22 chapter

Video tips & tricks

66 Anyone who tries to make a distinction between education and entertainment doesn't know the first thing about either. **99**

Marshall McLuhan, author of *Understanding Media*

Watch your favorite movie any time, anywhere

All you need is your computer, as long as you set it up right. The software you need is probably already on your computer, since you can use Windows Media Player to watch movies — it's for more than just listening to songs. Beyond that, you just need a movie. You can get one in three ways.

Insert a DVD. That's right, most computers can play movies on DVD — just like watching it on your TV.

Buy or rent online. Many locations on the Internet offer full-length movies you can download to your computer to watch. Two popular sites are **www.iTunes.com** and **www.blockbuster.com.** They both offer new and classic movies to rent for about $3 or buy for about $10 to $15. You'll also find recent episodes of your favorite television shows.

Get in the stream. Oodles of free films, both homemade comedies and high-quality documentaries, are available to watch on the Internet as streaming video.

That's a technology that lets you start watching a video clip before the file has downloaded completely. It's useful for large sound and video files that would take a long time to download. Try these popular sites for finding videos.

SnagFilms	*www.snagfilms.com*
YouTube	*www.youtube.com*
Veoh	*www.veoh.com*

Unfortunately, sometimes streaming video looks jerky, or the picture seems to stop and start. This may be due to a slow Internet connection or because there are lots of visitors at the Web site you're using.

Another cause could be incorrect settings in your Windows Media Player. Here's how you can fix the settings.

1. Open Windows Media Player, click on TOOLS, and then OPTIONS.

2. Click on the PERFORMANCE tab.

3. Under CONNECTION SPEED, be sure the DETECT CONNECTION SPEED option is selected.

4. Then, under NETWORK BUFFERING, check that the USE DEFAULT BUFFERING option is selected.

5. Also, be sure the VIDEO ACCELERATION slider is set to FULL.

6. Click on OK.

You're having trouble playing a DVD, and Windows Media Player says there's a decoder problem. A decoder is a piece of software that's needed to play DVDs. Most new computers with a DVD player also have a decoder, although Windows XP doesn't always come with one. If you need a decoder, you may be able to download it from the DVD manufacturer's Web site. See the instructions on your DVD. Otherwise, you can buy a decoder for about $15 to $50. Different decoders offer different features, so read the fine print. Check out **www.cyberlink.com** or **www.intervideo.com**.

Download home movies quickly and easily

Garbage in, garbage out. That's an old saying among computer programmers who knew if they gave a computer the wrong instructions, the machine couldn't get the job done right. Same thing goes when you input home video into your computer for editing. If it comes in at a low quality, the final product will never look good. Use the best connections for high quality from the start.

Before you can edit your home movies, you have to get the video off your camcorder and into your computer. There are several ways to do that, but the choice depends on what kind of cables your camcorder has and what ports your computer has.

Triple cable. You can use RCA cables — the familiar cable with three plugs in red, white, and yellow. But your computer needs to have a compatible video card on the back, with the RCA input ports, or an adapter box for the RCA connection. This will work, but the quality of the video may suffer because it's moving through an analog — not digital — feed.

Digital. Newer digital camcorders should let you connect with either USB or FireWire cables. These are better choices than RCA since the feed is digital, and you won't lose quality in the process of moving your data.

Memory card. If you have a new digital video camera with a memory card, you're in luck. The quickest method of moving video is getting it straight from the memory card to the computer.

◆ You'll need a memory card reader that attaches to your computer. You can buy one to connect to your computer's USB port for as little as $15.

◆ Take the memory card out of your camera. It looks like a small, square, flat piece of plastic.

◆ Insert the card in the reader, and Windows XP will recognize the new piece of hardware. You can then copy each video clip onto your computer's hard drive so you can work with it in the Windows Movie Maker program.

Have fun with home movies

Windows Movie Maker is a great video editing program, and it comes bundled with Windows XP.

There are other video editing programs, like CyberLink Power Director, Corel Video Studio, and Pinnacle Studio, but they're not free. The most popular programs cost around $60 to $100. See how far you can get with Movie Maker before you spend money.

Some experts say the newer version of Movie Maker, called Movie Maker 2, is head and shoulders above the original version, and it may do everything you need. Be sure your computer has this newest version. If not, you can download it easily online at **www.microsoft.com.**

With Movie Maker 2, putting together a nice home video about a recent trip, your grandchildren's roller-skating abilities, or your recent golf tournament is easy. Here are the basic steps in the process.

◆ Capture video from your camcorder.

◆ Gather video, still photos, sounds effects, and songs into a COLLECTION folder within the Movie Maker program.

347

◆ Drag video clips, photos, and sounds from the COLLECTION pane at the top of the screen into the TIMELINE bar at the bottom of the screen. Then you can arrange, trim, and edit the images.

Make your movies even more fun and professional by livening them up with music. You can use songs you downloaded into your computer using Windows Media Player.

1. Go to ACCESSORIES and click on WINDOWS MOVIE MAKER.

2. In the MOVIE TASKS pane on the left, click on IMPORT AUDIO OR MUSIC.

3. Navigate to find the song you want. If you downloaded it into Windows Media Player, it's probably in your MY MUSIC folder.

4. Once you find the song, highlight its name, then click on the IMPORT button. The song is then added to a COLLECTION at the top of the screen in Movie Maker. If you've already put video or photos into the project, they're also in that collection.

5. Notice the TIMELINE bar at the bottom of the screen has several layers. Drag the music clip you want to add from the COLLECTION pane at the top of the screen to the AUDIO/MUSIC layer of the TIMELINE bar. Place it wherever you want it to play — start the music at the beginning of the video, or halfway through so it stops at the end. As always, don't forget to save your video when you're done.

Don't see the TIMELINE? Then you're already in it. The pane at the bottom of the screen in Windows Movie Maker lets you switch between STORYBOARD view and TIMELINE view. The STORYBOARD view lets you see all your video pieces in a row, like links on a chain. The TIMELINE view is helpful to see how many seconds each video clip lasts and how it fits with the sound. You can toggle between the two views by clicking on the SHOW STORYBOARD and SHOW TIMELINE buttons.

Help for choppy videos

Playing a video on your computer is a complicated job for the machine to handle. Your computer has to work with words, sounds, animation, graphics — all at once. Problems can happen, like the picture stopping and starting, jerkiness, or lines on the screen.

Check the hardware acceleration setting to make your video look great. Hardware acceleration helps your computer control how graphics, video, and other programs are processed. To change the setting, click on START → CONTROL PANEL → APPEARANCE AND THEMES → DISPLAY. Select the SETTINGS tab and click on the ADVANCED button.

Then click on the TROUBLESHOOT tab. You can move the slider for hardware acceleration all the way to the left to turn it off, or decrease it to somewhere in the middle. If your video still doesn't look good, you may need to update your computer's video device driver.

For information on updating your device drivers, see page 126 in the *Fast fixes you can do yourself* chapter.

Create photos from your home movies

It's hard to get good action shots with your digital camera. The soccer ball moves too fast, the sailboat turns suddenly — and you've lost the shot. But you can use your video camera to film sports or other activities that feature lots of movement, then pick out just the right frame for a great action shot. It's easy with Windows Movie Maker software.

Here's how to pull out the photo you want from a video clip in a Movie Maker collection.

◆ Select the clip you want by clicking on it. It will appear in the preview pane — the top, right-hand portion of the screen.

Press the play button just below the preview pane, and the clip will begin to play.

✦ While the video is playing, watch for the image you want to capture as a photo. When it appears, click on the photo button. This is a small button at the bottom right of the preview pane with a graphic of a camera on it.

✦ The video will freeze at the frame you're saving, and the SAVE PICTURE AS dialog box will open. Then you can name the photo, change the folder it's saved to, and click on SAVE.

Your new photo is saved in JPG format, so you can use it like any other digital photo. Print it on your photo printer, attach it to an e-mail message, or upload it to an Internet photo-sharing site.

Share your home movies the easy way

Back in the day, you'd invite your family and friends over, hang a sheet on the wall, and start your film projector. They'd pretend to be entertained during an entire evening of watching vacation movies. Now, you can share videos from your computer — no popcorn or hassle involved. There are several methods of sharing homemade videos.

Save it for later. It's easy to save your video onto your computer's hard drive. Then you can watch your movie, invite your family in for a viewing, or make copies to share. To save your video in Movie Maker, select FILE, then SAVE MOVIE FILE. Pick a spot on MY COMPUTER to store the file.

Burn a DVD. Once your movie is on your computer's hard drive, you can burn it onto a DVD if you have a DVD burner. Then you can send copies to family and friends, and they'll be able to play it on their PCs or DVD players.

Send by e-mail. You can also share your movie by sending it as an attachment to an e-mail message. Friends can open the attachment when they receive your message, watch your movie, and save it or send it on to others. But if you have a slow Internet connection, this method may slow down your e-mail system or jam your computer.

For information on attaching files to e-mail messages, see page 299 in the *E-mail essentials* chapter.

Post online. You may want to share a larger video file by posting it to an Internet sharing site. Best of all, you can tell your friends where to look for your movie, and they can watch it when they're ready. You've probably heard of some of these popular Web sites.

YouTube	www.youtube.com
Blip.tv	www.blip.tv
Jumpcut	www.jumpcut.com
MSN video	www.video.msn.com

Sharing your videos online is free or cheap, depending on which Web site you use. Videos are posted in a format that almost anyone can view, and it's also a great way to find an audience if you're a budding filmmaker.

Yet, if you don't want the whole world watching your video, pick a sharing site that lets you protect your videos with a password. That way, only people you give the password to can watch. A site like **www.snapfish.com** lets you post both videos and still photos, and it's password protected.

Make the most of your digital images

66 A picture may be worth a thousand words but it uses up a thousand times more memory! 99

Author unknown

See your photos as soon as you snap

Your PC and digital camera team up for fast photo fun. Now you don't have to wait to finish and develop a roll of film to see the results of a photo session. Just upload the pictures to your computer, and you can look at them, make changes so they look even better, and share them with family. It doesn't get any better than this.

Upload your photos. First, you'll need to move the photos from your camera to your computer. You can do this easily by connecting your camera to your computer with a USB cable, or take the photos straight from the camera's memory card — a small, square piece of plastic that holds the picture files. You'll need a memory card reader attached to your computer, but this is the fastest way to move your photos. Some cameras come with special software to help you move photos to the computer, but you could just use a wizard in Windows XP to do the job. The Scanner and Camera Wizard is a program that'll walk you through the steps.

After you connect the camera or memory card, Windows XP will detect the new piece of hardware and ask what you want to do. If you're using a USB cable, select MICROSOFT SCANNER AND CAMERA WIZARD, then click on OK. If you're using a memory card reader, select COPY PICTURES TO A FOLDER ON MY COMPUTER USING MICROSOFT SCANNER AND CAMERA WIZARD, then click on OK.

Follow the steps in the wizard, making sure to name the group of photos something you'll remember, like "Florida holiday" or "Jeff's graduation."

Enjoy the show. Then you'll be able to view your photos in a slideshow on your computer screen. The quickest way is simply to select the VIEW AS A SLIDE SHOW option within the folder where you stored your pictures. They'll open as a full-screen slideshow. Move your mouse to reveal a toolbar that lets you pause, restart, or end the show.

Don't stop there. For a fancier slideshow, download free software that helps you make changes to the photos, rearrange them, add music, or burn your slideshow to a CD. Check out these options.

Windows Live Photo Gallery	*www.get.live.com/photogallery*
IrfanView	*www.irfanview.com*
Picasa	*www.picasa.com*

For information on how to use your photos as computer wallpaper, see page 64 in the *Control panel: customize your PC* chapter.

Oops — you accidentally deleted a photo that was on your digital camera, but you really want it. Act fast, and you may be able to get it back. Download a free trial version of the software File-Rescue Plus from **www.softwareshelf.com**, and you may be able to undelete that photo while your camera is connected to your computer. You can use the trial version to bring back two photos, but you'll need to buy the full version for about $40 to keep using it. It's a lifesaver when your finger is too quick on your camera's delete button.

Bring old photos into the digital age

Got some old photographs you'd like to include in a slideshow or put on CD for storage? All you need is a scanner attached to your computer, and you can turn paper prints into digital photos.

Your computer has a helpful piece of software to do this job. It's the Scanner and Camera Wizard, and it'll open automatically when you first connect the scanner to your computer.

If the hardware is already attached, you can access the wizard through START and MY COMPUTER. Under PRINTERS AND OTHER HARDWARE, click on SCANNER AND CAMERAS and double-click on the name of your scanner. The Scanner and Camera Wizard will open.

Check out these settings in the wizard to see if you want to make changes.

Resolution. You want this number to be high enough so the photo will look sharp and not grainy. Some experts recommend you stick with at least 150 dots per inch (dpi), and 200 dpi is best. You can change the resolution in the wizard under CUSTOM SETTINGS.

Color. For a more artsy look, you can turn a color photo into black and white. Make that change on the CHOOSE SCANNING PREFERENCES window in the wizard.

File format. The letters at the end of your file name indicate what format it's in. You have choices for photos and other graphics, depending on how you plan to use them.

♦ JPG or JPEG. This format, short for Joint Photographic Experts Group, is designed for photos. Using it will help your colors stay true, but some quality may be lost due to file compression. It's a good option if you plan to use the photos on the Internet. JPG is the default option in the wizard, and you're probably safe choosing it.

♦ TIF or TIFF. Short for Tagged Image File Format, this option is meant for all types of graphics. The file size will be large, but it's a good choice if you plan to archive or edit your photos — and you want the absolute best quality.

You can also scan in your old photo negatives or slides if you have the right equipment. Don't try placing the slides directly onto the glass of a regular document or photo scanner. You'll need a scanner with a transparent materials adapter to hold the slide correctly.

Get photos off your phone for free

You can send photos from your camera phone to your e-mail address, then open them on your computer to edit or print. You can also use picture messaging to send them. But either way, your cell phone service provider will charge you money to move your photos. Instead, connect directly to your computer to get your photos for free.

First, you'll need a USB cable that fits your phone so you can hook it up directly to your computer. This cable may have come with your phone, but if not, you can probably buy one. Take your phone with you to the store to be sure the cable will fit.

Second is software, which you'll need to get the photos from your phone to computer, called syncing the phone. This may also have come with your phone, so check the documentation. If not, you can buy software to do the job. For free software, check out

BitPim, available at **www.bitpim.org**. This program doesn't work for all types of phones, but you can see if your brand is on the list of supported items.

If your phone and computer are equipped with Bluetooth, you're in luck. You can send photos wirelessly from the phone to your computer. Check the TOOLS menu on your phone.

Rename your photos for easy finding

The best way to organize your photos on the computer is with a keyword that relates to the event or person, like "Jamaica trip" or "Ron's concert." But your photos may already be named by code numbers, so they're hard to find. Here's how to rename them easily.

Select a group of pictures to rename by clicking on the first picture in the list and holding down the SHIFT key. Then click on the last picture in the list. Right-click on the first picture, and select RENAME. Type in a new name for the picture, including the correct file extension, like .jpg. Press the ENTER key. All the photos in the list will be renamed, each with a number added to the end.

Free and easy way to edit photos

Don't buy expensive, hard-to-learn software to edit your photos. There's a free option already on your computer — Microsoft Paint. But even this little program can be tricky to use, and it won't let you do too much.

Instead, try Picnik. It's a free photo-editing Web site that'll do all you need. There's no need to download software to your computer. Experts love the features it offers — plus it's easy.

Whether your photos are on your PC or posted to a photo-sharing Web site, you can work with them using Picnik at **www.picnik.com**. You'll choose the option to upload photos, then the easy step-by-step help guide will walk you through locating and working with them. There's a lot you can do to make your photos look better — without knowing much about photography. With Picnik tools you can:

◆ crop images

◆ rotate photos

◆ fix colors

◆ banish red eyes

◆ sharpen fuzzy images

◆ adjust brightness/darkness

When you're done, you can save your photos back to your computer or sharing site, or e-mail them to a friend. All these great features are free, but you can buy a subscription for upgraded services.

A premium membership lets you upload large batches of photos at once, stash away your photos for later, skip the advertisements, and more.

For more information on software that helps you edit your photos, see page 175 in the *Top tips for popular programs* chapter.

Outsource photo printing for great results

Viewing your digital photos on your computer is fine, but eventually you'll want to put some in a photo album or hang them on the wall. For that, you need to print them. There are several options to do this job cheaply.

Print at home. If you want photos to take to a family reunion tonight, you'd better print them yourself on your computer's color printer or photo printer.

This option puts you in control of every step of the process. But the cost is rather high at 17 to 30 cents per print — not including the cost of the printer. Using a home printer won't be the best choice for printing photos when speed is not so important. It's difficult to get all the elements just right — best ink, high-quality photo paper, right size print — and your results probably still won't match what a professional can do.

Carry them to a photo shop. If you can wait a day or so, take the photos on CD or your camera's memory card to a local photo shop or kiosk to print or have them printed. You've probably seen photo kiosks at drugstores, grocery stores, or big box stores, like Target.

Most use either Kodak or Fuji processing and paper. Typically, you have the chance to do a bit of editing — like cropping or getting rid of red eyes — pick the print sizes you want, then either print them immediately or order from the store's photo lab. Prints can be ready in an hour if you order from the store's lab.

Order prints online. When time is not an issue, upload your photos to an online photo service and place an order. They'll be shipped to your house in a few days, or you may have the option to pick them up at a local store, like Target or CVS. You'll find good deals this way — sometimes as cheap as 9 cents per print — and most of the well-known services do a great job.

Kodak Gallery	*www.kodakgallery.com*
Shutterfly	*www.shutterfly.com*
Snapfish	*www.snapfish.com*
Wal-Mart	*www.walmart.com*

Create photo CDs for safe storage

Computers crash, files are lost, and photo prints can be damaged by light, heat, or water. Save your precious memories with a digital backup by putting important photos on CD.

You'll need a blank CD-R that's large enough to hold the photos you want to store. Look on the CD to see its capacity — it probably holds between 640 and 720 megabytes (MB).

For information on selecting the right kind of blank CD, see page 9 in the *Hardware nuts & bolts* chapter.

Check your photos for size. If the total is less than what your blank CD holds, you'll be fine. If not, you'll have to select fewer photos. Then you can put the rest on another CD.

1. Click on START, then MY PICTURES. Double-click on the folder of pictures you want to copy.

2. In the EDIT menu, click on SELECT ALL.

3. In the FILE menu, click on PROPERTIES. Click on the GENERAL tab and look at the SIZE field.

4. Click on OK.

What you see is not always what you get. For the best results in digital photos, calibrate your monitor. That way, you know what you see on the screen is what you'll see on paper. To start, order some photo prints from the service you plan to use. When they arrive, hold one up next to your computer monitor, while the same photo is displayed on your screen. Notice how the colors or shading compare, and adjust your monitor so it most closely matches the print. Then you know what you'll be getting next time you order.

Copy photos to the disc. Insert your blank CD into the computer's CD drive.

1. Under PICTURE TASKS, click on COPY TO CD. Windows XP will open a message balloon that reads, YOU HAVE FILES WAITING TO BE WRITTEN TO THE CD. Click on the balloon to see the files or folders that will be copied.

2. In the CD WRITING TASKS area, click on WRITE THESE FILES TO CD.

3. The CD Writing Wizard will open. Follow the instructions in this handy, self-help program.

4. When the process is complete, the CD will be ejected automatically.

Pick a safe place to store your backup CDs, like your safe deposit box or a fireproof safe. At the very least, ask a friend to keep your backup CDs at his house. In case of a fire or flood, your CDs are in a separate location.

You can get digital photos even if you don't have a digital camera. Next time you take in film to be processed, ask to have the photos put on a picture CD. It'll probably cost less than $10 for a roll — maybe as little as $3. Then you can move the photos from the CD onto your computer and use them like any other digital images. You can e-mail them to friends, make your own greeting cards, or post them on an Internet photo-sharing site. Plus, the CD is great backup storage for your precious memories.

Share your photos online

Don't make your family and friends wait while you get around to printing and mailing photos of your latest adventure. Post your digital photos to an online photo-sharing Web site, and friends can see them the same day.

Here's how photo-sharing works. You'll need to get your digital photos onto your computer. Then you can upload them directly to a photo-sharing Web site. The site will give you step-by-step instructions to follow, so the process is easy. Depending on which site you choose, you may be able to edit or arrange your photos into groups or albums and add captions.

Invite friends and family to see your photos on the Web site. You'll send an e-mail with an invitation, and friends will simply click on a link to see the photos. There are many photo-sharing sites, so decide on the features you're looking for.

Online editing. Some sites give you the ability to make changes to your photos after you post them.

Ordering prints. Compare prices if you want to buy prints of the photos you post.

Gifts. You can also purchase items like photo albums, T-shirts, coffee mugs, or mouse pads with your photos printed on them. Check out the offerings at the site you're considering.

Privacy. If you don't want the world to see your photos, pick a site that requires an invitation from you with a password before guests can enter.

Community. Sites that let you view and comment on other people's photos function like social-networking Web sites.

Rules and restrictions. Will you need to make a purchase through the site every so often to keep your photos stored there?

Cost. Some sites are completely free, while others offer a free version and more extensive subscription options.

Of the numerous photo-sharing sites available, these have earned good reputations from users and reviewers.

DotPhoto	www.dotphoto.com
Flickr	www.flickr.com
Kodak Gallery	www.kodakgallery.com
Photobucket	www.photobucket.com
Picasa	www.picasa.com
Shutterfly	www.shutterfly.com
Shwup	www.shwup.com
Smilebox	www.smilebox.com

SmugMug	www.smugmug.com
Snapfish	www.snapfish.com
Windows Live Spaces	www.homelive.com

For information on sharing photos with friends using e-mail, see page 299 in the *E-mail essentials* chapter.

Get your friends together to see your vacation photos. They can gather around your television to watch. One easy method is to connect your digital camera directly to the TV. If it comes with an RCA cable that connects to the TV, this will be simple. The other approach is to load your photos — in JPG format — onto a blank CD or DVD. Then you can pop the disc into a DVD player and start the show. Most DVD players will play these just fine.

Show off your pictures in a digital frame

Digital photography lets you do lots with your photos. But as long as the photos are on your computer, you're not enjoying them. Put them on display fast — no paper, printer, or CDs required. Get a digital photo frame for you or someone you love.

A digital picture frame looks like a regular frame, but the pictures show on a screen. That lets you change the photos in your living room whenever you want, even every few minutes — if the frame has a slideshow feature — because a frame can hold more than one photo.

You can probably find a digital frame for as little as $75 or pay as much as $350. Features vary, so consider these issues when you shop.

Screen size. Digital frame screens range from 3 inches to 15 inches, measured diagonally. You'll pay much more for the larger LCD screens.

File formats. You definitely want a frame that'll display JPG picture files, but some will also play audio or video files, like WMV or MP3 formats.

Transfer method. Photos can be moved from your computer to the picture frame by USB cable, through a wireless connection, or on a memory card.

Resolution. This feature is important so your photos look good — not fuzzy — in the frame. If you're choosing among frames of similar size, pick the one with the highest resolution.

Fancy features. You can find frames that let you edit your photos, play a slideshow, or add music. But you'll pay more for those features.

Recently, there were reports of certain models of digital frames — along with some other devices that connect using a USB port — that carried dangerous computer viruses. Avoid the headaches this could cause by keeping your computer's anti-virus software up to date.

Shortcut keys

These quick ways of performing common functions can make you a computer wiz. The plus sign (+) indicates you press all keys at the same time.

To do this fast	Try this shortcut
Copy	CTRL + C
Cut	CTRL + X
Paste	CTRL + V
Undo	CTRL + Z
Save file	CTRL + S
Select all	CTRL + A
Open File/Open window	CTRL + O
Display the Start menu	CTRL + ESC
Open Windows Task Manager	CTRL + ALT + DEL
Move cursor to next word	CTRL + Right arrow key
Move cursor to previous word	CTRL + Left arrow key
Move cursor to next paragraph	CTRL + Down arrow key
Move cursor to previous paragraph	CTRL + Up arrow key
Select from cursor to end of word	CTRL + SHIFT + Right arrow key
Select from start of word to cursor	CTRL + SHIFT + Left arrow key
Select from cursor to end of paragraph	CTRL + SHIFT + Down arrow key
Select from start of paragraph to cursor	CTRL + SHIFT + Up arrow key
Close the active item	ALT + F4 key
Switch between open items	ALT + TAB
Open Run dialog box	Windows key + R
Open Windows Explorer	Windows key + E
Open Search function	Windows key + F
Minimize all open windows	Windows key + M
Expand all minimized windows	SHIFT + Windows key + M
Show your desktop on top	Windows key + D

Speed up a slow computer

Use this quick reference as a reminder of ways to work faster and more efficiently.

Try this	See details on page
Upgrade random-access memory (RAM)	7
Clean your computer tower	27
Add a second hard drive	43
Change settings for color depth	68
Specify draft-quality printing	70
Change settings for visual effects	73
Enable indexing for searches	108
Defragment the hard drive	112
Set Windows XP to get automatic updates	116
Update device drivers	126
Roll back system changes	128
Install anti-virus protection	151
Keep anti-virus protection updated	154
Uninstall unwanted programs	167
Remove programs from startup folder	169
Connect to Internet via DSL or cable modem	195
Test modem connections	197
Delete temporary Internet files	198
Tweak broadband Internet connections	199

PC maintenance schedule

Keep your computer running smoothly with a little TLC. Don't call expensive computer support. Follow this schedule of basic maintenance tasks and solve your computer problems for free.

Do these tasks every day	See details on these pages
Clean out unnecessary & junk e-mail messages	309
Run Disk Cleanup	111
Back up just your important files on CD or an external hard drive	114
Have anti-virus protection, spyware blocker, and firewall get automatic updates	145–163

Do these tasks every week	See details on these pages
Manually update the security tools that don't do so automatically	154
Run a full system scan using anti-virus protection and spyware blocker	151
Run Check Disk to scan the C drive for problems and fix them	114
Defragment the C drive	112

Do these tasks every month	See details on these pages
Check for operating system updates & updates for non-security programs like Microsoft Word	116
Make a backup copy of your entire C drive	114

Index

A

AARP 261
ActiveX 166, 223
Add-ons. *See* Plug-ins
Adobe Reader 191, 206
Adware. *See* Spyware
AOL Instant Messenger
    (AIM) 318
Auctions, online 241, 252
Autocorrect 186

B

Banking
    credit cards 290
    Internet-only bank 291
    online benefits 288
Blogs 322
Blue Screen of Death 133
Bluetooth 13
Bookmarks. *See* Favorites
Books, classic 276–278
Botnet 308
Burning a CD 335

C

Cable Internet connection 196
Cable modem 42
Calendar 173, 188
Carpal tunnel syndrome 25
Cars, buying online 242
Category view 62
CDs (compact discs)
    burning 335
    copying to computer 333
    drives, types of 9
    scratched, fixing 10
Central processing units
    (CPUs) 6, 7
Charities 264
Check Disk program 114
Classic view 60–62
ClearType 69
Clip art 181, 273
Clipboard 102
Coin collecting 267
College degree 274
Color depth 68
Computer
    accessories 13, 35, 244

T

WordArt 180
WordPad 173, 177
Worms. *See* Viruses

Y

Yahoo! Messenger 319
Yellow Pages, online 233

Z

Zombie. *See* Viruses